WOMEN, RITUAL, AND POWER

WOMEN, RITUAL, AND POWER

Placing Female Imagery of God in Christian Worship

ELIZABETH URSIC

SUNY PRESS

Cover art: "The Creation of Adam" (1511–12) by Michelangelo Buonarroti, Sistine Chapel, Rome © creedline / Fotolia

Published by State University of New York Press, Albany

Printed in the United States of America

For information, contact State University of New York Press, Albany, NY
www.sunypress.edu

Production by Eileen Nizer
Marketing by Kate R. Seburyamo

Library of Congress Cataloging-in-Publication Data

Ursic, Elizabeth.
Women, ritual, and power : placing female imagery of God in Christian worship / Elizabeth Ursic.
pages cm
Includes bibliographical references and index.
ISBN 978-1-4384-5285-2 (hc : alk paper) 978-1-4384-5284-5 (pb : alk paper)
1. Women in Christianity. 2. Femininity of God. 3. Worship. I. Title.

BV639.W7U77 2014
264—dc23 2013040989

10 9 8 7 6 5 4 3 2 1

Contents

ACKNOWLEDGMENTS

This book has evolved over many years, and I am grateful for the financial and institutional support provided to see it develop. The research on the Catholic Daughters of Wisdom began while I was a graduate student at Yale Divinity School as the Louise H. MacLean Scholar awarded by the Yale Institute for Sacred Music. The Norton Grant for Women's Studies in Religion and a graduate fellowship at Arizona State University allowed the work to expand to include the Methodist and Lutheran communities. A visiting fellowship at the University of Edinburgh New College and a concurrent sabbatical leave granted by the Maricopa Community College District provided much appreciated time and space to conduct the research on the Church of Scotland and to complete the book manuscript.

The theoretical framing for studying the Daughters of Wisdom was presented in a paper titled "Feminist Theories and the Study of Contemporary Nuns" at the 2006 National Women's Studies Conference. A portion of the chapter on the Church of Scotland was shared in the paper "Ministers' Wives and the Motherhood of God Controversy" at the 2012 Women, Language, and Worship Colloquium at the University of Edinburgh New College. I discussed the concept of strategic emplacement during my keynote address at the 2013 Feminist Theology Facing Tradition Conference hosted by Liverpool Hope University.

I have benefited greatly from ongoing discussions with a variety of scholars of religious studies, gender studies, and theology, some of whom began as my teachers and many of whom have remained friends. The interdisciplinary collegiality in this field of gender and religion is something I value, and I appreciate those who stimulated my thinking at critical junctures of this research. My profound appreciation goes to Linell

Cady, who supervised my PhD dissertation, which was the real beginning of this book. I also want to thank Tracy Fessenden, Tisa Wenger, Mark Woodward, Sarah Amira De la Garza, Hava Tirosh-Samuelson, Robert Orsi, Carolyn Sharp, Jaime Lara, Margaret Farley, Diana Swancutt, David Stayner, Yolanda Smith, Jenny Daggers, Cecelia Clegg, David Fergusson, Elizabeth Koepping, Ian Bradley, Keith Crudup, and Mary Hunt. In addition, I am grateful to Joseph Subbiondo, Jennifer Hammer, Beth Luey, and Christine Szuter for their invaluable help and advice in my development as a writer. Finally, I am delighted to be published by SUNY Press, and I thank Beth Bouloukus, Eileen Nizer, and Kate McDonnell for their wise counsel and guidance through the publishing process.

I owe my deepest gratitude to the religious communities that participated in this study. I particularly want to thank the individuals in these communities who literally opened their attics, diaries, and other personal archives to substantiate and augment the church files and public records, as well as to many more who shared their lived experiences of prayer, ritual, faith, and church. You have shown me the value of living life in community. To that end, I thank my personal community of family and friends who have loved and supported me through the process of research and writing. This book is dedicated to my mother, Margaret Volk Ursic, my first teacher in the ways of Wisdom.

Introduction

Strategic Emplacement

> She is more precious than jewels, and nothing you desire can compare with her. Long life is in her right hand; in her left hand are riches and honor. Her ways are ways of pleasantness, and all her paths are peace.
>
> —Proverbs 3:15–17

The Sunday morning service at Ebenezer Lutheran Church in San Francisco was about to begin. Individuals, couples, and families with children were finding their seats while last-minute preparations were being made on the altar. The back of the altar held a large cross and a painting of a female face surrounded with roses. The organist began to play, and the congregation sang the first hymn. Pastor Stacy Boorn, wearing a floor-length robe and stole, welcomed all and presided over the service. After the Gospel reading, Pastor Boorn preached a sermon on how Jesus advocated for women in his teachings and actions. During the service, she referred to God as "She," "Mother," and "Holy Other," along with "Jesus" and "He." Girls as well as boys helped on the altar, and the congregation formally honored the older women in attendance as the "grandmothers" of the community. During the announcements, Pastor Boorn gave an update on the scholarship the community had given to the first female to attend a Lutheran seminary in Ethiopia. The service concluded with another hymn.

This book is about Christians who worship God with female imagery and language. We examine why certain Christian communities since the 1970s have included female references for God in congregational settings, and we explore how these communities successfully managed to place these new images into their communal rituals and prayers. Worshipping God with female imagery challenges both church and society to reflect on their gendered assumptions about women, men, and God. In some cases, congregations who celebrate God-as-She prompt claims for keeping God-as-He, and they reveal internal debates over gendered church practices and social customs. More broadly, this book is a study of gender and power as we explore what happens to Christian religious communities and individuals when *femaleness* is expressed in their central symbols of God.

Many people are unaware that the Bible contains female imagery for God. Most notable is Sophia Wisdom, a female character who appears in the first nine chapters of the Book of Proverbs as she leads and instructs the Israelite people. Proverbs Chapter 8 tells us she existed before the world was created. The Gospel writers referenced Sophia Wisdom when claiming the divinity of Jesus because she portrayed God's actions among the people. Matthew 11:19 and Luke 7:35 even use female pronouns to make this connection. Today, the overwhelming majority of Christians still do not know about female images of God in the Bible despite a fair amount of scholarly writing on the subject.

One reason for this lack of awareness is the lack of liturgical expression and sermons on the subject during Sunday worship. To understand what might be done to correct this deficiency, I have been studying Christian communities that have managed to sustain female imagery of God in their worship. As the stories in this book reveal, their success has depended upon utilizing four key resources: leadership, personal prayer experience, community, and evangelization.

I first became interested in the topic of gender and God while I was a graduate student at Yale Divinity School. I was studying how people expressed their devotion and belief in God through the arts, and I was fascinated by what their artistic expressions communicated about God, themselves, and the world. My interest in gender was piqued during a national art competition called *Jesus 2000: Images of Jesus for the Third Millennium* sponsored by the *National Catholic Reporter*. Artists from around the world submitted more than sixteen hundred images, reflecting a global Christianity. The new images of Jesus were more racially diverse than the predominantly light-skinned European images from centuries past. Moreover, the reviews about the competition celebrated this change. I was intrigued by the fact that the model for the winning image, *Jesus for All People*, was African American and a *woman*. It made me wonder if Christian perspectives on gender and God were beginning to change, just as attitudes about God and race had expanded over the past century.

Certainly one area of change had been language. Spurred by the 1960s women's movement, many churches began using words such as "human" and "humankind" instead of "man" and "mankind" when referring to both male and female. *Inclusive language* became the term used in church circles for these revisions. Some denominations rewrote hymns and liturgies as well as revised Bible translations. Other denominations added new hymns and prayers that linguistically reflected their new sensibility. These actions often brought about discussion and even controversy regarding what some perceived as tampering with tradition.

Adjusting words for people has been far less contentious than adjusting words for God. Today, most Christian churches continue to use exclusively or predominantly male terms for God, including "Jesus," "Father," "Lord," "King," "He," and "Him." Some critics claim that Christianity has intentionally downplayed the feminine aspects of God, but that explanation is too simple. Most Christian denominations worship Jesus as all-man and all-God, so it makes sense that Christians image God with a male body in paintings, statues, and stained glass. This is in contrast to Judaism and Islam, which view Yahweh and Allah, respectively, as solely God. Jews and Muslims never visually depict God in worship because they believe that humans could never completely imagine God, nor should they try. Christians, on the other hand, have produced so many images of the man-God Jesus for thousands of years that no other figure has been more represented in Western art.

At the same time, it is important to remember that most Christian denominations believe in God as the Trinity, meaning three "persons" in one God, commonly referred to as Father, Son, and Holy Spirit. Only one of the three, Jesus, was biologically male. Jesus had a human body during his life on earth, but after resurrection, few Christians claim that this aspect of God retained a human body. The two other aspects of the Trinity were never biologically male because they never had human bodies.

God the Creator is usually referred to as male with the gendered title "Father" because of English translation of gospel scripture. In Matthew 6:9 and Luke 11:2, Jesus teaches his followers how to pray with the Aramaic word "Abba." English-speaking Christians are usually taught that "Abba" means "Father," even though in Aramaic, "Father" may be better translated with the more formal "Ab" or "Av." "Abba" translates to something more like "Daddy" or "Papa," a more personal term that a child might use. Some Christian denominations believe that Jesus intentionally used "Abba" to teach his followers about their intimate bond with God more than the gender claim that God the Creator must always be referred to as male. As for the third aspect of God that remains on earth after Jesus is resurrected, the Holy Spirit is typically represented as a dove.

So why have Christians thought of God as exclusively male despite this theology? Even the first chapter of Genesis includes the statement "in the image of God he created them; male and female he created them" (Genesis 1:27). A significant factor has been how Christian congregations express their faith through liturgy, art, hymns, and prayers. When churches worship God with predominantly male language and imagery, their rituals communicate that God is male, even if their theological understandings are broader. New Testament scholar Sandra Schneider summed up the problem when she perceptively wrote, "God is more than two men and a bird."[1]

If churches try to expand beyond this traditional imagery for God, they often do so through language more than through visual art. The most common way is to de-emphasize male language for God by replacing "He" and "Him" with "God." While some might consider "God" to be a male term, these communities tend to view it as gender neutral. This substitution has helped worship leaders make their liturgies more linguistically inclusive even when their worship aids were not. It has also given individuals a way to make their own changes. I have sat with congregations where I could hear individuals say or sing the word "God" while the rest of the congregation said or sang "Him." One reason why gender-neutral language is popular in worship is that it provides those who want to imagine God in new ways to do so without directly challenging those who do not; all can say "God" with whatever images the word evokes for them.

If churches occasionally add female references for God, they are often presented as metaphors or adjectives for God rather than as direct address. It is possible on Mother's Day to hear sermons stating "God is like a mother" or to learn about "the mothering" of God. A minister may include "Mother" along with "Father" when saying a prayer, such as "God, who is both Mother and Father."

The most noticeable expression is when a female term alone is used to address God, such as when God is directly referred to as "She." This declaration stands out in contrast to the male norm, and it directly challenges any internal male images of God that worshippers may have.

Christian prayer and worship services have experimented with this language. Some of the most innovative groups, such as Woman-Church and the Grail, organized outside institutional church settings. They were inspired by the early church and formed communities from the ground up, meeting in each other's homes and developing prayers and rituals that spoke to the needs of their local community. Foundational books in Christian scripture, history, and theology that inspired and grounded these efforts included Rosemary Radford Ruether's *Woman-Church* in 1985, Elisabeth Schüssler Fiorenza's *Discipleship of Equals* in 1993, and Elizabeth Johnson's *She Who Is* in 1993. Today, many women's spirituality or Bible study groups now include female language and imagery in their studies and prayers, but this expression has not always translated with the same frequency or visibility into the larger rituals of their main religious communities.

For this book, I have been interested in the institutional church impact of ritualizing female imagery of God. For this reason, I have chosen particular congregations of established Christian denominations where the entire community is introduced to female imagery of God. All of the members, not just a subgroup interested in the practice, have had to wrestle with the issues of gender and power that these worship rituals evoke. As a result, each location produces a diversity of opinions about the practice, reflecting larger conversations happening within their denominations as a whole.

To explore these issues, I have focused the book on four Christian communities. They represent large, established Christian denominations: Methodist, Catholic, Lutheran, and Presbyterian. These communities were chosen because they all had formal recognition and authorization to operate within their particular denomination. In addition, these communities were led by ordained or vowed leadership. Three are located in the United States, and one is located in Scotland. Finally, all worship God with female imagery as an important image in their communal prayers and community identities.

Christian congregations that celebrate God with female imagery are uncommon. They provide fruitful locations, nonetheless, for exploring gendered assumptions about God. These communities jump off the pages of theology books into the practice of expressing female imagery of God in public settings, they provoke individual reactions and institutional responses, and they publicize internal debates in unexpected and unintended ways. Communities that assert their right to refer to God-as-She can expose strident claims for maintaining God-as-He. Published minutes of church meetings, editorials, denominational newspapers and magazines, and even general media often reveal the larger tale.

I met these communities through personal introductions and referrals. I did not undertake a search to identify all relevant Christian communities who worship with a significant amount of female imagery, and there could well be others. It is still fair to say, however, that denominationally recognized Christian congregations who are led by ordained clergy or vowed religious and who celebrate with female imagery of God as a central ritual focus and identity are rare.

The first community I met was an order of Roman Catholic sisters. The Daughters of Wisdom celebrate feminine attributes of God based on a three-hundred-year-old theological treatise written by their founder, St. Louis de Montfort. In *For Love of Eternal Wisdom*, St. Louis de Montfort expounded upon Old Testament scripture where Wisdom appears as a female character. He connected these passages with New Testament scripture, calling Jesus *Wisdom Incarnate*. The Daughters of Wisdom today seek Wisdom as the unique calling of their order, and they commemorate feminine aspects of the divine in their prayers, teachings of their founder, and community formation through the female imagery of Wisdom contained in the Old Testament.

The Daughters of Wisdom introduced me to United Methodist ministers Susan Cole and Hal Taussig. These ministers co-pastored a United Methodist Church in Philadelphia in the early 1980s and introduced their congregation to a female face of God through their sermons, Bible study, and liturgies. They wrote one of the first congregational worship instruction books on the topic, *Wisdom's Feast*. As my research progressed, I also learned about Ebenezer Lutheran Church in San Francisco. In 2003, under the direction of Pastor Stacy Boorn, this Evangelical Lutheran Congregational Association (ELCA) parish embraced the nickname "herchurch," emphasizing the use of female language and imagery in worship. Last, I learned about the Church of Scotland Motherhood of God report while I was a Visiting Fellow at the University of Edinburgh.

The four communities are predominantly white and middle class. These common characteristics may suggest that Sophia is ritualized more by Christian communities for whom gender is the primary and sometimes only named form of discrimination experienced by a significant portion of its members. In support of this view, later we will hear an African American theologian and a Latin American female theologian explain to the Lutheran herchurch community why they prefer ritualizing with other biblical figures who speak to their experiences of race and class along with gender. A notable exception can be found in theologian Grace Ji-Sun Kim's book *The Grace of Sophia: A Korean North American Women's Christology.* She does not include rituals, but Kim does see Sophia Wisdom as a relatable biblical figure for Korean North American women because of her parallels with Asian wisdom figures.[2]

I conducted the research for this book over a ten-year period. I made multiple field visits to members of these communities, located primarily in New York, Pennsylvania, and California, in the United States as well as Scotland. My field visits were followed up with telephone interviews with key participants, generating more than one thousand pages of field notes and interview transcripts. I also researched and analyzed archives, worship aids, and media coverage of key events at divinity schools in both the United States and Europe.

During this research, I became aware of other Christian worship communities who engaged female imagery of God in less dramatic ways or in less contested settings. Some congregations used female language for God in the rotation of their worship services. Some churches had special interest groups that used female images of God in their study, worship, and prayer. Other groups began under the auspices of an institutional form of Christianity, but they later left their denominations. There were also groups who always operated outside traditional church structures, sometimes identifying themselves as Christian and sometimes not.

Learning about these other communities and the challenges they face suggests to me that there is a desire for more female imagery of God in Christian worship than is currently available in formal settings of institutional Christianity. This book sheds light on what has enabled the communities profiled here to include female imagery in their Christian worship. As such, their stories are relevant for other religious communities interested in grassroots ritual reform.

Female Imagery of God in the Bible and Historical Uses

Much of the biblical justification for imaging God as female comes from Wisdom texts. The Hebrew word for wisdom, *Hokma*, appears throughout the Hebrew Bible, and more than half of the wisdom references occur in three books: Proverbs, Job, and Ecclesiastes. Hellenized Jews wrote the books of Sirach and Wisdom of Solomon in Greek, with more than one hundred references to *Sophia*, the Greek word for Wisdom.[3] Later, scholars coined the term "Wisdom literature" to refer to the five books of Proverbs, Job, Ecclesiastes, Sirach, and Wisdom of Solomon, where wisdom is a predominant theme.

Unlike earlier Jewish texts where God performs miraculous acts such as the parting of the Red Sea, the later Wisdom literature finds the wisdom of God in the immediacy and ordinariness of life.[4] The teachings in these books are practical, often drawing on the natural world to offer insights into God's instruction for living. For example, Pete Seeger's popular song "For Every Season" drew heavily from Wisdom literature: "To everything (turn, turn, turn), there is a season (turn, turn, turn), and a time to every purpose, under Heaven. A time to be born, a time to die. A time to plant, a time to reap. A time to kill, a time to heal. A time to laugh, a time to weep."[5]

Wisdom literature communicates lessons about wisdom in multiple ways: through the description of nature, the use of proverbs, as well as stories about wise people. Wisdom also appears as a female character. Contemporary writers often use the Greek word Sophia when referring specifically to this female-personified wisdom because Sophia is also a woman's name.

Scripturally, Sophia's first appearance in the Bible is substantial. She acts and interacts with the Jewish people throughout the first nine chapters of the Book of Proverbs. Sophia calls from the gates, instructs the faithful, counsels sages and kings, and places her value higher than silver or gold. Her divine actions are echoed in stories of Goddesses from nearby cultures, including the Egyptian Maat and Isis:[6] Even the Genesis story of creation is retold in Proverbs, chapter 8, where we learn that Sophia existed before the world was created. Some scholars claim that this creation account is depicted by Michelangelo in the ceiling of the Sistine Chapel (see image on the cover of this volume). The iconic God image has one arm outstretched, touching fingertips with Adam. God's other arm hugs a female figure, presumably Sophia.[7]

Sophia also figures prominently in the sacred books of Sirach and Wisdom of Solomon. All Roman Catholic and Orthodox Bibles include these books in their canon of Old Testament Holy Scripture. Because they were originally written in Greek and not Hebrew, Jewish and Protestant Bibles consider Sirach and Wisdom of Solomon apocryphal or deuterocanonical, meaning highly valued but not sacred canon. Some Protestant Bibles, such as the Revised Standard Version (RSV), the New Revised Standard Version (NRSV), and the original 1611 King James

Bible, include Sirach and the Wisdom of Solomon in a separate apocrypha section.[8] In this passage, King Solomon describes Wisdom:

> For Wisdom, the fashioner of all, taught me. There is in her a spirit that is intelligent, holy, unique, manifold, subtle, mobile, clear, unpolluted, distinct, invulnerable, loving the good, keen, irresistible, beneficent, humane, steadfast, sure, free from anxiety, all-powerful, overseeing all, and penetrating through all spirits that are intelligent, pure and altogether subtle. For Wisdom is more mobile than all motion; because of her pureness she pervades and penetrates all things. For she is a breath of the power of God, and a pure emanation of the glory of the Almighty; therefore nothing defiled gains entrance to her. For she is a reflection of eternal light, a spotless mirror of the working of God, and an image of his goodness. Although she is but one, she can do all things, and while remaining in herself, she renews all things; in every generation she passes into holy souls and makes them friends of God and prophets . . . She reaches mightily from one end of the earth to the other, and She orders all things well. I loved her and sought her from my youth; I desired to take her for my bride, and became enamored of her beauty. She glorifies her noble birth by living with God, and the Lord of all loves her. For she is an initiate in the knowledge of God, and an associate in his works. (Wisdom of Solomon 7:22–27, 8:1–4)[9]

Jesus was born during the Second Temple period, the same period when both Palestinian and Hellenistic Judaism produced much of the Wisdom literature. Jesus was well versed in Jewish sacred texts, and the Gospel writers were, too. Bible commentaries connect the words of Jesus in Matthew 11:28, "Come to me, all you that are weary and are carrying heavy burdens, and I will give you rest," with Wisdom's words in Sirach 24.19, "Come to me, you who desire me, and eat your fill of my fruits," and Sirach 51.23, "Draw near to me, you who are uneducated, and lodge in the house of instruction."[10] Scholars have also noted the parallels between John's prologue and Wisdom texts.[11]

At least once, the femaleness of Wisdom is included in a gospel text describing Jesus. "The Son of Man came eating and drinking, and they say, 'Look, a glutton and a drunkard, a friend of tax collectors and sinners!' Yet wisdom is vindicated by her deeds" (Matthew 11:19). The NSRV Study Bible explains, "Jesus seems to be identified with *wisdom*, though the latter was mythologized as female (see Proverbs 8–9; Wisdom 7:22–8:21). Thus *her deeds* are actually his."[12] Various contemporary Bible scholars have identified this connection of Jesus with Old Testament Wisdom as Sophia Christology.[13]

Other historical uses of Wisdom scripture have also highlighted the femaleness of Wisdom in relation to Christianity. When the Roman Emperor Constantine moved the capital of the empire from Rome to Constantinople in the fifth century, he named the cathedral he built Hagia Sophia. The cathedral served as the seat of the Christian patriarch of Constantinople for more than nine hundred years. Sophia continues to be revered as the Mother of God in Eastern Orthodox churches. Most images of Sophia in Christian churches today are in branches of Orthodox Christianity.

Medieval Christian commentaries occasionally referred to female images of Wisdom. For example, the twelfth-century abbess Hildegard of Bingen created artwork and described Sapientia (Wisdom) as a divine feminine prefiguring of Jesus.[14] Also, Meister Eckhart, a fourteenth-century German Dominican priest and theologian, imaged a fertile God who gave birth to the Word in all of us.[15]

Sophia has also figured prominently in certain offshoots of traditional Christianity. In the early church, Christian Gnosticism celebrated Sophia as the feminine complement to the masculine Christ and even named one of its sacred texts *Pistis Sophia*. Beginning in the nineteenth century, European metaphysical and Christian esoteric movements, including Sophiology, Theosophy, and Anthroposophy, drew upon gnostic texts regarding Sophia to develop understandings of an everlasting feminine divine.[16] The United States was touched as well. The eighteenth-century Shaker community in Oneida, New York, claimed that Mother Ann Lee was the second coming of Christ, citing Sophia Wisdom texts.[17]

Yet Wisdom texts have also been used in ways that have ignored the female personification of Wisdom. In the thirteenth century, theologian and philosopher Thomas Aquinas used Wisdom texts to prove God's existence, but he did not focus on Wisdom's female personification. Also from the medieval period, Jewish Kabbalism included "Hokma" in the Tree of Life—but on the masculine side of the tree. In contemporary Jewish worship today, the Jewish Renewal Movement and other Jewish worship communities are more likely to use the term "Shekhinah" when referring to the feminine side of God,[18] an ancient name for God's presence associated with God's feminine characteristics as a light or a radiance coming into the world.[19]

Until the 1970s, few Protestants or Catholics were aware of biblical female Sophia Wisdom; if they referenced Wisdom, they considered the female personification merely a literary convention. The most that an academic biblical scholar might claim before the 1970s was that Sophia Wisdom was a hypostasis, a created intermediary to serve between heaven and earth, much like an angel. And even this proposition was contested.[20]

SOPHIA FEMINIST THEOLOGY: IMAGES OF GOD AND WOMEN'S EQUALITY

It is important to remember that until the women's movement in the 1960s, churches largely restricted women from studying and serving as Christian theologians, ordained ministers, and Bible scholars. In the early 1960s, theologian Mary Daly went to Switzerland to pursue her doctorate because Catholic universities in the United States would not allow women to study theology at the highest levels.[21] It was during Daly's European studies that she went to see the Second Vatican Council in Rome in the fall of 1965. The Catholic Church was receiving kudos worldwide for opening its doors to the modern world, but Daly saw a huge discrepancy between the sexes. This experience spurred Daly to write *The Church and the Second Sex*, published in 1968. Her title was a play on the title of Simone de Beauvoir's 1949 *The Second Sex*, a decisive work in the beginning of the women's liberation movement. Daly pointed out that while hundreds of highly adorned male bishops and cardinals vigorously debated issues at the council, only a small handful of women were invited to be observers. Most of these women were veiled nuns wearing all black. They looked on silently, as no woman at the council was allowed to speak.[22]

While Daly's first book called for reform of Christianity, her next book, *Beyond God the Father* (1973), articulated a more radical critique. She questioned if a religion predicated on a Father-God could ever value and treat women with the same dignity and respect given to men. She penned a quote that became famous for succinctly describing a prevalent feminist attitude of the day, "If God is male, then male is God."[23] This critique about religion resonated across the women's movement, but there was little agreement about how to respond. Three general views were represented by secular feminists, Goddess feminists, and religious reform feminists.

All three views held a feminist perspective, meaning they all believed in and were advocates for equal political, economic, and social rights for women. Secular feminists tended to reject religion altogether, claiming that religion and patriarchy were both culturally constructed to preserve a certain social order of men over women and to protect those in power. Many leaders in the women's movement took this stance. In this view, religion was its own invention, creating the myths and stories that normalized the second-class treatment of women.

Goddess feminists agreed that male-dominated religions perpetuated patriarchy, but they did not reject religion itself. Goddess feminists claimed that Goddess religions had existed for a long period in history, predating Father-God monotheism. In this view, patriarchy was not the inevitable progression of society, but an anomaly for five thousand years after twenty thousand years of Goddess religions. Both Goddess and secular feminists vehemently opposed the existing patriarchal religious establishments.

Religious reform feminists, however, believed that the male-dominated religions were not hopeless to reform. These feminists, mostly Christian and Jewish, were seeking religious reform. They acknowledged the sexist historical overlays in their religions, but affirmed the religious truths of these religions as well. In their view, these religions became sexist not because of what God ordained, but because of what men had done in the name of God. These women and men believed that their religious traditions could be reformed just as society could be reformed. Many felt that what these religions needed was a good vetting to dismantle the man-made harmful aspects from what they saw as essentially good and holy religious beliefs and practices.

While secular and Goddess attitudes became identified as the dominant positions of American feminism regarding religion, many women in the movement continued to participate in the religions of their birth. Religious participation was at 59 percent of the US population in 1952 and continued to slowly rise to 62 percent in 1980.[24] Despite media hype that included the 1966 *Time* magazine cover "Is God Dead?," a record number of women continued participating in their religious traditions even as they began to critique them.

Also, despite skepticism from secular and Goddess feminists, the 1960s women's movement helped to create the largest gender reform of Christianity. Women's ordination became the most visible sign of success, giving women access to the same sacred roles as men for leadership positions within their churches. While not all Christian denominations made the change to allow ordained female worship leaders, many did so, including the Protestant denominations featured in this study. The Presbyterian Church of Scotland was the first national church to allow ordination of women in 1969. The Evangelical Lutheran Church formally approved ordination of women in 1970, and the United Methodist Church nationally implemented the decision to ordain women in the 1970s, a decision made two decades earlier.

The education of Christian women in the fields of theology and Bible studies also had a major impact on churches, as the women's movement opened doors for women to pursue advanced degrees in all academic fields. Women were finally given broad access to the most sophisticated techniques of language study, systematic theology, and philosophy needed to develop theology, *theo-logos*, or knowledge of God. They were also educated in related fields of archeology, literature, and history that could be brought to bear when interpreting ancient texts for the modern faith believer.

The term "feminist," despite its lessened social use today, continues in academic circles to describe scholarly research on power from the perspective of gender. Christian feminist theology and feminist biblical studies make explicit the power and gender claims implied in various church teachings. These feminist interpretations for biblical texts and theological categories have been useful and inspirational for both women and men, and they have offered insights and critiques of previously unexamined patriarchal church teachings.

Feminist theology, like feminism in general, was initially critiqued for addressing mostly white, middle-class women's concerns. Today, feminist theologies have significantly multiplied as it has been acknowledged that gender is inextricably tied to race, ethnicity, and class. Two of the more widely known theologies are womanist theology and mujerista theology, which speak to the unique experiences of African American and Latin American women, respectively. There are also Asian and African feminist theologies and many others. All seek to advance and understand gender equality from moral, social, and religious perspectives.

Another criticism of early feminist theology was that it assumed gender to be a fixed binary of male and female, and heterosexuality to be normative. Today, there is more acceptance of lesbian, gay, bisexual, and transgender (LGBT) people. Queer theology emerged in the 1990s, reclaiming the derogatory slang word "queer" to create a positive theology that acknowledges, informs, and supports the faith needs of these communities.

Since the 1970s, feminist theology has grown to become an established subfield within theology. There are now many strands and movements within it that address such topics as ethics, sin, and creation. Feminist theologians reconceptualize these topics in ways that are life giving and not oppressive to women's experiences. The growth of the discipline was documented in a 1996 *Dictionary of Feminist Theologies* that included 350 pages of specialized terms and definitions written by more than 180 contributing scholars considered leaders in the field.[25]

Sophia feminist theology developed to focus on female images of God in scripture, passages that had largely been overlooked. Feminist theologians noted that right after Jesus teaches the parable that God is like a good shepherd searching for the lost sheep (Luke 15:3–7), he describes God as a woman searching for a lost coin (Luke 15:8–10). They questioned why the first parable had become iconic while the second was virtually unknown. They also noted other scriptural female metaphors for God, including "mother hen" references in the Gospel of Matthew 23:37 and Luke 13:34.

These biblical references opened the door to female language and images as innovative ways to communicate the mystery of God. United Methodist Bishop Susan Morrison agreed: "We can sing to God as a mineral ('Rock of Ages,' for instance), but we create a crisis when the feminine dimension of God is lifted up. What is it about the feminine that evokes such feelings?"[26]

Sophia theology continues to be one of the most identifiable feminist theologies in worship settings because it deals with images and language; Christians are encouraged to use female images and references for God in prayer and worship. Christians are also encouraged to celebrate so-called "feminine" qualities of God, such as hospitality, inclusiveness, and cooperation, along with these images. According to Sophia theology, when imagery for God overemphasizes maleness, "masculine" characteristics of judgment and righteousness predominate in churches. This imbalance can result in power struggles, noninclusive thinking, and misinformed decision making. In this view, imaging God as female becomes essential for balancing Christianity as well as helping Christians conceptualize full gender equality in God and humanity.

Sophia theologians disagree with more traditional interpretations of Sophia as a literary invention, a hypostasis, or the first of God's creations.[27] They claim that a patriarchal bias colored these earlier interpretations of Wisdom and diminished the importance of her femaleness and her divinity. They assert that Sophia is a scriptural way to explore the feminine face of God, or God Herself.[28]

Other feminist biblical scholars and theologians, however, have raised serious historical and theological objections to valorizing "Lady Wisdom." Rosemary Radford Ruether has advocated for a more critical and historical reading of the Sophia texts. Ruether points out that while Wisdom in the book of Proverbs does call from the gates, she only calls the men, and she appears to be created by male writers to encourage men to be faithful to their religious instruction and behavior. Other scholars have questioned whether the various Wisdom literature authors all shared the same perspective. The Wisdom literature spans approximately six hundred years, and it was originally written in two different languages. The debate continues among biblical scholars on whether Hokma/Sophia/Wisdom was written to be a liberating or enforcing presence of existing patriarchal religious practices.

These historical textual debates are not the only ongoing conversations regarding Sophia. In her book *Goddesses and the Divine Feminine: A Western Religious History*, Ruether claims that she was misinterpreted as opposing the use of these images today for feminist agendas. She points out that she supports efforts by modern-day women to explore ancient female symbols and images for use today, but she cautions against implying that their current use mirrors their use historically.[29] Theologian Elizabeth Schüssler Fiorenza concurs, acknowledging the critique other feminists have made of the Wisdom texts, but arguing that the imagery is inspirational for Christian women today.[30]

Despite these endorsements, a relatively small portion of female imagery for God has made its way into Christian ritual. For some Christian feminists, this lack of female imagery needs remedying. For many secular and Goddess feminists, this lack of female imagery simply affirms their long-held positions that Christianity can never be fully reformed of embedded patriarchy. To return to Mary Daly's quote, "If God is male, then male is God. The divine patriarch castrates women as long as he is allowed to live on in the human imagination."[31] Implicit in this statement is the belief in the connection between ritual and social reality. Today, ritual theorists may challenge the idea of a direct cause and effect between ritual and social reality, but there is no question that those who advocate for female imagery of God seek rituals that better reflect their view of God and the world.

In many Christian churches, communicating feminist theology through sermons or rituals, particularly Sophia theology, has become difficult, even professionally dangerous. Male and female ministers who feel personally enriched by feminist theology are sometimes wary of challenging their congregations with feminist theological insights in their sermons or using inclusive language and imagery for God in their worship services. Many female Christian ministers believe that they already challenge worshippers' sensibilities around gender and God. Consequently, they do not want to openly confront worshippers' beliefs about women or their gendered images of God out of fear of losing their church positions.

These fears are justified. One of the largest waves of firings of paid professional churchwomen in America occurred around the use of female imagery for God. In 1993, a Re-Imagining Conference was held in Minneapolis to support the World Council of Churches initiative titled "Ecumenical Decade of Churches in Solidarity with Women, 1988–1998." Experimenting with female images of God in worship was a main feature of its liturgical celebrations as a way to "reimagine" Christianity with regard to women. More than 2,200 people attended the event, including a significant number of women who held paid leadership positions in their church denominations. For many, the Re-Imagining Conference deepened their Christian faith, their relationship with God, and their understanding and celebration of each other.[32]

Unknown to conference organizers, groups who opposed the event sent reporters as attendees. They used their conservative Christian media outlets to cast the experimentation with God-as-She in Christian ritual in the most negative light possible and successfully attracted national media attention to cover the "controversy."[33] Having lost the battle over women's ordination in their various Protestant denominations, these conservative coalitions focused on female imagery of God as a galvanizing issue to motivate their base in order to stem the tides of change that women's leadership was bringing to their churches, and they were successful.

The negative coverage of the Re-Imagining Conference resulted in arguably the largest wave of firings of professional churchwomen in America, including the executive director and others who had planned the conference. This had a chilling effect on Christian Sophia ritual innovation, even for those who did not participate in the conference. None of the main worship leaders profiled in this book attended the event, but each encountered his or her own aftershocks and reverberations, highlighting the severity of the backlash. Even today, imaging God-as-She in many Christian denominations is considered an extreme and even heretical act.

Strategic Emplacement of Female Imagery in Christian Worship

Most Christians today who do not know that Christian feminist theology exists have never seen it or learned about it in church. Gender reform of Christianity has stalled in part because of a lack of ritualized enactment. While it must be acknowledged that there are many ways and locations to practice and produce religion, it is hard to imagine how a reconceptualization of God could occur in the lives of everyday Christians without a reform of Christian worship.

Current ritual theory supports the notion that sacred worship is often a location for protest and reform of religion. Unlike earlier ritual theorists who focused on sacred ritual as primarily providing social stability, ritual theorists today emphasize a more dynamic and contentious process known as "ritualization." In contrast to viewing ritual as static, ritual scholar Catherine Bell and others proposed a strategic and power-laden process of differentiation. In her work *Ritual Theory, Ritual Practice*, Bell showed how rituals are "concerned with distinguishing local identities, ordering social differences, and controlling the contention and negotiation involved in the appropriation of symbols."[34] She encouraged scholars to widen their lens and examine the process of ritual making, or, in her terms, the "ritualization of activity." Far from being a smooth, harmonious process, ritualization is often more about contesting and negotiating power.

Because feminist rituals deal with power, protest, and counternarratives, ritual theories that highlight action or performance have often been helpful for investigating their creation and impact. Ritualizing as a negotiation of power specifically applies to the worship locations in this book because these communities have challenged systems, both religious and social, that have troubled them. Religious studies scholar Bruce Lincoln supports this view. "Women in oppressive circumstances have means, creative and powerful, to react against the processes that victimize them. Among these are the disruption of existing rituals and creation of novel rituals."[35] Ritual theorist Ronald Grimes also agrees. "In many respects the most effective ritual criticism is the development of an alternative rite. Some of the best examples of criticism in this kind of context are feminist and countercultural."[36]

Ritualizing Sophia theology in Christian contexts is one part of a larger trend of feminist women ritualizing their interpretations of their histories and traditions. As Grimes noted in 1990, "[f]or the last twenty years or so, feminism has been a consistent source of ritual creativity; it provides an ongoing context for ritual experiment unparalleled in any other sector of North American society. This phenomenon is regularly, and I think, wrongly ignored by most theorists of ritual."[37]

While more attention has been given to feminist ritualizing in recent years, there is still relatively little investigation of this practice in Christianity. Theology and prayer books encouraging Christian feminist worship proliferate, but little analysis has been published on the impact of actual Christian feminist ritualizing within the religious institutions they were meant to reform. As a consequence, this Christian practice is not well known, and the assumption among many is that it does not exist. While preparing this book, I was often asked two main questions: "Where are these communities?" and "How do they manage to do it?"

To explain how they do it, I use the term "strategic emplacement" to describe the intentional act of placing ritual in strategically significant locations. Ritual theorist Jonathan Z. Smith first brought attention to the context of place when interpreting ritual in his 1987 book *To Take Place: Toward Theory in Ritual.* In this landmark work, he argued for the primacy of place when analyzing ritual. While place included geographic location and physical built space, Smith also extended the category of place to include concepts and mental classifications as well.

Current scholarship on sacred place now recognizes that ritual and space are more contested and less determinative than was once believed. There has also been a significant move away from formalized ritual space to the study of lived religion, where the religion is examined within the context of a faith believer's life. This reconceiving of place has resulted in more studies of women's ritualizing, as women traditionally have had more agency in rituals away from formal liturgies and formal built church spaces.

In this book, however, I focus on institutional worship settings to explore questions of gender and power. Scholars of religion and culture David Chidester and Edward T. Linenthal explain in their work *American Sacred Spaces*, "Sacred places are arenas in which power relations can be reinforced, in which religions between insider and outsider, rulers and subjects, elders and juniors, males and females, and so on, can be adjudicated. But those power relations are always resisted. Sacred places are always highly charged sites for contested negotiations over the ownership of the symbolic capital (or symbolic real estate) that signifies power relations."[39] Religious studies scholar Greg Johnson extended this idea in *Sacred Claims* to include tradition itself as both the means and the product of power protests. "Tradition is not located outside of disputes; it is a means and vehicle for waging them and is itself a product of them."[39]

Strategic emplacement focuses attention on place as a significant if not dominant component for understanding certain types of ritual action. Strategic emplacement is not a claim that place is always the most important aspect of ritual, nor that formalized ritual space is "holier" than other places. It does not even assert that categories of sacred and profane are necessarily created with strategic emplacement, either. In fact, the Christian communities featured in this book enjoy blurring these supposed categories in the rituals they create. Rather, strategic emplacement examines the act of placing ritual. It provides a lens when place or space is one of the most contested aspects of ritual making.

It is worth noting that the majority of feminist ritualizing in the United States today is not being performed on Christian altars. Within the branch of Goddess feminism, place can be defined anywhere in Wicca when casting a circle or setting up a personal altar, and neo-pagans prefer natural settings for worship. The broader women's spirituality movement has protested women's restriction and exclusion from formal built ritual space by making rituals where access to place is readily available and where they have freedom to innovate, such as private homes and public lands. In his provocative work ***Deeply into the Bone: Reinventing Rites of Passage***, Ronald Grimes included examples of American women's alternative rites for menopause and divorce, none of which occurred in institutional Christian settings.[40]

This lack of focus on formalized ritual space for women's religiosity has been compounded by what religious studies scholar Mary Farrell Bedarnowski identifies as "ambivalence" in the religious imagination of American women, particularly around religious traditions.[41] Some might say that these alternative rites and alternative spaces reflect American women's preferences for ritualizing. Even women who continue to attend traditional Christian church worship may augment their faith life with these types of expressions.

I would argue, however, that these ritual choices may also reflect women's voices being shut out from the main religious power centers of ritual performance in which these women were raised or in which they continue to ambivalently participate. This book shows that emplacement of Christian feminist rituals in more formalized ritual place or space has mattered a great deal to the participants involved as they sought to integrate feminist theology into their church's accepted ritual tradition. In this view, performing a Christian feminist ritual down the hall or in a private home does not have the same denominational impact when compared with enacting these ceremonies on the altar during Sunday morning worship. In fact, I would claim that performing feminist theology down the hall reifies the position that feminist theology is a special interest theology relevant only to a small special interest group, rather than reinforcing the larger message that all human and godly power must be understood in terms of gender, race, and class. Performing feminist theology during main communal rituals sends a message that all church ritual and teachings must celebrate everyone as equals in the eyes of God.

The communities profiled here offer examples of how women's ritual needs have been addressed within Christian church worship. Both those for and against female imagery of God are well aware that they are competing for who gets to control the communal worship message. This type of ritual making is a highly political and contested act.

Some may say that this perspective puts too much attention on congregational public worship, but controlling a church's look and message can be of paramount concern, particularly for large denominations. Religions compete for members, financial resources, political leverage, and social power. This concern is particularly acute today, when Christianities face unprecedented competition on Sunday mornings, making the particulars of the worship more important than ever.

Communal religious rituals are also powerful touchstones for church members that inform and instruct their daily reality. The sound bites that characterize a denomination's religious beliefs are often preached and performed in weekly religious communal rituals that connect communal identity with personal identity and social directives. It is during communal rituals that selected scripture passages are heard, and particular interpretations of those passages are preached, prayed, and sung. From an institutional perspective, Sunday morning Christian worship generally simplifies, streamlines, and edits a robust and complex tradition into what church leadership hopes will be the official version believed by its members.

The downside of this strategy is the potential for the tradition to be perceived as only what is presented on Sundays. Some of the most highly emotional and most organized negative reactions to new forms of ritual worship come from people in the pews because Sunday morning worship *is* the tradition for them. When ritual innovation occurs, church members can feel that their tradition has been tampered with, if not blasphemed. It is not uncommon for church institutions to benefit from unofficial lay groups to police church orthodoxy without having to appear heavy-handed themselves.

While power exists in many church arenas, public communal rituals continue to be critical for shaping and shifting the practice of the religion and mobilizing special interest agendas. This is a significant location where tradition becomes a tradition through the repetition of formalized, sacralized activities. Theological discourse becomes concretized into religious and denominational distinctiveness through the act of ritualizing, and expressive acts often meld with the agendas of interest groups.

So how did the communities in this book successfully change their ritual practice? In my research, I found that four resources were essential. First, there was a leader who had institutional church authority to direct a local Christian community and who was committed to using female language and imagery in worship. For the Protestant cases, this meant an ordained minister or deacon. In the case of the Catholic sisters, the provincial (a term that replaced Mother Superior) held this position. These charismatic leaders held positional power, but they also knew how to be effective agents of change within their denominations. In all four cases, the leaders displayed a deep love and commitment for their particular Christian denominations despite being advocates for reform. They were also theologically and politically savvy enough to negotiate their efforts within their local communities as well as their larger denominational organization.

Second, these communities had members who spoke about their personal prayer experiences of God as female. The testimonies were deeply felt and at times otherworldly, adding legitimacy to the biblical references and theological explanations of the practice. These members spoke about their experiences informally with friends or more formally in public settings, including communal worship. These encounters also offered opportunities for individuals to tell their personal stories along with experiential God encounters, placing these acts of testifying in the realm of identity politics. In their witnessing, community members often shared personal stories of experiencing gender prejudice as a way to explain why female images of God have been inspirational for them.

Third, there were core members of the worship community who were as committed as the worship leaders to seeing female language and images of God in worship. These community members served a significant role in shifting community opinion, advocating for female imagery in worship among members who were less taken by the practice, and doing so in more personal and informal ways than those in leadership could. This worship topic gave them a forum to speak about broader gender justice issues within the church and society. In addition, these community members often enthusiastically participated in helping to create and perform the new prayers and worship expressions.

Fourth, all of the communities had a strong commitment to evangelize. The leadership teams of these worship communities saw themselves as prophets within their own church traditions to express and promote the truth about God-as-She. While some communities were better than others in getting their message out, this prophetic commitment to call their larger church community and society into account gave these local communities the impetus and courage to publicly innovate prayer and worship in dramatic ways. Creating this type of worship took a great deal of effort, and the call to evangelize provided the drive to dedicate the time, talent, and resources needed to create this liturgical reform.

Finally, being *strategic* in their ritual emplacement meant that the communities consciously coordinated the essential resources of leadership, personal prayer experience, community, and evangelization with a long-term view for larger church and societal reform. These communities saw resistance and failures as small setbacks and valuable learning opportunities rather than insurmountable roadblocks. Without a strategic perspective, these incidents could have stopped progress toward their larger goal of mainstreaming gender equality in Christian worship. Instead, these events reinforced the need for change and became pivotal moments in coalition building for their cause.

CHAPTERS AND SIGNIFICANCE

In the chapters that follow, we examine the development of and resistance to female imagery for God in prayer and worship within the contexts of both Christianity as well as the women's movement. We investigate how strategic emplacement of female imagery of God in Christian ritual has been accomplished within the particulars of a denomination's theology and institutional organization. We learn about the four essential resources of leadership, personal prayer experience, community, and evangelization, and how the profiled communities employed them to innovate worship.

In Chapter 1, we explore the role of church leadership in advancing female images of God in worship. In the early 1980s, Reverend Susan Cady felt called as an associate pastor of a United Methodist parish in Philadelphia to combat sexism. She used her leadership position to introduce her congregation to new understandings of gender and God-as-Sophia through preaching, teaching, and leading small groups. Along with Hal Taussig, her co-pastor, and Marian Ronan, a Catholic lay associate, she published *Wisdom's Feast*, explaining how to foster acceptance of Sophia theology in parish life and worship practice.

In this chapter, we investigate how positional power was used to initiate and protect ongoing strategic emplacement of female imagery of God in prayer and worship. Later, when a disgruntled parishioner organized alliances with conservative United Methodist priests and bishops, Rev. Cady and Rev. Taussig were both targeted by critics for censure and charged with heresy. Rev. Cady bore the brunt of the push back, but she was protected by her own female bishop and was promoted instead. Although the charges were dismissed, the formal charges of heresy and a theological inquiry by United Methodist bishops showed the extent to which patriarchal push back could be organized and targeted at individuals in major struggles between liberal and conservative wings within a Christian denomination. This chapter highlights the type of early triumphs and setbacks experienced with this liturgical reform.

In Chapter 2, we focus on the connection between personal prayer experience and worship expression. Like many Roman Catholic women's religious orders, the US province of the Daughters of Wisdom went through many changes in the wake of 1960s Vatican II and the women's movement. By exploring their namesake, *Wisdom*, as a feminine face of God, the Daughters found a way to create a group identity and purpose after many of the sisters left the order in the 1970s. Using the Vatican's language of male and female gender complementarity, the Daughters have claimed the feminine attributes of God as their unique calling to bring balance and help correct problems in the world today.

The Daughters of Wisdom have explained the femaleness of God in terms of Catholic mysticism, where God can be experienced in a variety of ways. The primary focus for the Daughters has been on understanding and expressing their personal prayer experiences of God, particularly when God is experienced as female or feminine. These God encounters have helped them find freedom and agency in a life that has continued to be constrained by the Catholic Church primarily along gender lines. While they do not ritualize on a parish altar, they have used their separate space to create Wisdom prayers and rituals for group gatherings as well as their ministries. They have also conducted Wisdom education for their international order worldwide, finding ways to communicate their moderate message of expanding God imagery in other national contexts.

In Chapter 3, we examine the role of communities in advancing or resisting worship innovation. Anne Hepburn, president of the Woman's Guild, said a prayer to "God Our Mother" at the 1982 annual meeting, and many of the hundreds of Guildswomen were shocked and upset. The controversy was so great that the Church of Scotland General Assembly appointed a committee to study and prepare a report on the "Motherhood of God." Over the next two years, coalitions both for and against female imagery of God advanced their causes in national newspapers, radio, and BBC television interviews as well as church circles.

The worship controversy became a way for different factions within the church to organize their communities and make their voices heard. When the report was complete, the controversy was still so great that the General Assembly voted not to debate the issue or even to receive the report. Twenty years later, when a new hymnal was compiled, six hymns included female imagery of God, thereby approving its use and practice. Today, the worship controversy continues to be remembered and repeated in liturgies and prayers as a way to reinforce alliances and to continue the debate and extend its reach to shape future worship design and expression.

In Chapter 4, we consider the role of evangelization in the creation of Christian worship with female imagery for God. In 2002, Lutheran minister Rev. Stacy Boorn was serving an aging ELCA Swedish parish in San Francisco that was in need of attracting new members in order to survive. When she referred to God as Mother-Father during a baptism, the parish leadership council tried to fire her. Treating the incident as a justice issue, she successfully fought back and refashioned a new parish community with feminism as its mission. The parish adopted the nickname "herchurch," and it began using female images of God on the altar. To emphasize its vision of egalitarianism, herchurch is never capitalized.

In expressing a feminine face of God, herchurch combines many strands of feminist theology, using many terms for God, including God/dess as well as Sophia, and celebrating Mary Magdalene and other women in church history in elevated roles. It also embraces current theories of gender and sexuality. Liturgies reflect this perspective when God is referred to as Holy Other, and the herchurch Web site welcomes LGBT members in its open and affirming community. To evangelize its message, herchurch has placed banners on the outside walls of the church building, hosted Faith and Feminism conferences, advertised God/dess rosaries on its Web site, and uploaded worship videos on YouTube. The congregation has also bridged its work with other feminist spiritual communities, including mujerista organizations, womanist networks, and various Goddess groups.

Just as the communities surveyed here had to make decisions regarding how to describe themselves and their image of God, I too had to make choices. I use the New Revised Standard Version (NSRV) translation for Bible verses. I have chosen to capitalize both Goddess and God, as some of these communities embrace Goddess as their name for God. I have mostly used the correct term, "sisters," for the Daughters of Wisdom because they are an apostolic order, though I occasionally use the term "nuns" because that is how Catholic women religious are commonly referred to in public discourse. Finally, I use the term "feminist" in an explanatory sense when describing those communities who embrace theologies and causes that emphasize the equal rights and worth of women. Many individuals within these communities, however, particularly members of the Daughters of Wisdom and the older members of herchurch, would not personally describe themselves as feminists.

The aim of this book is to explore feminist liturgical reform as a lens to investigate gender and power dynamics in churches. This work contributes to the existing theological, historical, and psychological studies on female divine imagery in worship by examining what happens when these approaches are engaged in concrete Christian locations. Because the study sits at an intersection of ritual studies, Christian theology, religious studies, and women's studies, the significance of the findings will vary by discipline.

With regard to ritual studies, we learn about the enormous effort needed to get a new understanding of God enacted in a power location of an existing religion's sacred stage. The first generation of a new worship expression necessitates a coalition of forces co-creating and cooperating both on and off the altar. It also requires attention to the behind-the-scenes negotiations as much as the ritual itself to ensure public expression.

The communities in this study have participated in strategic emplacement. They have all participated in coordinated efforts between worship leaders to create and enact the new expression, theologians to explain and justify the practice, ecclesial bodies to formally or informally allow or promote its use, and community members to participate in creating its sacred performance. Strategic emplacement has also meant that these communities took a long-term view and intentionally engaged all possible resources for their goal of emplacement, including intellectual, financial, theological, organizational, political, and human capital.

This coordinated effort helps us to explore substantial questions of when and why strategic emplacement matters. One answer is that strategic emplacement in ritual helps to advance a version of tradition during times of conflict and debate. For these communities, communal ritualizing offered the potential to normalize and control the image and message of the community. This study of strategic emplacement allows us to explore how the act of placing fits within broader action-oriented theories of ritualization.

With regard to theology, we explore how a theology develops, flourishes, or dies within its lived context. Theology is not just an intellectual enterprise, but also an exploration and development of faith. Only when a theology moves off the written page into the hearts and minds of believers does it come to full fruition. While new theologies need to be vetted intellectually among theologians, there is another type of vetting that occurs when the theology is ritually expressed and taught to the faithful. Theological innovation, particularly liberation theologies such as feminist theology, needs full congregational expression to be deemed relevant beyond the believers who identify with the liberating claims. Without full congregational participation, marginalized groups can become further marginalized when they express their liberating theological views among themselves because this highlights their difference from the main body of worshippers. Feminist theology has suffered this fate in a variety of ritual locations. Without acceptance and integration into communal worship, a new theology may be judged as heresy in the court of public opinion, even if it has denominational support from theologians and leaders working within the church.

Moreover, understanding what happens when a particular theology is engaged as lived religion allows reflection on further development of the theology and may spark the next questions to be theologically explored and addressed. Because this book engages feminist Christian theology in practice, it offers the opportunity to address one of the greatest challenges for theologians today: engaging the sociocultural context. By tracking a new theology's use across specific communities of worship and then including this information in further reflection of the theology's development, this study offers one way in which theology and culture can interact.

In addition, because these communities are admittedly rare, we revisit the historiography of writing women's history. The first generation of books written on women and religion in the 1970s, like women's studies more generally, were about exceptional women in religious scripture and history. These works were eventually critiqued for their triumphant narratives and for obscuring the range of women's experience. Some scholars responded by looking at the complexities within larger trends in American women's religiosity, such as women's continued participation in conservative churches. As R. Marie Griffith, a scholar of women and religion, noted in 1997, "older models that analyze conservative forms of religion as intractable bastions of male privilege and female subordination are being supplanted with richer and far more complicated frameworks for interpreting female religious activity and women's power within organizational bounds."[42]

In this book, we return to the exceptional norm-breaking histories of women and religion. Unlike the earlier exceptional histories, however, we learn that locations of Christian feminist activism are as complex as their conservative counterparts. Because these communities claim to be consciously operating out of principles and perspectives of women's equality, they offer another layer to the analysis of how blurred categories of agency and constraint, oppression and submission really are. By studying locations that overtly engage in feminist ritual norm breaking, we have an opportunity to examine how feminist protest and women's agency are both supported and subverted individually, congregationally, and institutionally.

These communities have managed to stay connected to their religious institutions while asserting their right to express their feminist critiques. This can be uncomfortable, difficult, and challenging for both their life of faith and their sense of justice. Sometimes these individuals and groups exhibit the most cherished ideals of what women imagine they would do if given the leadership power to transform their religious traditions. At other times they fall short, even exhibiting behavior that negates the ideals they purport to extol. In short, they are human, and unlike a theological treatise or an academic theory, they demonstrate how messy religion and feminist activism on the ground really is.

From a women's studies point of view, we examine current patriarchal push back in churches. We also investigate locations that still benefit from special interest group politics around a category of "female." Because the women's movement identified religion as a major contributor to sustaining sexism in society, assessing how far female images and female language of God have progressed within Christian denominations is one way to examine sexism in church contexts today.

In addition, we examine locations where feminist women and men have been the leaders in all aspects of this Christian theological movement, from writing the theology, to enacting it in worship, to consuming it as congregants. The fact that they are doing so within the religious and cultural context they have inherited allows for evaluation of how patriarchal policies and practices are being deconstructed or reasserted in new ways. Imaging God-as-female in prayer, worship, and teaching within traditional Christian settings has produced dramatic contested sites to interrogate these questions.

These particular religious communities are attempting to bring forward a full equality of femaleness in heaven and on earth. They are not only locations of analyses but also locations of activism and protest. As an assessment of this activism, we uncover the complexities and opportunities facing women's equality within Christianity today with possible insights for future efforts. Religious feminist activism might not be the preferred route for change by all feminists, but these religious locations are important because a significant portion of women continue to believe in God and develop their sense of self influenced by their religious context.

Finally, our analysis of these communities reveals a blurring of categories used in feminist critique. We see slippage between various theories of gender, whether performed in ritual or in justifying other initiatives in the community. These communities hold an ideal of communal power sharing, but how these communities actually work shows a variety of decision-making models and leadership styles including hierarchical power, particularly in the role of pastor. These findings raise interesting questions about what type of power is needed to innovate ritual within religious institutions and if the ends justify the means.

Why focus on Christianity? In the 1960s, Christianity was the primary expression of religion that the women's movement critiqued, and Christianity is still arguably the power religion in many parts of the world. It is true that non-Christian religions in the Americas and Western Europe have grown significantly in the last fifty years with waves of immigration from Asia, Eastern Europe, and the Middle East, as have emerging New Religious Movements. Nonetheless, Christianity continues to be the dominant religious presence in both politics and media, particularly in the United States. Put another way, it is difficult to imagine how the women's movement could change social perceptions and practices of religion in the West if it did not influence Christianity.

Let us not forget that religion continues to be one of the strongest sectors in society where patriarchy remains publicly enacted and socially tolerated. There are religions practiced today in which only men are allowed to lead worship, touch the holiest items, or perform the most sacred ritual acts. There are still religious customs in which women and men are segregated during worship, with men always in the better seats; and there are still worship spaces where women are not allowed, except to clean them. While some call this tradition or God's directive, others see it as sacred theater for privileging the male. Efforts to show alternative ways to worship God that honor both female and male believers have strong social implications.

Let us now turn our attention to Methodist ministers Susan Cady and Hal Taussig, who were among the first American Christian pastors to venture down this road with their West Philadelphia congregation in the early 1980s.

1

The Resource of Leadership

Wisdom's Feast and United Methodism

> By me kings reign, and rulers decree what is just;
> by me rulers rule, and nobles, all who govern rightly.
> I love those who love me, and those who seek me diligently find me.
>
> —Proverbs 8:15–17

Driving through the leafy suburbs of Philadelphia, I was finally meeting Rev. Susan Cady (Cole) and Rev. Hal Taussig after a series of long-distance phone calls and correspondence. Both had been United Methodist ministers for more than thirty years. She was a full-time retreat leader and spiritual director, and he was a professor at Union Theological Seminary as well as a pastor at Chestnut Hill Methodist Church. Their current work, however, was not the reason for my visit. Twenty years earlier, they wrote one of the first books on Sophia theology for parish life. Published in 1986, *Wisdom's Feast: Sophia in Study and Celebration* described how Sophia theology was being used in sermons, rituals, and Bible studies in church. Their book provides a window into how Sophia ritualizing began at the parish level in the early 1980s. The backlash to their book reveals how emplacement of Sophia theology became politicized during the latter part of the twentieth century. As worship leaders, Cady and Taussig demonstrated commitment and dedication when educating and ritualizing Sophia in church worship. As we shall see, church leadership is an essential resource of strategic emplacement of Sophia in worship.

DISCOVERING SOPHIA

As we settled in with our mugs of hot tea, Cady began by describing her upbringing in Mentor, Ohio, in the late 1950s and early 1960s. Methodism had deep roots in this small town, and her first memory of church was as a small child, drawing on the church bulletin while the congregation sang "Holy, Holy, Holy" and "Jesus Loves Me." Cady loved going to church and never questioned the significant part it played in her life. I asked if she had always wanted to be a pastor. She replied "No" because she had been taught while growing up that only men could be pastors. The most she imagined was becoming a pastor's wife.

I found her answer curious because Methodism had a relatively long history of ordaining women. Founder Charles Wesley licensed Sarah Crosby to preach in England in 1761. The first woman in America to be ordained was Anna Howard Shaw in 1888, with a few women continuing to be licensed or ordained on an "exceptional" basis over the next seven decades by local bishops. In 1956, when Cady was ten, the United Methodist Church granted women full clergy rights on a national level, making it one of the first mainline Protestant churches in America to do so.[1] How could Cady not know?

The answer was that her local church leadership chose not to tell her. Bishops who did not agree with women's ordination resisted the decision by not appointing female clergy in their geographic areas. Uneven implementation of the new policy among bishops in the 1950s and 1960s meant that many United Methodist women and men were not aware that women could be ordained.

Cady had accepted the teachings of the church as they were presented to her. After graduating from a Methodist college in 1967, she did marry a Methodist, but not a pastor. It would be seven years before Cady's "call" would surface. During that time, she embraced married life, moved to Philadelphia, had a child, and expanded her horizons by teaching in a racially mixed urban school.

Then one Sunday Cady went to church and saw a woman of similar age installed as associate pastor of her parish. It was the first time Cady actually saw a woman placed in the pulpit, and it moved her deeply. Her personal call to ordained ministry was awakened in that moment. Cady identified with the woman on the altar, not just with her femaleness but also with her age. For Cady, it was seeing the woman perform sacred ritual that changed her perception of who could serve God as ordained leaders. Within a year, she started the process to become an ordained United Methodist minister herself.

Her first major step was to attend Union Theological Seminary in New York City. Just three months after Cady began her seminary studies, the December 1974 cover of *Ms.* magazine featured a picture of Carter Heyward, a Union alum. Heyward and ten other women were being "irregularly" ordained to protest the exclusion of women in ordained ministry in the Episcopal Church. The article described the ordination struggles that women were facing in certain denominations.

Cady came to Union inspired by these times. She was interested in studying women and female imagery of God in the Bible. The progressive social environment, however, did not always transfer into the classroom. "There were enough women at school to question a lot and begin to stand up a bit, but the professors certainly did not do much. What I got from my Old Testament professor was to look at Near Eastern texts for some of the myths there."[2] I asked Cady why she had not been directed to the Wisdom texts at that time. She replied that it was as if no one had noticed Sophia yet. Cady wrote her master's thesis on mother Goddess imagery in baptism rites and in exodus scripture instead.

Cady's thesis helped her embrace her professional and personal call after being told her whole life that God never meant for women to lead Christian worship. While women in many professions in the 1970s and 1980s had to figure out their new roles, female ministers also had to reconsider how they related to God as women as well as pastoral leaders. For some, this reassessment included radically different images of God. As Cady recalled, "That's pretty much when God the Father dropped out. It just totally dropped out for me. And Jesus—I found I related to Jesus more as brother than as savior. All that happened during seminary. The only image I had was of God as a desert."[3]

Today, Cady has more insight into what was happening during her seminary years. "I am a spiritual director, and now I know all about this. It is basically a transition in God imagery, reflecting a transition in how one relates to God. That's all it is. I mean honestly, spiritually it's not a big deal. It just means your spirit is in transition. Today I help people with that kind of transition all of the time. But then I didn't know what that was. All I knew was that God the Father was no longer of any use to me, and whatever was yet to emerge had not yet appeared. When you are in-between things, you don't know if something will emerge or not. So it was a very hard place to be."[4] Today, many Christian seminaries require seminarians to engage in monthly spiritual direction sessions where they reflect on their changing images and deepening understandings of God. Spiritual direction was not part of Cady's seminary program in the 1970s, however, and she had to handle this unexpected turn in her prayer life alone.

THE CHALLENGES OF PASTORING

Despite the changes in her prayer life, Cady continued with her training to become an ordained minister. Her first Methodist parish assignment was Calvary United Methodist Church in West Philadelphia. She had been a member of Calvary before she attended seminary, and she periodically returned during her studies. It was located on the edge of the University of Pennsylvania campus. West Philadelphia was one of the poorer sections of the city, an area providing low-cost housing for city residents and students alike. According to Cady, this mix of Ivy League students with the local neighborhood encouraged new thinking, yet it also challenged the congregation to allow for diversity of thought and expression and still remain in community with one another.

It was during her seminary days that some younger women in the congregation formed a feminist study group. They had begun reading feminist theology and asked to present their discoveries during worship. The parish leadership agreed, and one Sunday they presented a panel during worship where they discussed Mary Daly's book *Beyond God the Father*, particularly the quote "If God is man, then man is God." Cady recalled that it created quite a stir but that no controversy endured.

Hal Taussig was already a pastor there at the time. He did not initially relate to their interest in feminism and religious imagery, but he wanted to support the group in their theological quest. He remembered having read a paper written in German by the chair of his PhD dissertation committee that referred to a feminine face of God in Proverbs and other Old Testament Wisdom books. He encouraged the group to look at the Wisdom texts for scriptural support for their inquiry. The group became so inspired by the Wisdom Sophia texts that when Taussig went on a two-year sabbatical in 1979, he decided to explore the scriptures himself.

While on sabbatical, Taussig did extended meditations on the Sophia material, using *lectio-divina*, a Christian contemplative technique where he imagined himself in the scripture stories. The imagery was compelling, and he found the experience deeply moving. He returned to the parish as an enthusiastic supporter of the group's Sophia work.

During this time, Cady was appointed as one of the four co-pastors at Calvary. Cady was learning to cope with the intense demands of pastoring, and she noticed that she was treated differently than her male colleagues. She recalled how during all her years at Calvary, she was never approached to baptize a baby, while the male pastors were frequently asked. This experience spurred her in new ways. "For me it was clear. Even though Calvary was one of the most progressive churches in the conference, it was still biased in favor of men. It just was. So part of the spirit that crept in there at that time was noticing that there was no place better than this, and this still wasn't good enough. So that was all in the mix. It was all part of it."[5]

Cady's early ministry experience reflected the awkwardness of the times. The problem, according to Cady and her fellow clergywomen, was that their congregations still favored men in pastoral ministry. In response, they formed a Methodist clergywomen group to deal with the unique challenges they faced. Gathering weekly, sometimes with their babies, they would do some form of spiritual exercise for spiritual and collegial support. Cady recalled that when pastors held large conferences and gatherings, men would make comments that the women were separating themselves from the men. Cady remembers, however, that she was never invited to join the men's circles, and this exclusion was why she reached out to her female colleagues.

THE SERMON: A PUBLIC TURNING POINT

In January 1982, Cady delivered a Sunday sermon that revealed the complications of pastoring as a female minister during the late 1970s and early 1980s. She also presented a vision of God that offered her comfort and hope. The New Testament gospel reading was Mark 1:14–20, where Jesus calls the apostles to follow him to "fish for men." The Old Testament passage was Proverbs 8:1–11, a text widely quoted in Sophia theology, in which Sophia stands at the gates and calls out to the faithful to follow her (see the scripture at the beginning of Chapter 4 of this volume).

Cady began her sermon by referring to her "call" to follow Jesus. She admitted to the congregation that she had been in the midst of a crisis for some time. She described how much she loved the scriptures, but now felt the scriptures were cut off from her experience as a woman. She knew about the feminist reinterpretation of the Bible, but it was not enough. "The parts we'd been able to liberate still seemed so small, so insignificant compared to the patriarchal immensities that remained untouched."[6] She said that this insight about scripture also applied to her experience of the United Methodist Church structure.

While many women were battling sexism as they entered new professions, for female pastors this problem was amplified because they were expected in their new positions to reaffirm the power of exclusively male sacred symbols, images, and language with their embodied actions. Secular feminists had already critiqued Christianity for this, claiming that the emplacement of exclusively male imagery perpetuated sexism and patriarchy by making it holy, natural, and self-evident. Cady and her female colleagues, however, had become ministers believing this would not be as troubling as it later became for some.

For Cady, the discord occurred once she became a central agent in the ritual act. During the sermon, Cady told the congregation how much she loved celebrating the Eucharist, but had recently felt uncomfortable with the ritual. "All of my theological grounding gave way. And I kept trying to talk myself out of it: "But you know that in Christ there is no male or female—you know that the body of Christ includes us all. But it made no difference. All I could see was that this central act of the church was the celebration of the life, death, and resurrection of a man—and I felt on the outside." In despair, she wondered if she would ever feel at home again in the church. Her internal anxiety continued to build as she began preparing the worship for the following week. She described her vision of Sophia for the congregation:

> I was in the middle of writing one of the prayers for the service, when there she was, looking at me through a window in the door, and she was calling out to me, "What are you afraid of anyway? Do you think I care about your old theology? Do you think I care what name you name me? Do you think I care if people think I'm legitimate or not? Haven't people always refused to listen to me? But that doesn't make me any less real—and that doesn't make you any less faithful." And then, laughter. Much laughter. Mocking laughter, laughing with me and at me, all at the same time. And dancing. "I've been here all along. Come on out and dance with me,

> and sing. Come on out—open the door. I've been waiting for you for so long." . . . In my vision, Sophia was looking at me through a window in a door. I wasn't sure where the door led; I was afraid it led out of the church. This week I found the courage to open it, and it opened out into this great, wide, airy expanse—a huge, seemingly endless dome full of light. I looked back at the door through which I'd come, and saw that it was a church whose door I'd opened—a tall, narrow, Gothic structure; it was dwarfed by the immensity of the vast dome. But the church building was inside the dome, not outside it. In opening the door, I hadn't left the church behind. It was still there, but now as a part of a much larger reality. In following Sophia, I opened the door, the door that opened up perceptions and possibilities to a much wider sphere—a sphere that includes my past and new possibilities for the future.[7]

For Cady, these interior experiences of God were real, profound, and life altering. She did not think of them as figments of her imagination, but as experiences of God. Her epiphany was that God not only had feminine characteristics, but also could have a female form. This image not only spoke to her inner discomfort, but also dynamically released it. It was while crying for joy that Cady discovered the depths of her need to see God in this way:

> The inside of my head hadn't changed with a mere shift in vocabulary. My imagination was so formed by my tradition that I couldn't see God in any other way. And now I can, and that has made a tremendous difference—all the difference. The change is so immense that it's hard to talk about it coherently. But let me try. It's changed who God is for me. God is no longer just a he—no longer a male God who occasionally acts motherly but is still male just the same. . . . And now that God has opened up to include the feminine, so has my whole perception of what is possible opened up . . . I always identified with the women around Jesus, experienced his power second-hand, never directly. But I can identify with Sophia. No problem at all. She is like me. She can dwell deep within me and call out to me. She is laughing within me, and I laugh along with her.[8]

The identification with Sophia did more than resolve the tension of being a woman experiencing Jesus secondhand. Sophia was an image of femaleness representing traits that Cady herself wanted to cultivate, and she felt God's presence in supporting her in them. She connected Sophia's experience with her own:

> We're ignored a lot and often not taken seriously. Much of the time, our opinions and experience don't carry the same weight as those of men. Sophia knows what that's like—she's experienced it too—but she keeps on calling. Following her doesn't end the pain of being on the edge of our tradition. It doesn't change the reality of being on the margins of power. It doesn't end the very real possibility of being thought foolish and silly. Matter of fact, following her just about assures that all of that will be the case. But what makes it worthwhile is that she is with us in the wandering. That her strength, her laughter, life itself, is there, too. For women on the verge of a new era, when the past is crumbling and the future has not yet emerged, she leads us through a long period of wandering and keeps us going in a world in which male privilege will not be relinquished without pain and struggle and hurt for many of us. She's strong enough to keep us going, and she leads me in the certainty that she leads towards life—fullness of life, not just for me, but for all people. A life that is whole and complete. A life that, like my vision of that vast dome, allows for a lot of variety, a lot of difference, all accepted, all loved, all a part of life with Sophia.[9]

Cady's experience of Sophia placed femaleness in the center of power, as God is the ultimate source of power for Christians. This image of Sophia also affirmed an internal reworking of female identity as primary, not secondary to power. This image of Sophia reaffirmed Cady's divine and public right to be on the altar and to lead God's people. "She's also the strong one. She's full of power. In the Book of Wisdom is a passage describing Sophia leading the Hebrews through the sea. She was their shelter by day, and she led them by starlight at night—and she slew the pursuing Egyptians. Sophia brings salvation that is full of power—power for me to share, strength for me to use. Because she is strong, so is it possible for me to be strong." The image of the dome reframed Cady's anxiety about potentially falling out of her tradition into seeing her Methodist faith as being contained within something bigger and grander, something that invited exploration. It affirmed the wonder, not the fright of being on the edge of her tradition. It was a hopeful perspective, which allowed her to see new possibilities in her Christian faith.

After this sermon, Cady and Taussig began teaching and preaching on Sophia when Sophia Wisdom texts appeared in the Sunday scripture readings. They viewed their Sophia work as a pastoral response to the currents of change that were running through their congregation because of the women's movement. Their approach moved debate around women's roles and women's rights in the parish away from the temporal, earthly, and political realm to the eternal scriptural realm. They were going to God's Word to support the entire congregation in embracing new understandings about life. For Cady and Taussig as pastors, the biblical figure of Sophia was a touchstone for those wanting to see more equality for women and at the same time a corpus of scripture that provided new but firm footing for others who were bewildered by the amount of social and liturgical change happening around them.

This incorporation of feminist spiritual ideas and focus on Sophia was only possible because Cady and Taussig were in leadership positions as pastors. To create the amount of change in the parish that they sought also required motivating others within the parish community to help make it happen. Cady and Taussig found that beginning with the feminist spirituality group was the best way to start, letting the group slowly develop in its relationship with Sophia, and letting the group call some practices of the larger parish community into question. The biblical basis of Sophia was key to providing validation for the larger congregation to listen to the women's concerns.

Ritual played a significant role. In the spring of 1986, the feminist study group had been reading about the close connections between Sophia and Jesus Christ in the New Testament, and the group had been experimenting with placing female imagery as the central character in the life and teachings of Jesus. As Easter was approaching, the group asked Cady to lead alternative Holy Week liturgies, and Cady agreed. The ceremonies did not replace the main liturgical events at the church, as they were scheduled one hour before the main worship occurred, allowing the women the opportunity to participate in both ceremonies. The group developed a foot-washing ceremony in which, instead of Jesus washing the feet of his disciples, "Sophia Washes Her Followers' Feet." There was a Good Friday ceremony, "The Trial and Crucifixion of Sophia"; and for Easter, "A Sophia Resurrection."

Cady's leadership role as a pastor allowed her to create such ritualizing. Without her participation, it would have been impossible for the group to ritualize these understandings as United Methodist Holy Week liturgies. The legitimating presence of her position also elevated the activities of the group and endorsed the new Sophia theology it was exploring.

The result was profound for the participants involved. Cady had shared in her sermon that she and other female pastors felt like spectators watching Jesus, only relating to Jesus through the female characters around him. The members of the feminist spirituality group felt the same. They wanted a ritual to experience what Christ experienced, and making the central character female in these well-known gospel stories brought new meaning and new perspective to the participants. Just as Jesus was the sacrifice to end all sacrifices, Sophia became emblematic of the sacrifices of women. During the Good Friday reenactment of the crucifixion, Sophia stood trial. The group was invited to say things that both women as well as female deities have been accused of throughout the ages. A partial list included:

> You're just a woman . . . you're getting out of hand . . . you don't know your place . . . you participate in witchcraft and the work of the devil . . . you don't have any place in the church . . . you're not as strong or as powerful as the male God . . . you are trying to usurp God's power . . . you are heresy . . . you're a slut . . . you're a cheap broad . . . you're a castrating bitch . . . you're not a real Goddess . . . you're too minor . . . you're not important enough . . . who do you think you are, acting like an equal to God? . . . you're silly and foolish . . . you're evil . . . you're the gateway of the devil . . . God can't be a woman.[10]

For the crucifixion, materials for drawing, painting, and sculpture were provided, and each woman created and shared her art. Most pictures included murder, which might have been expected in relation to the crucifixion narrative, but Cady recalled that almost all the pictures included rape. Afterward, candles were lit, and all were invited to pray as they periodically said names of women who had suffered and died. The evening ended in silence and the candles were blown out. Connecting rape with the crucifixion of Jesus was a powerful act of creative ritual making. The liturgies transformed the histories and tragedies that these women either symbolically or literally endured, from shaming secrets to holy moments.

At Easter, the resurrection was retold as Sophia. In their ceremony, Mary Magdalene encountered the empty tomb, and Sophia instructed her to tell her sisters and brothers the good news. Then the group sat in a circle as the scripture in the upper room was read with Sophia showing her wounds. Continuing on the theme from the night before, names of women who had been wounded were invoked, with the group responding, "We touch your wounds. We rejoice in your presence with us" as they touched each others' hands. The worship continued with a reading of the end of John's gospel with Sophia appearing on the shore, sharing a meal with them, and asking, "Do you love me?" based on John 21:17. The group then meditated on the scripture and was encouraged to use prayer and imagination to experience the gospel story in a new way. The Saturday Easter vigil evening ended with a festive meal.

Years later, when these liturgies appeared in print, some would accuse the group of blasphemy for not imaging God as male and calling him Jesus, but these women saw themselves as following the invitation of the scripture to view God with both genders. They wanted the freedom to experiment, to see what new insights about God and themselves could be called out if they ritualized the passion of Christ with female imagery.

PUBLICIZING SOPHIA

While their work at Calvary continued to develop, Cady and Taussig began to share their Sophia Bible teachings outside the parish. There were many who found the message of a feminine face of God in the Christian tradition inspiring, and their work quickly expanded. As early as 1984, just two years after Cady's sermon, the United Methodist Commission on the Status and Role of Women of the Eastern Pennsylvania Conference invited them to give a workshop on Sophia at Philadelphia's main United Methodist Church on Arch Street. As the chairwoman of the event explained, "It is not sufficient simply to seek to improve the social and professional status of women in the church. We need to see the evolving new roles of women and men in a larger perspective of growing in relationship to the biblical witness. . . . Wisdom/Sophia may be of particular help to women today in finding a way to affirm themselves within their relationship with God and the church."[11]

For the conference, Cady and Taussig invited Marian Ronan, author of *Image-Breaking, Image Building*, to give a response to their talks. Ronan was a staff member of the Grail, a Catholic laywomen's community, and she provided additional insight from her own work on images of God for Christian women. After the conference, Ronan suggested that Cady and Taussig consider writing a book. She arranged for them to meet her publisher, a small, liberal Catholic press.

The publisher suggested making two editions: the first would be on the theology, and the second on the worship and study aid materials. In a fortunate turn of events, before the first edition was complete, the small publisher was bought by Harper & Row, which was contractually obligated to fulfill the existing agreements. This gave their book much more publicity and distribution than they had anticipated. *Sophia: The Future of Feminist Spirituality*, by Susan Cady, Marian Ronan, and Hal Taussig, was published in 1986 by Harper & Row and publicized on its "Academic Announcement List for Oct/Nov/Dec 1986" in the Sociology and Women's Studies section.

The book was described in the Harper & Row press release as "a fascinating study of the biblical figure that could unite feminism and Western religion."[12] *Sophia* appeared along with five other new titles that all celebrated the exceptional histories and contributions of women in a variety of fields. The description of the books gives a snapshot of the subjects, themes, and debates regarding women in 1986 in American publishing. *Hypatia's Heritage: A History of Women in Science from Antiquity through the Nineteenth Century* highlighted "outstanding scientists whose names have been left out of the history books." *Jaguar Woman: And the Wisdom of the Butterfly* "celebrates the crucial role of women in Indian society." *The Economic Emergence of Women* illuminated "the economic and social origins of women's new roles, including changes in the job structure and technology, birth and divorce rates, education and ideas about sex roles and the family." *Women's Way of Knowing: The Development of Self, Voice, and Mind* was about women who "struggle to be heard in schools and families that value neither a woman's voice nor her ideas." *Psyche as Hero: Female Heroism and Fictional Form* expounded on "woman as hero (autonomous initiator of change), rather than heroine (assistant to male hero)."

These themes reflected popular and academic interest in women's new roles. The small cluster of new books also reflected the beginnings of gender analysis before it was widely recognized that race and class were entwined with gender. The economics book privileged gender over class, with no mention of race in its description. The book written about American Indian culture placed the white author, Lynn Andrews, as the protagonist in the narrative. Even the book on historical scientists reflected the focus on privileged women who had been "exceptional" in their fields. Like *Sophia*, all the books assumed that gender was a binary of male and female and that the ideal woman was an independent autonomous individual, equal to and as capable as men in all actions.

When *Sophia* was published, Cady and Taussig hosted a party and invited their bishop and his cabinet, along with many of their colleagues in ministry. The response was positive. Their supervisor, Superintendent Arthur Bradenburg, wrote a glowing review for the *United Methodist Reporter for Eastern Pennsylvania*, echoing the perception of gender as the prime liberation movement and tying the book in with the famous Christ/Christa crucifix controversy that was occurring at the time:

> Recently a crucifix with a crucified female figure was displayed in New York's Cathedral of St. John the Divine, long known for its avant-garde experiments in theology and liturgy. Cries went up, special meetings were called, and the female crucifix went down. Somehow I have a feeling that incident is a key to this astonishing little book . . . Patriarchy is that interlocking system of oppression—racial, sexual, political and economic—which aims to subjugate and control the earth, the poor, females, people of color, feeling and spontaneity. Patriarchal spirituality is the extension of that into our hearts and minds. The emerging feminist spirituality movement may be the most powerful liberation movement of the twentieth century. It cuts across all the other liberation movements and calls into question the basic patriarchal assumptions of Western civilization and at least three of the world's religions: Judaism, Christianity, and Islam. Cady, Ronan, and Taussig argue that the feminist movement will be a saving dynamic for the post modern world only to the extent it finds a set of myths and symbols which enable it to ground itself in the Ultimate Reality."[13]

This expansive view of Sophia, not just as a remedy to combat sexism, but as a way to deconstruct all social inequalities, would continue to be echoed in other reviews at the time along with the call for new images of God. The image of Sophia, however, blurred the distinction between Christian and Goddess groups, which often benefited from clear demarcations between the two. Some reviewers expressed uneasiness in co-locating Goddess imagery within Christianity. This critique came not just from Christian sources, but from the growing Goddess movement as well.[14]

After the book came out, interest in Sophia grew beyond Calvary United Methodist Church. Cady and Taussig helped form a Philadelphia Sophia Group that met in people's homes for ritual, prayer, and fellowship. Eventually, Taussig, Cady, and two others also formed Sophia House, offering courses and retreats on Sophia designed for both college and retreat settings that led to more ecumenical collaborations. An order of Roman Catholic nuns, the Daughters of Wisdom, invited Cady to speak to them about the biblical origins of their namesake. For years afterward, the predominantly Methodist Philadelphia Sophia Group would go on joint retreats with a small group of sisters from the Daughters of Wisdom to explore their shared understanding of Sophia.

THE BACKLASH BEGINS

In 1987, one year after *Sophia* was published, Cady was reassigned to be pastor of Emmanuel United Methodist Church, a small, predominantly white, working-class congregation in Roxborough, a section of Philadelphia where many families had multigenerational roots in the neighborhood. In a congregation that valued tradition and stability, Cady represented change. Not only was she the church's first female pastor, but she was also the first female clergy to serve in any church in that section of the city. The following year, Cady would also become the parish's first divorced pastor, and many in the congregation struggled to accept her divorce. In addition, the top position in the Eastern Pennsylvania Conference, which covered half of the state of Pennsylvania, was now held by a woman, Bishop Susan Morrison.

Yet for all of the challenges around women's leadership in the church, there was little initial resistance to Susan Cady's authoring a book on Sophia. She told the lay leadership team about the book when she arrived, and there were minimal questions or comments. Cady did not start a parish group around Sophia when she saw it did not serve a pastoral need, though she continued her activities with Sophia House and the Philadelphia Sophia group outside the parish. Then a new edition of the book titled *Wisdom's Feast: Sophia in Study and Celebration* was published. This edition included more than fifty worship and instructional aids, including sermons, Bible studies, rituals (including the Sophia Passion), hymns, retreat formats, and formation of Sophia circles. The book also included advice on how to successfully develop and integrate Sophia awareness and worship into a parish setting. The overall message was that introducing a new theology took time, pastoral preparation, and care, particularly when introducing new images of God based on scriptural references that were not well known. These words of caution were prescient for what happened next.

Up to this point, publicity about Sophia gatherings, retreats, and coursework, even the first edition of Cady and Taussig's book, seemed to have received positive feedback in the church, mostly from friends within the Eastern Pennsylvania Conference. The fact that their superintendent and their bishop supported their work gave them significant institutional support to explore Sophia theology in ritual. At the same time, Cady and Taussig were now doing most of their Sophia work in voluntary gatherings outside parish structures. Cady's decision not to form a Sophia group at her new parish may have been a wise pastoral decision, but soon she could not keep her Sophia work outside the parish separate from her life as a church pastor.

On February 19, 1989, the front page of the Sunday edition of the *Philadelphia Inquirer* featured an article titled "Women creating ritual to fill religious void." There was a picture of Cady, Taussig, and two others watching a woman in the foreground lifting a potted plant over her head in a residential setting. A second picture on an inside page showed the five seated in front of a table set with candles, challah bread, wine, and dishes, with a caption below indicating that they were "singing their own hymn." Cady was quoted in the article as saying that women's ritual was "very personal, and almost always includes at least an invitation to sharing and storytelling."[15] The article described this as a movement of "religious feminists," some who made these alternative liturgies their only form of worship, while others attended them in addition to regular church services.[16]

Eric M. Umile, a white male lay leader of the Roxborough Emmanuel United Methodist congregation, read the article and was shocked to see that his Methodist pastor was engaged in such activity. He accused Cady of heresy, but he got little support from the rest of the congregation. In fact, the parish, which had openly struggled with her divorce, was now coming to her defense.

Frustrated, Umile began to write letters. He wrote Cady's superintendent, bishop, and finally the president of the national United Methodist Council of Bishops, but no action was taken. Next, he wrote to the *United Methodist Reporter* newspaper. His article was published on October 6, 1989, in the series *Here I Stand* under the title "Why silence about heresy?" There was a picture of the cover of the book *Wisdom's*

Feast, which had been published just a month before, along with the subhead "Mainstream the goddess?" His writing would provide the core narrative of the anti-Sophia material generated within United Methodism over the next three years:

> The *Philadelphia Inquirer* ran a front page story earlier this year on "feminist spirituality." Bread, milk, fruit, and a potted plant were used in place of the traditional Eucharistic elements of bread and wine. Among the celebrants were two United Methodist pastors, who along with a third, have co-written a book, recently released in paperback, which maintains that a goddess named Sophia is at the heart of the Judeo-Christian religious tradition . . . In fact, it tells us that she and God were lovers and created the world together. Moreover, it says that Jesus was not the Messiah, but actually the incarnation of the divine Sophia herself. The authors regard patriarchy as a "demonic aspect of classical Western spirituality." In their view, Christianity is patriarchal in spirit and, hence, unacceptable and dangerous to the feminist cause. They say the reason we know nothing about Sophia is because male-dominated religious institutions have deliberately ignored and suppressed her since the early days of Christianity. Consequently, the authors feel that their main task is to "mainstream the goddess" into the lives of all women. In fact, they tell us that some religious feminists are conducting experimental worship services that involve such things as substituting Sophia in place of Jesus in the Easter account. One church leader has told me that our church is blessed in its "diversity and openness to new theological perspectives." Does that mean that we should sit passively by while self-seeking special-interest groups infiltrate our churches and play fast and loose with the religious symbols that we hold sacred? . . . That professed Christians including our top church leaders are choosing to be silent when confronted with heresy in their very midst is portent of the dark future that awaits this denomination. I pray that people will come to their senses before the walls come tumbling down.[17]

When the article appeared, Cady was shocked that the editors had allowed the *Here I Am* column, which published personal accounts of Methodists and their faith, to be a place for tearing down the faith position of another Methodist. Taussig, for his part, photocopied the article and typed in the inaccuracies and half-truths he found: "Very few of the texts dwell on the love affair between Sophia and the Lord of All . . . She is mainly pictured as the lover of human beings . . . There was practically no way that the early churches could say that Jesus was not the Messiah."[18]

A significant point of debate was whether Christianity had been corrupted by the human overlay of patriarchy, as Christian feminists surmised, or whether Christian patriarchy had been given by God as a significant and unapologetic part of the tradition, as Umile and others claimed. Taussig found Umile's short editorial to be an expression of his anxiety around a range of issues that Taussig saw as interconnected: feminism, sexuality, sacredness of symbols, diversity of voices, and denominational boundaries.[19] All of these themes were points of change that, taken together, appeared to be disrupting Umile's sense of holy patriarchy.

Cady and Taussig's supporters, inside and outside the church, rallied to lend their support, writing letters to the editor of the same newspaper and providing positive book reviews of *Wisdom's Feast*.[20] Umile's reaction to their work convinced Cady and Taussig that their ministry of Sophia was needed more than ever. Their new Sophia House brochure described a place "where women and men can celebrate and integrate the spiritual dimension of feminism."[21] Their legitimacy and positional power as ordained Christian ministers helped them to expand their work. There was enough interest and resources that a quarterly newsletter was added to complement the monthly study meetings and workshops they were holding.

Bishop Susan Morrison was not deterred by Umile's complaints either. In March 1990, she had the opportunity to make her first appointment to one of the most prestigious churches in her conference, Arch Street United Methodist Church. Located on the historic and exclusive Rittenhouse Square in the heart of Philadelphia, she chose to appoint Cady to be its new associate pastor. Without responding to the controversy, the bishop's placement of Cady communicated her position.

Umile responded by forming the Lay Coalition for Doctrinal Integrity. The title gave an impression of a much larger group than the two couples listed as founding members. Proceeding on his own crusade, Umile sent a letter to all 600 parish lay leaders of the Eastern Pennsylvania Conference, encouraging each to "[p]in your pastor down and find out what his or her position is." He asked for signatures to an attached petition stating that the signed were aware of *Wisdom's Feast* and believed the theology incompatible with orthodox Christianity in general and with beliefs and practices of UMC in particular. During this time, Umile and his wife left Emmanuel parish. They joined another parish whose pastor shared their views.

Upon their arrival, Rev. Paul Beck issued a letter urging his parishioners to contact Bishop Morrison regarding *Wisdom's Feast*, characterizing it as "pagan" and inviting them to reaffirm their commitment to Jesus Christ, not Sophia. This anti-pagan framing would appear in subsequent issues of the UMC Huntington newsletter, where *Wisdom's Feast* would be continually attacked. "We must not allow pagan idolatry to be given equal footing with Christian doctrine."[22]

TAKING SIDES AND GOING NATIONAL

As the debate heated up, the Eastern Pennsylvania Annual Conference, where ordained and lay leadership would meet to discuss and vote on issues, was quickly approaching in June. The Sophia controversy was well known by then. Both sides scheduled worship services to spiritually affirm their positions. Supporters of Cady and Taussig organized a worship service on June 8, 1990, the eve of the conference, in which participants were invited to show their support for Cady and Taussig by bringing objects to "empower and encourage them." Even though the UMC bishop and council were solidly on Cady and Taussig's side, the controversy had obviously taken a toll on the group. The gospel reading was about Mary Magdalene and the other women witnessing the empty tomb yet being rebuffed by the male apostles. Later in the liturgy, the worship leader read a statement that reflected the frustration and weariness of those who were the vanguards for bringing feminist reform into United Methodist worship:

> The hearts of the leadership of Jesus' followers had turned to stone. The hearts of the women were heavy as stone because nobody would believe them, stone cold, stone deaf, stonewalled. Words that are all too familiar to us. Words that break our hearts. Words that break our spirits. Words well known to women and men who are witnesses to something coming to new life. Words that create immovable, stone cold obstacles at every turn. Stones are the tests of believers. Do

> we believe our Mother-Father God can so empower us and give us courage that we can roll away any stone?[23]

The reality of being at the center of such a controversy was now a burden for Cady, Taussig, and their supporters. In contrast, the Jesus Christ is Lord (JCIL) Task Force was happy to report that three hundred people attended their rally of support. Their service held before the conference was titled "Jesus Christ is Lord," with only male pastors officiating and music provided by the all-male Huntington Valley Boys choir.[24] During the conference, study and discussion groups met regarding Sophia, but no official resolutions or actions regarding Sophia teachings were passed.

Undeterred, Eric Umile's efforts soon found national support. His complaints were picked up and broadcast nationally by the conservative, evangelical United Methodist magazine *Good News*. The July/August 1990 cover simply read in bold letters: WHO IS SOPHIA? AND WHY ARE SO MANY UNITED METHODISTS WORSHIPPING HER? Inside was a six-page article titled "Wisdom's Feast or Gospel's Famine? The brewing storm over Sophia Worship." The article recounted Eric Umile reading the *Philadelphia Inquirer* article and chronicled his struggles to stop Sophia theology in the United Methodist Church. The author of the article felt that integrating feminist theology into church ritual was particularly threatening. "These books synthesize Sophia scholarship and offer it to the common person. Suddenly it's not just speculation at some seminary; it's something you can try in a church Bible study." The author of the article acknowledged what Cady and Taussig had already realized: that Cady in particular was being targeted. "It is unfortunate that Cady has borne the brunt of most of this controversy. She is actually the most conservative of the three authors."[25] Yet editor James V. Heidinger II did not hold back his personal attacks. He wrote that Cady's sermon acknowledging her discomfort with celebrating the experience of "some man" reflected "unhealthy, if not seriously affected, attitudes toward the male gender."[26]

This criticism of Cady as an angry, prideful woman in theological crisis was echoed in a 1990 Christmas petition titled "An Open Letter about Our Common Crisis of Faith as United Methodists." Signed by forty-four laity including Umile, the letter also questioned her sexual identity. "If a personal crisis of sexual identity began this crisis of faith . . ."[27] The sexual innuendos were well known; Taussig had heard male pastors derisively call Cady a lesbian. This allowed critics to bring up homosexuality, another issue being contested in the church at the time.

Cady was being cast as norm breaker: breaking the sanctity of marriage through her divorce, preaching on scripture in abnormal and heretical ways, and challenging the tradition of an exclusively male clergy to lead the United Methodist flock. Calling her a lesbian in this context just added to her offenses. It was character assassination.

The names Cady was called and the boundary-breaking improprieties she was accused of committing characterized her as a heretical woman, a tradition that had ancient roots. In the same year Cady was enduring these personal attacks, *Harvard Theological Review* published the article "The Heretical Woman as Symbol in Alexander, Athanasius, and Jerome." It described the symbolic figure of the heretical woman described by early church fathers:

> The fourth-century figure of the heretical woman, who is almost invariably identified as sexually promiscuous, expresses the threatening image of a community with uncontrolled boundaries. Just as she allows herself to be penetrated sexually by strange men, so too she listens indiscriminately and babbles forth new theological formulations carelessly and without restraint: all the gateways of her body are unguarded. She furthermore ignores both woman's physical restriction to the private sphere and her corresponding social subordination to the public sphere of men; the heretical woman is a wanderer—a "gadabout," as English translations of ancient texts—she is notoriously indifferent to the authority of her male superiors. The figure of the orthodox virgin is the counterpoint to this figure of the heretical woman.[28]

Cady's actions—speaking out as a Methodist pastor, standing on the altar, expressing new theological understandings, replacing male images of God with female ones, and then publicizing this through writings and workshops—fit neatly into this old trope. The female body itself had become a symbol for church boundaries.

Because of these personal attacks, Cady and Taussig decided that Taussig would be the primary speaker to defend and explain the book in public. Some opportunities were educational. In January 1991, Taussig and Claudia Camp presented on Sophia at the Annual Conference's continuing education for clergy. The presentation occurred without incident, while other engagements were more contentious. In March 1991, a mandated theological forum in the Eastern Pennsylvania Conference took place where Sophia was the major topic of discussion. Taussig prepared a paper, as did John N. Oswalt, professor of Old Testament and Semitic Languages from Asbury Theological Seminary, who had written a twenty-one-page critique of *Wisdom's Feast.* Oswalt acknowledged the mistreatment of women by men in the Abrahamic "religions of continuity," but objected to Sophia as a remedy; only a transcendent God, not an "alien" Sophia-God, could make things right. JCIL was very active, hosting pre-forum rallies and recruiting forum audiences to make its dissatisfaction known during the debate.

In April, JCIL published its first newsletter, produced on a typewriter with the heading "Jesus Christ is Lord!" written in marker across the top. The newsletter explained that the purpose of JCIL was to protest *Wisdom's Feast*, which "teaches the existence of a female goddess, Sophia, who is present at creation, makes all things new, is a co-creator with God, a heavenly queen and God's lover."[29] JCIL listed four officers including Eric Umile. Showing the level of coordinated effort the group was putting into protesting *Wisdom's Feast* and its authors, JCIL had formed five committees to advance its cause, each with a specific mission. The research committee documented the spread of Sophia doctrine and contacted bishops of other annual conferences. The search committee identified potential delegates for voting church positions who would stand firm in JCIL convictions. The apportionment committee recommended that churches withhold their September monthly apportionment and send it one month late, informing bishops and others of their stand against "Sophia the Goddess" as well as their objection to promoting any pastors and teachers who supported Sophia theology. JCIL also formed a Communications Committee to mail the newsletter to every United Methodist lay leader, superintendent, and bishop nationally. The Resolutions committee was to design resolutions for the annual conference that would forward its aims.

At the 1991 June annual conference, Cady and Taussig hosted a question and answer forum on Sophia. A coalition of the Daughters of Wisdom Catholic nuns also came to show support for Cady and Taussig and hosted a session to express support of Sophia theology. Both events were well attended. Sophia supporters had a display table with a video and printed material explaining their religious views. JCIL also had a display table with information. Meanwhile, JCIL received a boost from the western side of the state. In an article in the Pittsburgh Press, the headline read "Methodists to probe heresy allegations against bishop." It reported that during the Western Pennsylvania Annual Conference, a resolution had been submitted to investigate alleged heresy in *Wisdom's Feast* and Bishop Morrison's response to it.

Taking its complaints to a national level, JCIL partnered with its western Pennsylvania allies to create a petition at the 1992 United Methodist General Conference, asking that a task force be appointed to study Sophia theology and determine if it was compatible with United Methodist doctrine. Upon review, the Faith and Missions Committee recommended that the petition be rejected, as the claims were "ridiculous," with not enough information provided. The General Conference defeated the proposal 621 to 290, but JCIL was heartened that it had received substantial support. This national vote showed that while JCIL was not a majority opinion among the United Methodist leadership, it was not a small remnant group, either. Umile had accomplished quite a lot in a short amount of time.

These formal votes also reflected a larger debate occurring within United Methodism at the time regarding what the vision of the church should be and what theology would undergird it, as well as who would get to lead the denomination as a result. To have the western and eastern Pennsylvania bishops represent such different views showed how this schism reached into the top leadership of the church. The United Methodist polity allowed such divergent views to be present within the denomination because of the relatively autonomous power bishops had over their own conferences. At the same time, as attacks against Bishop Susan Morris by other bishops increased, those underneath her became emboldened to attack her leadership as well.

THE FORMAL CHARGE OF HERESY

On January 4, 1993, a recently ordained junior clergyman in the Eastern Pennsylvania Conference took up the banner to attack *Wisdom's Feast* and challenge his own bishop. He filed a seventy-four-page grievance with Bishop Morrison against Cady and Taussig for heresy.[30] The stakes were high. If approved, Cady and Taussig would be stripped of their ordination and lose their jobs. This initial grievance was dismissed by Bishop Morrison, but Cady and Taussig continued to feel the wrath of the conservative wing of the United Methodist church.

In March 1993, Cady was invited to Drew Theological Seminary to deliver a lecture on Sophia and to lead a communion service using Wisdom scripture. A male minister and faculty member at Drew attended the worship service and wrote a disparaging article published by *Christianity Today* titled "Encountering the Goddess at Church."[31] That October, the same junior clergyman who had filed the grievance against Cady and Taussig filed another grievance with the United Council of Bishops against his own bishop, Susan Morrison, for not disciplining Susan Cady for her actions at Drew. That was also dismissed, but the fact that a junior clergyman felt emboldened to file a grievance against his own bishop showed the extent to which Morrison's authority as a female bishop was being undermined and challenged.

A WIDER BACKLASH AT THE 1993 RE-IMAGINING CONFERENCE

Then an event occurred in 1993 that moved the focus off Cady and Taussig personally but heightened the Sophia controversy nationally and broadcast it to a much larger audience. It began with an event in Minneapolis in November 1993 called the Re-Imagining Conference. The conference had grown out of an initiative by the Geneva, Switzerland–based World Council of Churches (WCC), one of the largest ecumenical organizations in the world, in which the United Methodist Church held membership. In 1988, the WCC launched a ten-year program titled "Ecumenical Decade of the Churches in Solidarity with Women." The program aimed to provide a framework within which member churches could reflect on women's lives in society and stand in solidarity with them as well as examine their own church teachings, structures, and practices with a commitment to full participation of women.

For its part, the North American leadership of WCC Ecumenical Decade of the Churches in Solidarity with Women decided to host a conference to celebrate the midpoint of the decade. A national Re-Imagining conference was held in Minneapolis on November 4–7, 1993. The Presbyterian Church USA had the highest attendance, with 409 of the 2,200 mostly female attendees, but the next largest group was United Methodist with 391 attendees, including 36 United Methodist directors of staff.[32] Neither Cady nor Taussig attended the conference, though Bishop Susan Morrison did.

During the conference, feminist theology was central to many of the sessions, and Sophia was included in some rituals as an example of reimagining God. Conference organizers would later remark that their intention was to create a safe place to explore new images, language, and thoughts about Christianity in light of women's experience, as this was the WCC initiative. Unknown to them, a few reporters from conservative Christian journals were also in attendance to monitor and publicize what they found disturbing and heretical. Susan Cyre, writing for *Christianity Today*, critiqued many aspects of the event, including when attendees blessed, thanked, and praised Sophia using milk and honey. "Sophia, we celebrate the nourishment of your milk and honey . . . at the banquet table of Creation." In response, Cyre said, clergy and laity of the United Methodist Church, Presbyterian Church USA, Evangelical Lutheran Church of America, and American Baptist Church were galvanized to protest participation by their denominations.

As we will see in the other cases, Christian denominations that allowed women to serve as ordained clergy still had members who resented that decision. These conservative coalitions were now regrouping and seeking other ways to voice their protest and stem the tide of change in their churches. Because they had lost the fight over women's ordination, they now sought to stop emplacement of new theological understandings regarding female imagery on the altar.

Cyre succeeded in generating controversy. On May 24, the Re-Imagining conference became the topic of ABC's *Nightline*. The segment opened with the voice-over introduction, "In many of America's mainline Protestant churches, a holy war is raging over a feminist movement to rethink not only masculine concepts of God, but bedrock Christian doctrine."[33] Ted Koppel interviewed feminist theologian and conference speaker Rita Nakashima Brock as well as Susan Cyre. Koppel asked if they thought the event could lead to schism in the churches. Brock affirmed the right of women to remain and contribute to the changing understandings in the church, while Cyre's position was that women who could not accept the orthodoxy of the church should not belong. UPI Radio covered the event on May 13, and the *MacNeil/Lehrer NewsHour* ran a segment on June 16, 1993, as well.

The controversy surrounding the conference revealed how contestations over power were being played out on the ritual stage. The more extreme the rhetoric became, such as "splitting the denominations," the more media attention it received. As media scholars Hoover and Clark pointed out in their analysis of this event, only when conservatives who were fighting to regain positional power within their denominations could cast the issue into its widest, most dire possible consequence did the event become newsworthy. It became what ritual scholar Victor Turner termed "social drama." Instead of being a weekend of experimental worship exploration, the event was characterized as a showdown between "Christian versus pagan" and "orthodox versus heresy."

A high proportion of women in attendance held staff positions in newly created women's ministry offices. There were also ordained female ministers and even female bishops in attendance. The controversy was a bonanza for the conservative wing of the churches represented. Casting the Re-Imagining rituals as a "breach" of tradition and theology could remove these women from their jobs or at least compromise their work, and the effort of the conservative coalition was successful. As a result of the national coverage of the "controversy," many women who attended the event were fired from their church positions.[34] Because Cady and Taussig had not attended, they were not involved, but Bishop Morrison and the Women's Division of the Board of Global Ministries for the United Methodist Church were targeted.

The *Good News* organization played a major role in trying to shut down or severely weaken United Methodist women's leadership. One month after the event, all United Methodist bishops received a letter from *Good News* editor James V. Heidinger III stating that the Women's Division of the Board of Global Ministries had "betrayed the trust with United Methodist women and should rightly disavow the radical substance of the conference and apologize to the church for supporting such an event."[35] In the January/February issue of *Good News*, Heidinger called the conference "the most disturbing news story we have ever published . . . the most theologically aberrant I have ever read about, far removed from the Christian tradition." In a show of financial and political might, the magazine was then mailed out to every pastor and lay leader of every United Methodist congregation in the entire United States.

Because the *Good News* organization represented an unabashedly conservative voice within United Methodism, few were surprised that they would object to the conference, but when the more neutral *United Methodist Reporter* began to participate, many became concerned.[36] During January and February, at least fifteen articles and editorials weighed in on the event with a variety of perspectives. The newspaper's own editorial weighed in, calling Sophia a "centuries-old idol with a fresh coat of paint" and directing the reader to an accompanying article on Gnosticism.

The result of the negative publicity and the ongoing debate forced the United Methodist Women's Ministry as well as Bishop Morrison into defensive positions, requiring them to justify their participation. The Women's Ministry took a contrite stance and produced a fact sheet in January 1994 that highlighted the limits of its participation in the event.[37] In February 1994, Bishop Morrison and eight other Methodist clergywomen issued a bolder response. From their statement titled "A Time of Hope—A Time of Threat":

> This is a time of hope. The partnership of women and men in the United Methodist Church is growing—in the Council of Bishops, in Annual Conferences, in local congregations, and in theological schools. Christian community and sharing of leadership are broadening across racial and ethnic lines. Globally, the voices of women are being heard, and cooperation among Christian women increases denominationally and ecumenically. In theological books, sermons, and liturgies, women are singing a new song.
>
> But this is also a time of threat. Hostility toward outspoken, creative, and courageous women of faith is not new, but it is now more sharply focused. Public attacks on the leadership, theology and funding of a recent conference call us to speak out. We are convinced that people frightened by fresh theological insights and by challenges to narrow orthodoxy are attempting to discredit and malign women. Constructive dialog is welcome, but irrational and distorted attacks increase an environment of violence against women.
>
> For years the United Methodist Church has been divided by controversy over the leadership of women, reproductive rights, inclusive language, and homosexuality. As women have addressed these issues, the clash of theological perspectives has intensified. At the heart of the conflict are diverse images of God, the meaning of a multi-racial, multi-cultural church, ecumenical commitment, equal participation of women, and the dynamics of control and power. What is at stake is who will name these issues, how these issues will be described, and who will set the agenda for the future of the church.
>
> We are clear that the verbal attacks on the Re-Imagining Conference in Minneapolis (November, 1993) are not isolated. While some naysayers have rushed to judgment on the basis of hearsay, others appear to be part of an ongoing design to split and weaken the United Methodist Church. . . . The use of the term "heresy" in our time, may be a way of refusing to hear the voices of those who have been marginalized in

> the life of the church. Today theological minds explore a whole range of issues, including the biblical meaning of God's Wisdom, Sophia (like God's Word, Logos). Similarly, in light of social experience, such as slavery and female sexual abuse, understandings of sacrifice, atonement, and martyrdom are being examined . . . Today's "reformation" holds the potential for life-giving renewal in the United Methodist Church and in the hearts and lives of women and men alike. We, the undersigned women, loyal and committed to the United Methodist Church, call on all sisters and brothers to join us in celebrating and living this movement of the Holy Spirit.[38]

By March 8, 1994, the names of 814 United Methodist women from across the United States supported the statement by adding their names. On March 11, 1994, Susan Morrison used her column "From the Bishop" in the *United Methodist Reporter for Eastern Pennsylvania* to reflect on the experience. "I have watched the growing controversy over the ecumenical event called "Re-Imagining" with astonishment and dismay . . . When over 2000 women and men gather from around the world plus a huge waiting list, it indicates there is a need that hasn't been met through traditional gatherings. Are we willing to ask the question, 'Why?' "

She identified two larger issues. Her first was theological. She believed the church had not created enough opportunities for theological dialogue and that "win-lose" discussions were the result. To that end, she asked for a task force to be put in place to plan events and ways theological debate could occur in the spirit of community. The second revolved around how women were being treated in the church, specifically Susan Cady:

> Another broader issue is the growing attack on women and women in leadership. It is not a coincidence that the major issues [of] the past decade in the church relate to women: inclusive language, reproductive rights, ordination of women. It is not a coincidence that the woman author, Susan Cady, has been much more attacked than has the male author, Hal Taussig, for the book *Wisdom's Feast*. We can sing to God as a mineral ("Rock of Ages," for instance), but we create a crisis when the feminine dimension of God is lifted up. What is it about the feminine that evokes such feelings? What does this say to our sisters, daughters, granddaughters and others?

> Lastly, the hostility and nastiness that has been evoked [by the Re-Imagining controversy] appalls me. The Women's Division has given decades of faithful service and mission, more than any other part of the church. How can we condemn them with such ferociousness for an event they didn't even plan? The character assassination and "negative labeling" of women in leadership who have given their lives in faithful commitment to the church is, in the least, unchristian. Shame on us. We do not reflect the love and grace of God in such actions. We also present an image of the church that no one is going to join.[39]

Morrison ended her column with a hymn used in the closing service at the Re-Imagining Conference praising Christ and God and speaking of the faithful as learners, seekers, and pilgrims.

As a result of the heightened controversy, a resolution was passed at the following General Conference that Sophia theology be investigated. The result was a ten-page report titled "Biblical Wisdom and Current Theological Ferment: Report of the Task Force on the Study of Wisdom, the Council of Bishops (Oct. 31–Nov. 4, 1994)." After years of turmoil and dissent, it all came down to this theological judgment, and the theological ruling supported Cady and Taussig's work.

The Council of Bishops task force endorsed the expression of female images of God as well as the importance of the wisdom tradition in Christianity. The task force concluded, "Feminine images for the expression of the fullness of God have both biblical and historical precedent and appropriateness." The task force also aligned Jesus with the wisdom tradition. "Jesus' teaching in the Gospels is in the form of the wisdom tradition more than the prophetic style." Finally, in regard to Sophia, the task force affirmed her place in the Christian faith. "Woman Wisdom is best considered to be a personification of an attribute of God and not a goddess or a being with separate existence from God."[40] Once this national bishop's theological inquiry ruled that Sophia theology was within the Methodist tradition, the controversy surrounding Cady and Taussig abated, and the heresy charges against them were dismissed.

It had been a long decade. In 1996, a ten-year anniversary edition of *Wisdom's Feast* was published. In the preface, the authors reflected on the controversy that had ensued since the first edition was released. Overall, they believed that the lashing out against *Wisdom's Feast* and the harsh treatment Susan Cady and Bishop Susan Morrison had received was, at its root, a reaction to the ordination of women. They also believed that the United Methodist process of bishops appointing pastors to churches rather than congregations choosing their local leadership also intensified the debate.

CONCLUSION

Many women of Susan Cady's generation experienced sexism in their churches during this era, but Cady's experiences were particularly dramatic. She grew up being told that women could not be priests when in fact her denomination allowed it. When she attended seminary, she received little professorial encouragement to explore feminine themes in the Bible. As an associate pastor, she was not invited by families to baptize their babies. When she was pastor of her own parish, she was eviscerated by one of her male parishioners in a national campaign. Finally, she was brought up on heresy charges by a junior male colleague.

For Cady, discovering and celebrating female imagery of God early in her ministry work gave her courage, passion, and purpose in spite of this treatment. Many also supported her when others tried to tear her down, and she benefited from being institutionally supported and protected by a committed group of colleagues and superiors. For Cady, speaking and ritualizing Sophia was a significant ministry for her as a young pastor. Only when she experienced God as the female Sophia did her connection to her Christian faith life become reenergized with creativity and momentum.

Many women and men demonstrated a renewed commitment to their faith during this era, even as they sought changes to improve gender equality in their churches. The picture of femaleness put forth in the Sophia rituals and sermons paralleled the gender claims in much of the women's movement that women were as capable as men to serve in public leadership roles. Sophia scripture gave biblical endorsement of this view.

Cady's leadership as an ordained pastor and ritual specialist gave her a way to create ritual and enliven the voices that were speaking out. Having the institutional positional power to direct and lead ritual was a critical piece of the strategic emplacement of Sophia on the altar. Cady could not have advanced feminist theology onto the altar without women's ordination. Religious studies scholar Richard D. Hecht concurs.

"Certainly place directs attention, but the rights to space are prerequisites to the rites that are focused in the lens of place . . . To take place requires the *right* to take place."[41]

I would also add "rights require rites." Cady had the right to be the pastor, but she was still slighted by congregation and colleagues alike, and even the traditional rite became a place that affirmed the patriarchal backlash she was experiencing. Sophia ritual became her protest, her claim, and her expression to legitimate both her femaleness and her authority on the altar. This insight has been echoed by others studying feminist ritualizing.[42] Catherine Bell explains: "As the symbolic equivalent of the right to vote and receive equal pay, such writers see the "right to ritual" as the appropriation of the power to define, mobilize, and nuance the images that shape their lived reality."[43]

Cady and Taussig explained in my conversations with them in 2008 that they found it unfortunate that Sophia theology had been stopped long before it had the opportunity to fully develop. Cady recalled that in the beginning, there was hope in the eyes of regular, good-hearted Methodist women as they heard about Sophia. As the years progressed, however, she noticed that they felt less and less safe to explore Sophia in their prayer life. The second book Cady never had the chance to write was on Sophia for these regular churchwomen. She noted that while the theological inquiry had ruled in their favor, the conservative element of the church may have won, making it too controversial and too dangerous for people, particularly women, to explore divine female images within mainstream United Methodism. Cady enjoys her ministry work now as a spiritual director and retreat leader where she can affirm people in exploring their changing images of God as a form of God-dialogue that can be probed for deeper connections to their faith, rather than being judged as heresy or crisis.

Taussig has continued working on Sophia scripture as a biblical scholar. He has published and participated in ongoing biblical debates that are now more than twenty years old on whether Sophia was meant to be a liberating agent for the Israelites or an extension of the patriarchal priestly class. He believes both to be true, varying by book. His seminary students now find the female Sophia who incarnates in the male Jesus to be a rich scriptural vein for exploring queer theology in the Bible. He enjoys being invited to join them on this next frontier.

Because little Sophia ritualizing can be seen on church altars today, we might think that it has rarely been attempted, but this chapter suggests that is not the case. If the study of women's religious history focuses only on the largest surviving trends, we will be gazing only at one set of stories. Only through recording exceptional histories such as these can we see the underside of religious political power plays around gender and understand the histories of what was lost. Learning where people struggled to ritualize new understandings of God gives us a glimpse into the diversity of expressions Christian churches might include today had more won the right to "rite" the wrongs of church and society.

Let us now turn our attention to the Daughters of Wisdom, an order of Catholic nuns who became friends with Cady and Taussig as a result of *Wisdom's Feast* and developed their own trajectory with Sophia Wisdom.

2

The Resource of Personal Prayer Experience

Daughters of Wisdom Catholic Sisters

> To fix one's thought on her is perfect understanding, and one who is vigilant on her account will soon be free from care, because she goes about seeking those worthy of her, and she graciously appears to them in their paths, and meets them in every thought.
>
> —Wisdom of Solomon 6:15–16

I met the Daughters of Wisdom in Litchfield, Connecticut, while playing cello at a local sacred music event. At the end of the performance, a woman with a big smile and salt-and-pepper hair came up to me. "We liked your music, but we really heard your prayer! We are Daughters of Wisdom." She pointed across the room, and a handful of older women wearing silver crosses were waving and smiling at me. "Why don't you come by our retreat house? I would be happy to give you a tour."

The next day, we walked the beautiful grounds of the Wisdom House Retreat Center. It was originally a farm estate that later served as the Daughter's novitiate where young sisters-in-training were taught the ways of the order. The sister explained that the Daughters were one of the few religious orders in the Roman Catholic Church to have Wisdom in their title and one of the only to have a mission set by their founder to "acquire Wisdom" as their order's purpose. She personally liked to use *Sophia*, the Greek word for wisdom, because it was also a woman's name, and she was most inspired by Wisdom passages in the Old Testament where Wisdom appears in female form.

As we walked into the chapel, I could see a large statue of a woman mounted on the wall behind the altar as if she were floating in space. Unlike the Protestant communities in this volume, the Catholic Daughters of Wisdom always had female imagery in their religious practice, but historically their attention had been on Mary. Their journey to include Sophia in their prayer life was intriguing to me. As I got to know the order better, the province's leadership team agreed to a formal study but requested that individual sisters not be named in order to protect their privacy. As a result, this chapter is different from the other communities profiled in this book, as only names of founders and past provincials are mentioned. This chapter, like the order itself, is a collection of voices expressing a variety of perspectives and experiences.

The sensitivity to privacy also fits with the theme of this chapter—how female images of the divine have been experienced in the personal prayer lives of the sisters, and how these prayer experiences provide a critical resource for strategic emplacement of female imagery in worship. As the Daughters have described it, a sister's relationship with God is by far her most personal intimate relationship. While Catholic sisters are known for their public ministries, such as schools and hospitals, I was interested in this more personal and equally significant dimension of their lives. The Daughters make time for personal prayer. Today, most Daughters begin their day with a private hour to be with God, and some gather with other sisters for evening prayer. They also listen and watch for God to direct their lives, and they see the world around them as a place where God's presence resides and is expressed. This belief that God's presence can be seen and felt is how they could come to the music concert and "hear my prayer."

In this chapter, we examine how the resource of personal prayer experience has been cultivated and understood during four significant chapters of the order's modern history: before Vatican II, as a result of Vatican II in the mid-1960s, during the exodus of sisters in the 1970s, and during the current rebuilding of the order in the last twenty years. As we will see, exploring their namesake of Wisdom through scripture and their founder's writings has brought the Daughters of Wisdom hope and a renewed sense of purpose. As we will see, personal prayer experiences have been an essential resource for emplacement of Wisdom Sophia in congregational prayers and celebrations.

I have chosen to present the accounts of the Daughters' prayer experiences simply. It is not my intent to explain the source or accuracy of these encounters or the interpretation these women voice about them.

Rather, my point is to show that their worldview includes these prayerful/mystical dimensions and that for them, these experiences are very real, interactive, and profound. Far from being ancillary or peripheral, daily encounters of God's presence as well as more mystical, rarely spoken of "holy moments" have been the touchstones of the Daughters' lives. They are the solid ground on which these women have understood themselves, God, and the world. Whether I believed them or not or whether I would have interpreted their accounts differently or not was not the point. For the Daughters, these experiences are as significant and real as anything that could be empirically measured. My interest has been to place these experiences within the context of their lives and to see how these experiences motivated their choices and actions.

The Daughters of Wisdom Before Vatican II

Perhaps it is not surprising that their founder, Saint Louis de Montfort, also lived his life simply, seeking direct experiences of God's love. Father de Montfort rejected the comfortable life offered a French eighteenth-century priest in order to live among the poor as an iterant preacher. Montfort wrote prayers, composed hymns, and developed devotions to help others experience God's love directly, too, often including female imagery. He is identified with the French School of Spirituality, which flourished during his time and emphasized, among other things, devotions and personal holiness. His most famous work, *True Devotion to Mary*, includes a twenty-eight-day prayer cycle, *Total Consecration to Jesus through Mary*. He established an order for women in 1703 and named it the Daughters of Wisdom. He also founded an order of priests, the Company of Mary, later known as Montfort Missionaries.

Father Montfort charged the Daughters to serve women, children, and the poor as well as to acquire Wisdom. He wrote a document that influenced the development of their order titled *Love of Eternal Wisdom*. In this work, he describes and encourages the seeking of Wisdom, much like King Solomon and others do in the Wisdom literature of the Bible (see the scripture passage at the beginning of this chapter).

The first Daughter of Wisdom, Marie Louise Trichet, spent her first ten years serving and living among the sick in an overcrowded poorhouse hospital in Poitiers, France. Today, she is recognized as the co-foundress of the order, beatified in 1993 by Pope John Paul II. Mother Marie Louise outlived Montfort by forty-three years and grew the Daughters to a substantial size, with thirty-five houses across France mostly devoted to teaching and nursing. During the French Revolution, when all Catholic orders were outlawed, many Daughters were killed. Later, Emperor Napoleon reinstated the order to provide nurses for his troops. When the order was restricted again by nineteenth-century French secularization laws, the Daughters sought to establish themselves outside France as a way to preserve the order.

The work of the Daughters of Wisdom in the United States began in 1904, ministering to French immigrants in St. Agatha, Maine. They would soon start high schools and hospitals in both Maine and New York, along with other supportive ministries. In 1926, an indoor pool for the treatment of polio patients was built at their hospital on Long Island, and St. Charles Hospital became known for innovative rehabilitation techniques gained from the Daughters' global nursing network. Initially, young women from French American families joined the order, but eventually the order attracted young Catholic women from a range of ethnic backgrounds.

Like most Catholic women's religious orders, the Daughters of Wisdom convents until the mid-1960s were strict. Not only were they following dictates from Rome on religious life, but they also had to prove to their leadership in France that American women could abide by rigorous French standards. As was the custom, Catholic religious orders wore the dress and followed the customs of their founders. Mother Marie Louise Trichet in the eighteenth century wore an unwieldy, floor-length gray wool habit and a white headdress that cut off her peripheral vision. Before Vatican II, the US Daughters wore exact replicas of this eighteenth-century dress and ate from pewter bowls with large wooden utensils.

Father Montfort had penned a Rule for the Daughters that was twice as long as the directives and rules he gave the men's order. The Daughters also had a book of Little Customs that instructed them on almost every aspect of their lives, including how to hold their hands. One phrase of the order was "Who sees one Daughter of Wisdom, sees them all." Individuality was minimized and "particular" friendships were discouraged. When Daughters encountered each other in the hallway, they were taught to address each other impersonally: "I greet you good angel."

Holiness was gauged by how perfectly one followed the rules. When the mother superior gave an order, it was to be obeyed without question. If you broke a rule by arriving late or speaking unprompted, you were expected to drop to the floor, admit the fault, and kiss the floor in front of Mother Superior. As one Daughter pointed out, sisters who were administrating schools and hospitals and dealing with life or death situations in their jobs had to ask permission to stay up past their designated bedtime. "Before Vatican II, you were only to think in your profession of teaching or nursing, but in the convent you were expected not to think and do what you were told. The less you thought the better." The vow of obedience reinforced this behavior. As one Daughter described:

> When you entered, the community changed you to fit into this life. Obedience meant never questioning—blind obedience. The poverty part wasn't bad, but blind obedience was different. Those who could keep quiet were the models, interpreted as having meek and humble hearts. It was a closed society—no radio, no TV. That was part of the mystique. Religious women were kept childlike by model. Decisions were made for them—where to live, what to wear, where to go and what to do. All was taken care of. No understanding of adult life, particularly for me because my days were spent teaching children. You did not choose your ministry. There was a kind of caste system—the smartest were made teachers, the next were made nurses and then there were household sisters who cooked, cleaned, and sewed. Your individuality was covered up by your habit and we thought it was wonderful! I was a child when I entered. I went from my mother to a mother superior. I entered at 18 and was teaching by age 20.

The sisters-in-training slept in a large dorm room under a crucifix that read, "Your sole master is Jesus Christ." God was an Almighty Father God who asked vowed religious to find the value in suffering, just as Jesus had suffered for the sake of humankind. Mother Mary was not God but a significant and necessary mitigating agent—a compassionate, loving mother who could hear prayers and even respond to petitions because of her closeness to Jesus and the Father. This gendered view of the heavens reflected prevailing attitudes of an ideal family where the father was in charge and the mother could influence the father based on her closer emotional relationship with the children.

The Daughters spoke of the instruction they were given to abandon themselves totally to God. To make sense of their lives, the ideal was to be selfless, and Mary was held up as their model. Using a consecration written by Montfort, they prayed to be "slaves" of Mary, with no will of their own except to do God's will, just as Mary had at the Annunciation.

In this pre–Vatican II setting, God's will was defined by the church and communicated by the mother superior, who oversaw their work and lives.

Details of their previous convent life made me wonder why anyone stayed, but the Daughters explained that the structure created its own reality. They had been taught that adhering to the rules kept them closer to God. This lifestyle was called "semi-cloistered" and entailed working full-time jobs in the world while maintaining a prayer schedule almost as rigorous as that of cloistered contemplative nuns. The Daughters were in prayer for three and a half hours a day and listened to spiritual readings during all three meals. They spoke freely for only two hours a day while maintaining silence for almost half of every twenty-four-hour cycle. While working as nurses and teachers, they were expected to silently repeat certain prayers every half hour.

Despite this intense focus on prayer, few sisters had particular images of God from this period. I was surprised because the Daughters in the convent had been exposed to techniques that actively engaged their imagination, including spiritual exercises of both St. Ignatius and St. Sulpice. Most Daughters said they received little instruction; what they remembered were sheets of paper to read. Some recalled falling asleep during meditation. When asked about their prayer life, most Daughters recounted the schedules, the rote prayers, and the teachings from the Montfort priests, who taught them using *True Devotion to Mary.* Wisdom was always male because Jesus was Wisdom Incarnate, and Mary was their female intercessor and role model for her total "yes" to God.

Only one Daughter shared a dramatic image with me. I asked her if she had read or seen anything to trigger such an unusual image. She said there was nothing special she could recall because everything was controlled in the convent:

> The Blessed Mother has always been important to me, but I had an experience in novitiate much different from what we were being taught about Mary through *True Devotion.* I had an image of the virgin priest offering the blood and body of her son on the altar. It happened during my first vows and I presented these images to the novice director. Her response was, "I think you should keep that quiet for a long time." Her comment has stayed with me all these years. She did not discount the image, nor instruct me to stop imagining Mary that way. She just wanted me to be private about it, and not even forever. Keeping quiet at the time was wise because I

> probably would have been excommunicated. Did she realize what she was saying? I have no idea, but her words were prophetic for me. I believe I had a glimpse of the mystery we were going to discover later about Sophia, Mary, and Jesus.[1]

For this sister, the vision was something deep, intimate, and ultimately prophetic for a wisdom she would later embrace. Her story also revealed how these experiences were often kept private. Prayer experiences were dangerous when they did not fit neatly into church dogma. This sister was grateful that at least she was not told to deny it, but merely to be silent about it.

This image was perilous because the priest was female. If her image had been of a male priest, there would have been no problem at all. Nor was having a female in the vision a problem; Catholics could interpret female visions as Mary. The problem was that she transgressed gender restrictions as a female officiating on the altar. Even Mary had her place.

Vatican II: Changing Images of God and Religious Life

Then everything changed. In 1962, Pope John XXIII convened the Second Vatican Council, calling all Catholic bishops around the world to Rome to reconsider significant aspects of the Catholic faith. The council met four times between 1962 and 1965. The dramatic changes brought about by the Second Vatican Council cannot be underestimated.[2] These changes included liturgies delivered in the language of the people, increased roles for the laity, and a focus on ecumenism. In the wake of Vatican II, Marian devotional practices declined as Catholics turned to Bible study and social action as ways to know and get close to God.

Many of the Daughters, particularly the younger ones, were excited by the changes. Unlike Mary Daly, who saw the all-male council as a reaffirmation of patriarchal control, the Daughters experienced the Second Vatican Council as initiating extraordinary freedoms and opportunities for them as women religious. Those who were students at the time credited the Daughters who taught them about Vatican II at Wisdom Academy High School as the reason they became Daughters themselves.

Life for vowed religious changed dramatically. One council directive was the call for all religious to renew their orders by going back to their origins and rediscovering their original charisms—their original spiritual call and purpose. Some Daughters felt women religious in the United States took this council directive more seriously than the male orders. It could have been the times. Catholic women's religious orders were being given the opportunity to define themselves in bold new ways as American women more generally were seeking greater voice and self-determination through the women's movement.

The Daughters of Wisdom embraced the change and went from being one of the more conservative religious orders in the United States to one of the more progressive ones in a very short time. Many Daughters credited their mother superior, Mother Mary, with moving the order into the modern age. One sister described the reforms as "catapulting the order twenty years over a three year period." Mother Mary arranged for a priest to teach the Daughters how to study scripture for the first time. For many, these classes were where they learned of Lady Wisdom in the Old Testament. Priests were also brought in to help Daughters begin to question, making it good to question after living in a culture of blind obedience. Why wear the habit in the house? Why call each other "sister"? Many of these questions resulted in reforms that undid much of their way of life. Questions were also sent by their own Daughters of Wisdom general council in Rome for discussion. Mother Mary brought in a psychologist priest to give the sisters someone to talk to as they personally adapted to the changes.

The questioning had both a corporate and individual purpose. On a corporate level, the Daughters were exploring for themselves what it meant to be a Daughter of Wisdom. On an individual level, the Daughters had never been individually asked what they wanted to do in their ministries, and now they could propose new initiatives. Sisters began living in smaller communities of twos and threes to be closer to these new ministries, and many participated in new types of service work. One nursing sister moved into Brooklyn to help train and find work for immigrants, securing housing, teaching English and advocating for immigrant rights. "That is where I first saw Sophia, as hope among the people."[3] After much discussion, the order also voted to wear a modified habit that was more practical, and later to reject the habit altogether in order to be closer to the people they served.

A reorientation to God was also happening for the Daughters as scripture study and higher education were changing how they imagined God and the world. After years of absolute concreteness and certainty, education and study revealed the mystery of God. As one sister explained, "I studied scripture at Manhattanville and learned things I never heard before. My mental picture of God changed. Before it was an all-powerful God Almighty Father. Now I see much more mystery in God, and I am convinced if I can figure it out, it isn't God."[4] They were also given instruction on multiple ways to access God through different meditation and prayer techniques. One sister described taking classes in Zen Buddhist meditation given by a Catholic priest, with "Jesus" as the mantra to chant. Another sister found that prayerful dance helped anchor her religious vocation:

> I entered after the changes started as I had already been instructed in reading scripture during high school and praying more naturally. When I entered, some of the older sisters wondered if I had ever been taught to pray because there wasn't a formula at the end of my prayer. I didn't know the lock-step prayer program they had. During recreation one day, a sister was visiting who did interpretive dance to the Simon and Garfunkel song, "Sounds of Silence." She was wearing the shorter modified habit with black tights. I had never seen dance close-up before nor seen unstructured dance. I was fascinated. I took a portable record player to my room and played "Spirit of God" and created a dance privately. When I mentioned this to another sister, she wanted to see it, so during another recreation I danced even though I was nervous. She recognized that this was a special way for me to pray and encouraged it. I learned that I needed a physical way to pray, particularly because I was struggling with both a desire for marriage and the convent. After high school, I went to Fordham for college and had a boyfriend, but after my first year, I felt an intense need to experience convent life. Now that I was in the novitiate, I was struggling with no marriage, and would cry and cry because it was so hard to put into words. Dance was non-verbal and dancing was the best way for me to express these feelings and make a decision. I remember dancing the Annunciation with another sister. She was the angel and I was Mary. We danced to a song of Mary's fiat, her total acceptance of God's call. I found my whole body responding to whatever was being asked of me.

And that was when I knew my call was to religious life. That was when I knew I would stay.[5]

This sister's questioning of vocation was happening to many religious. The Catholic Church, particularly in the United States and Europe, saw a vast number of priests, brothers, and sisters leave their vocations after Vatican II, and the Daughters of Wisdom were no exception. In 1963, the first full year of the Second Vatican Council, the US province of the Daughters of Wisdom was at its peak, with twenty young women signing up to join 412 sisters and sisters-in-training serving in twenty-one different ministry locations in the United States and overseas.[6] Just two years later in 1965, the year Vatican II ended, no one had joined, and twenty-one had left. In a five-year period ending in 1970, more than 100 Daughters in the province had left. The statistics give only a surface account of the substantial organizational chaos, personal crises, and strained relationships that occurred during this turbulent time. "It was a shock and created a sense of panic throughout the province because these were good people. It was particularly traumatic for us because it appeared that the Daughters began their exodus at least one year earlier than most of the other orders in the area."

Much has been written about this exodus of vowed religious in the Catholic Church. Some scholars have suggested that when Vatican II called all Catholics the "priesthood of all believers," there was no longer the spiritual distinction and additional holiness to be gained for a vowed religious life that called for so much sacrifice.[7] Some of the Daughters agreed with this, but explained it in a different way. "There was so much external regimentation and rules for such mundane things. They were not essential for a religious life, but they made the rules the life, so when they were relaxed, one big reaction was why be a religious at all? Life was too difficult. The rules around religious life did change, but mostly after people left."[8] Many pointed to the fact that most entered at a young age and all the questioning and changes were a maturing process that made them think about their lives differently.[9] Others said that it was because the church was encouraging Catholics to find God in the world that the structure and justification of the semi-cloistered life no longer made sense.

When I met former Daughters who had left the order during this time, they said prayer and hearing God's call was what motivated them to leave. They felt God actively calling them to enter this larger world. Still, it was not an easy decision to make. "It was really hard to leave because I was walking out into the unknown. It was as if God was calling me to walk out onto a misty pier, not knowing where it would lead or if I would fall off the edge. All I could do was trust God because I had no idea what would happen to me."[10]

It was equally difficult for those who stayed. The sisters who had the unfortunate task of assuming leadership through the departures said it was an extremely hard time. "Imagine having to sit there as sister after sister comes to tell you she is leaving. Some even told me that I should leave too before it all died. I just listened. I myself did not believe that to be true, but that was not the time to argue."[11] Another sister explained, "I understand that many left to serve God better. They said they prayed about it, and maybe it was right for them. But not for us. It was a shattering experience for those of us who stayed."[12]

When I asked the Daughters why they did not leave, too, their responses were almost identical—they were not called to leave. Many of the Daughters who stayed noted that the turbulence made them even stronger in their faith because it forced them to confront what they really believed.[13] Others said they had prayed deeply about it, particularly when friends or mentors left, but they felt no call to leave themselves.

Most of the younger Daughters who stayed believed that even greater changes were coming. The women's movement was in full swing by the 1970s, and there was hope that the Catholic Church would begin ordaining women, as many Protestant denominations were doing. On the heels of Vatican II, anything seemed possible.

But as the 1970s and 1980s progressed, the possibility of women's ordination turned from an issue of hope to an issue of pain. In 1994, Pope John Paul II declared in *Ordinatio Sacerdotalis* that women would not be ordained. In 1998, *Ad Teundam Fidem* made further restrictions, declaring that the topic could not even be discussed, and anyone who spoke about it could be excommunicated. For some Daughters, these events only heightened how much the church was missing by not including women's voices in the leadership and decision making of the church:

> I was in parish ministry so I was expected to attend the special chrism mass where the bishop blesses the oils used for sacraments such as Anointing of the Sick. I sat down and looked around, and there was all this maleness. I had gotten my period and I thought, "We need a flow of blood in all this testosterone." I feel a call to this church, and a call to the ritual of the Mass and daily Eucharist. But when women's ordination was denied, I found it difficult to participate. It is something I mourn every day. I feel sad, angry, and betrayed.[14]

WISDOM SOPHIA: (RE) DISCOVERING A SENSE OF PURPOSE

For the Daughters who stayed, particularly for the younger ones who had watched most of their peers leave, there had been a deep searching for what a new vocational call might be for them individually as well as a group. Now it was up to the Daughters themselves to find deeper meaning for their lives, the kind of lives they believed God had called them to live.

The Daughters of Wisdom began taking more initiative and control of their spiritual development. A member of the Daughter's leadership team explained:

> From the very beginning, Montfort set forth both an interior and an exterior aim for the congregation. The exterior aim was to work with the poor, but the interior aim was always the acquisition of Divine Wisdom. After Vatican II, choices for our external ministries expanded, but our interior aim continued to be the acquisition of Divine Wisdom. In the past, the Montfort Missionaries gave all our retreats, so our understanding of *True Devotion* and our purpose always had their flavor. In the past the sisters did it in the living. But now we could bring our own understanding to articulation.[15]

To start this process, the Daughters brought in speakers other than Montfort priests to expand their understanding of Wisdom. Even before they were introduced to Sophia, speakers taught them about feminine characteristics of God. For many of the Daughters, redefining feminine characteristics in terms of leadership and not submission provided new focus for their mission and ministries and showed a new way to be Catholic in the world. A Daughter described how she was inspired to try out these feminine Wisdom values:

> I'll never forget a Catholic sister we brought in from another congregation to educate us. She was a professor of Old Testament studies and an expert in Wisdom literature. She was talking to us about the difference between the Way of Mastery and the Way of Wisdom. The Way of Mastery involved control, competition, independence, domination/submission, disdain, and offensiveness/defensiveness. The Way of Wisdom

> she showed us had a very different spirit. By drawing upon the Wisdom scripture, she identified seven characteristics of wisdom that she said were feminine values: collaboration, cooperation, compassion, interdependence, mutuality, and respect. I have always been very practical, and I wondered if this could really work. It was 1979 and I was principle of Montfort Academy in Fredericksburg, Virginia, at the time. I brought these Wisdom ideas to our staff meetings to see how we could do it. One lay teacher asked why they had not learned this before, and we told her that we were just learning it ourselves. Catholic schools always provided quality education, though much depended on the competitive model to accomplish it. Could we really accomplish quality education using a Way of Wisdom? I believe we did. We did some things that were radical for Catholic instruction at the time, such as eliminating the honor roll. Instead, we honored the unique giftedness in each of our children, be it academics, sports, arts, etc. . . . We started listening to the children more, and letting them show their gifts. Overall, the parents were satisfied because their children were learning and were happier with the process.[16]

The Daughter's assertion that certain leadership styles were considered feminine and that women understood these approaches better than men used the church's own teachings about gender to advocate for female leadership. Complementarity was the term the Catholic Church used to explain that women and men were complementary, equal but with different gifts and roles. It assumed that gender was a binary of male and female with inherently different masculine and feminine traits. The Daughters used this teaching to say that women, if given the chance, would naturally approach leadership in a feminine way. Having scripture to describe what this feminine way represented and how it could be enacted in the world was revelatory. The way feminine Wisdom revealed God's presence and love in the world gave the Daughters a template to emulate.

This line of reasoning also affirmed the lives that the Daughters were living. If wisdom dwells in experience, then the Daughters experienced femaleness—socially, professionally, and spiritually. Even after Vatican II, the Daughters continued to live in highly female-centered social environments, as only women could join their order, and many participated mostly in women's religious networks. Many also continued to engage in female-identified professions such as teaching and nursing and focused their social activism and spiritual work on women. All this was in contrast to a Catholic hierarchy that was exclusively male.

Soon the exploration of feminine values included the scriptural embodiment of Sophia as female. This shift affirmed both their female bodies as worthy of representing God along with their complementary "feminine" wisdom. The Daughter who introduced the order to a female-personified Sophia was a doctor in West Virginia. She had initially been trained as a nurse, and after Vatican II she felt that she could help more people as a doctor, serving the poorest of the poor. When she completed her medical studies, she contacted the bishop of West Virginia to serve the people of Appalachia and was given permission to start a clinic near the Kentucky border. She has served there now for more than thirty years and is currently the county's only pediatrician:

> It actually began when I was making final vows. I was intently reading the Wisdom books of the Old Testament in parallel with the Gospels. I recognized many phrases in the prologue of the Gospel of John that seemed to refer to Wisdom texts and wanted to know more. Then in the late 1970s I came across an article by Elizabeth Johnson connecting Jesus and Wisdom in a new way. Because of my interest, in 1986 someone brought to my attention Susan Cady's book, *Feminist Spirituality*, and I was very moved when I read it. I called the Methodist Session in Pennsylvania and got Susan's phone number. She couldn't believe there was an order of Catholic nuns called the Daughters of Wisdom! She had never heard of us. I invited her to present at a combination retreat and conference we had scheduled in Litchfield titled "Woman and Wisdom." Susan was great. It was a time when the women's movement was strong, and there was a lot of dissatisfaction in the Catholic Church around the oppression of women. For me, Sophia seemed to be a way out. It has been wonderful for my spiritual development. Sophia has been an inspiration for me as a physician as well. The image of a physician in this country is male. I am a female physician, and God who heals is feminine. This informs my professional life to be compassionate and understanding, something I don't see in many male physicians.[17]

Sophia theology was tremendously exciting for many of the Daughters, and the feminine face of God as Wisdom gave them renewed purpose and direction for having remained a Daughter. One sister saw herself and her peers with a divine destiny in the congregation's history. "The basic prayer of our order has always been, 'Oh Sagesse (Wisdom), come be with us.' The Daughters have been praying this for over three hundred years for Wisdom to come. I believe now she has done it. The question is now that She has come, what is She asking us to do?"[18]

A small group of Daughters decided to study Sophia and became known as the Sophia spirituality group. Susan Cady and Hal Taussig had their own Sophia group in Philadelphia, which was predominantly Methodist. In the late 1980s, the Catholic and Methodist Sophia groups met jointly a couple times a year. This interdenominational friendship benefited both groups and assisted both communities in dealing with their own denominational challenges. The Methodist ministers helped the Daughters find their own voice in their Wisdom identity.

In 1991, three Daughters attended the United Methodist Eastern Pennsylvania Annual Conference to defend their Methodist minister friends and the book they had written, *Wisdom's Feast.* When the oldest Daughter of Wisdom stood up to speak, "you could have heard a pin drop."[19] No one expected a Catholic nun with white hair to be endorsing Sophia theology. She let the conference know that the Daughters of Wisdom had been formed in 1703 and that the Sophia tradition had a long biblical tradition. The value of bringing Catholic sisters to the Protestant discourse was to verify that Sophia theology was more than a modern invention. Another Daughter sent a similar letter of support to the editor of the *United Methodist Reporter,* and it shows how the Daughters were explaining and justifying Sophia theology in the late 1980s. The letter was given the heading "Sophia has long history":

> The tradition of Sophia/Wisdom as the feminine personification of the Divine is as least as old as the books of Proverbs, Sirach and Wisdom. The understanding of Jesus as wisdom incarnate is as least as old as the gospels of Matthew and John. I am a Catholic nun and member of a Catholic Religious Order called "The Daughters of Wisdom." The order was founded in 1703, and is dedicated to the following of Jesus Christ, Our Lord and Messiah, who is also Incarnate Wisdom. The tradition of Sophia/Wisdom has a long history in Christian Spirituality. She appears in the writings of the

> Greek Fathers, the Orthodox tradition, St. Hildegard of Bingen, the Rhineland mystics, and the French school of spirituality. Even today she appears in Thomas Merton's poem, "Haggai Sophia." The authors of "Wisdom's Feast" and "Sophia" have done us a great service by reminding us of this lovely Judeo-Christian tradition. They have given us an historical account of this tradition, which can expand our search for the Divine. The remembrance of God as Wisdom can be energizing for Christians today, especially for women.[20]

Back in its own Catholic context, the 1988 Daughters of Wisdom General Chapter meeting in Rome issued a mandate calling all Daughter of Wisdom provinces worldwide to engage in "a thorough interdisciplinary study of the charism of Wisdom spirituality with a view to uncovering the basic inspiration of the Founders, freed from elements related to their time, and reinterpreted for today."[21] For the US Daughters, this institutional directive encouraged them to explore Sophia Wisdom theology with even greater fervor and to encourage greater province-wide participation.

WISDOM LEADERSHIP INITIATIVES

A Wisdom committee was established to explore and educate the province and others about Sophia Wisdom. Daughters were encouraged to give retreats where they worked and lived. The physician in West Virginia gave workshops at her clinic for Hispanic women, who found it very easy to pray with Sophia because they already had a deep devotion to Mary. Daughters noted how ironic it was that laywomen initially had an easier time with Sophia instruction than many of the sisters. Because "Wisdom dwells in experience," it was not difficult for laywomen to find God in their lived experience because that was what they knew, but the Daughters had to undo their pre–Vatican II semi-cloistered instruction that to be with God meant being separated from the world.

While some Daughters were obviously moved by the Sophia teachings, others were not, and it was beginning to fracture the community. For many of the older sisters, keeping a consistent image of God and prayer practice was their only anchor amid the Vatican II changes. They saw no reason to change from seeing Wisdom exclusively as the male Jesus. Out of this need to unify the province as well as create a pathway to accomplish what the international leadership had asked, the provincial leadership team developed educational programs to update the order's understanding of Wisdom.

One of their first initiatives was to organize Wisdom Circles. They invited Daughters to organize small study communities and include others from where they lived and worked; at least one Montfort priest participated in the first year. These small faith groups, ranging in size from a few members to more than a dozen, met monthly to discuss readings prepared by the Wisdom committee. A handout was prepared for each meeting by one or two Daughters and included simple ritual and prayer to open and close the meeting as well as questions for discussion based on the readings. Provincial leadership oversaw the new educational and spiritual development process, directing the themes to be studied and the messages to be communicated.

The program was a success. After its pilot year, most Wisdom Circles wanted to continue, resulting in 25 groups of 177 people participating in 1994. The desire to learn blossomed, as the province leadership had hoped. In feedback after year two, the circles asked for more instruction on Wisdom scripture, and Kathleen O'Connor's *The Wisdom Literature* was the chosen text.

In the archives, I found the first Wisdom Circle handout. For the inaugural Wisdom Circle meeting in October 1992, the scriptural commentary on the Wisdom of Solomon seemed to reflect how some Daughters felt about their current situation in the church and why they sought new inspirations for their faith:

> The tiny nation was displaced, conquered, controlled, exiled. They were dominated by foreign powers and were rendered powerless, seeing no help from their God who had favored them as the "chosen ones" . . . This Yahweh of their ancestors was letting them down . . . Their tradition no longer spoke to their experience. Their God no longer appeared to be actively involved in their everyday lives and so this empty belief was placed aside. It was evident to them that God no longer determined their history. And all they could do was ask why. In response to this question, the sages of the day paused to reflect. These learned Greek speaking Jews took their cue from the experience of the culture around them . . . The Israelite sages sought to incorporate this [Greek] wisdom into their Hebrew tradition, so that their more complex and

> mystifying situation would have meaning. Those who suffered at the hands of the oppressors would find hope and vitality in these unfavorable circumstances. As wisdom was welcomed into their lifestyle it became a way of guidance—and more. She became Guidance Herself, "a reflection of the eternal light, the untarnished mirror of God's active power, image of God's goodness" (Wisdom 7:26) . . . In our Wisdom Tradition, Montfort chose this as one of his themes in Chapter Six of *Love of Eternal Wisdom*. "The eager desire of Divine Wisdom to communicate (Herself) to (all) . . . In search of us, Wisdom runs by the highways . . . climbs the peaks of the highest mountains . . . sits at the gates of the cities . . . enters public places . . . crying out . . . You I wish for . . . You I seek . . . You I claim . . .[22]

A core message communicated in the early Wisdom Circle materials was that Sophia Wisdom herself called the Daughters to constantly learn and seek new understanding. "She is in fact the learning process itself. She calls us to a life of seeking understanding of the world in which we live. Since she is the One who participates in bringing everything into being, she is the natural teacher and the natural content. Because there is always something more to learn and to understand, she never stops calling people to herself. It is devotion to this process of continual learning which promises so many rewards. The more humans understand the world, the more success and contentment they will have, the Sophia texts seem to say."[23]

In addition to Wisdom Circle handouts, other materials were developed to help those in the order deepen in this new understanding of Sophia Wisdom. One Daughter wrote Wisdom Sophia reflections for the Daughters to pray with during Advent and Lent that tied Wisdom scripture in with the life and writings of their founders. In 1993, the Dutch province of the Daughters of Wisdom commissioned a study, *The Mystical Process of Transformation in Grignion De Montfort's "The Love of Eternal Wisdom": A Lover's Letter to Her Beloved*, which was used as the study guide for two years of Wisdom Circles.

Despite the new material being generated, there was still a major problem with translation of Montfort's original French texts. There had been only one English translation of *Love of Eternal Wisdom* completed years before by a Montfort priest in Britain. Once the order became aware of Sophia theology, they noticed that all of Montfort's references to Wisdom as "She" appeared in English as "He." The issue of translation became controversial within the congregation and reflected the larger disagreements regarding how to interpret Montfort's writings.

Some Daughters thought the English translation had intentionally suppressed the feminine character of the writing. Others defended the translation, saying that Montfort never intended for God Wisdom to be imaged as female. Still others pointed out that when Montfort referenced scripture where Wisdom was personified as female, he too must have been thinking of feminine attributes of God, especially when he used terms such as "maternity of the Father."[24]

At the very least, this attention to translation helped the order understand why they had not thought of female-personified Wisdom before, especially when reading their own document. Eventually, the order decided to commission a new translation, and they invited a former Daughter to do the work. When I examined both translations, the differences were striking, particularly regarding the images of Wisdom that were evoked. In this excerpt, Montfort is writing his reflection on the sixth chapter of Wisdom of Solomon, where Wisdom is clearly personified as female. Here is the original translation into English authored by the priest in Britain:

> How gentle, attractive and approachable is Eternal Wisdom who possesses such splendor, excellence and grandeur. He invites men to come to him because he wants to teach them with a smile. He bestows blessings on them many times over and forestalls their needs in a thousand different ways, and even goes as far as to wait at their doorstep to give them proofs of friendship. Who would be so heartless as to refuse to love this gentle conqueror?"[25]

When the Daughter's translation was published, Wisdom was again female:

> How sweet is Eternal Wisdom in Herself, how approachable and engaging—even in the face of her brilliance, her excellence, and her sublimity! She calls humans in order to teach them the ways of happiness; She seeks them; She smiles upon them; She fills them with blessings; She anticipates them in a thousand ways, even to the point of sitting at their doorstep and waiting for them, to offer them tokens of her affection.

> Could one have a heart and refuse it to such a winning Sovereign?[26]

Not surprisingly, the Daughters found the imagery of their own translation more identifiable and relatable. The document itself also provided new avenues for spiritual growth. In *Love of Eternal Wisdom*, Montfort detailed four ways to acquire Wisdom: ardent desire, continuous prayer, universal mortification, and devotion to the Blessed Virgin. Some of the Daughters explained that they were never taught the first three ways because the Montfort priests' had as their founding document *True Devotion to Mary*, which only highlighted the fourth way. The Daughters were originally taught that wisdom could only be acquired through Mary. Now they could explore the three other avenues as well.

Soon "Ardent Desire" became the preferred new method for many Daughters to explore Wisdom, and they linked this instruction with the Catholic tradition of mysticism. Mysticism also provided a way for the Daughters to explain what many others found difficult about the texts with regard to gender, namely to imagine Wisdom as a female who then incarnates as the male Jesus. The Catholic mystical tradition provided historical examples of saints' visions of God where gender was mutable, and these examples from church tradition informed and legitimated the Daughter's teachings on Wisdom.

EXPERIENCES OF WISDOM SOPHIA

Given the order's emphasis on mysticism and its core teaching that Wisdom dwells in experience, I wondered how many Daughters actually had experiences of Sophia Wisdom. In my interviews, the Daughters who first embraced Sophia theology described experiences that had already prepared them to accept a new message and image of God. As one Daughter described:

> I experienced her before I knew what she was called. It happened at a time when I was having a crisis of faith. The God I knew from my novitiate was dead. As far as I could tell it never existed. So what could I believe in? I wondered if I would ever believe in God again. This had gone on for months and I was very discouraged. So one day I decided to

> just walk out to a field and stay there until I figured something out. I set myself the task of finding something, anything, to believe in with certainty. I was out there for hours, most of the afternoon. It was wonderful laying in the sun, feeling a soft warm breeze on my skin and hearing the buzzing of nature in action, but I still had nothing for a belief. Then I looked over and saw a small yellow flower and realized that I could believe in that yellow flower. I was certain that it was created by God to become what it was. It wasn't much but it was a beginning. At least I could believe in something. Over the next few days I had a growing sense of how connected we all were. God was a spirit that connects all of creation. That spirit is creator and very feminine. For a few days after that, I would notice the color yellow and be reminded of God's presence.

Nature was a favorite location for many Sophia experiences that the Daughters recounted. Nature itself was experiential and helped some Daughters recognize Sophia once they started learning about her. "It was at the end of a week of silence, prayer and study about Sophia when I had my first experience of her. I had gotten up early to drive home from the retreat. It was five o'clock in the morning and there was still mist on the mountain, dark mist, and there were stars and the moon. It was exceedingly beautiful, and her presence was very strong. I felt her wonder, her joy, and her relationship. This was not something way out, but a closeness. I was so moved I spontaneously began singing a song as I drove, making it up as I went. First it was me singing to Sophia, and then it was her response back to me! It was simple, yet profound."

Sophia became known to these Daughters when the mundane physical world was transformed into a world of wonder. The biggest change seemed to be a change in perspective. The Sophia experiences assured a connection to God, particularly at times when that connection was not being felt. Nature also provided a mode of communication. As one Daughter shared:

> I feel closest to Sophia when I am in my garden. That is usually where I talk with her. One year I planted snow peas and they had just begun to grow up the vines. I couldn't wait to see the beautiful snow peas. Then I left for a two-week

> trip. When I returned, the teenage boy mowing our lawn had mowed down all the plants. I was so disheartened. Then I felt her saying, "they will come back in a couple weeks." This thought was so outside my own thoughts that I even argued with her, pointing out that all the plants had been killed. Well wouldn't you know, a few weeks later they sprouted again! A neighbor had an explanation and maybe it was true, but I certainly did not know it was possible and I would not have predicted it. That was Sophia for me. I am still astonished.

In addition to nature, some Daughters reported a spontaneous creative expression as the location for their Sophia experience. The Daughter who sang coming down the mountain was one among many; quite a few of the Daughters mentioned feeling moved to write, sing, or dance. It was striking to me because the Daughters as a congregation were not known for being artists. It was as if this Sophia creative impulse was bursting out of them in extraordinary ways. Music and lyrics created by two Daughters, such as "Wisdom, the Splendor" and "Wisdom Dream," became much-loved songs at gatherings of the order. "Wisdom, the splendor and fullness of God, has built herself a house and set for us a table."[27] "Go forward, go forward, go forward in faith. Believe in the dream, a world where Wisdom delights to play, a world where Wisdom plays in our presence."[28]

Occasionally the art inspired by an experience of Sophia Wisdom also created ways for others to experience Sophia, too. A few sisters mentioned a play that a Daughter had written to celebrate the fiftieth anniversary of the US province in 1999 as their transformative moment regarding Sophia. The play included vignettes from the Daughters of Wisdom history, starting with Marie Louise, as well as significant events for the Daughters in the United States and abroad. Lady Wisdom was a female character in the play. There was a video recording of the performance that I was invited to watch. The Daughter who acted the part of Lady Wisdom wore a shimmery white robe with a long, light blue scarf. During the play, Lady Wisdom provided comfort, instruction, and vision to the Daughters and was present in their history from beginning to end.

Some Daughters who were in the audience mentioned the play as the time when their hearts and minds were opened to the reality of Sophia Wisdom. The most dramatic account was from a Daughter who had been cast as co-foundress Mother Marie Louise, and she had her transformative experience while she was on the stage:

> I was asked to play the part of Marie Louise. I was terrified because I had never acted before and I had a health concern that was affecting my memory. At first I said no, but there was a lot of pressure because I was about the only one small enough who could still fit into the habit on display in the Heritage room. I had joined during the modified habit period, so others had to dress me at the performance because I did not even know how to wear it. I was petrified when I went onstage and froze. I felt empty. Then I felt Marie Louise with me, like she was really there. I was filled by her spirit and it was incredible. The Daughter playing Lady Wisdom was wise as well as funny. She was a natural comic playing the lighthearted foolishness of Wisdom and had us eating out of the palm of her hand. While we were onstage together, I saw the face of Lady Wisdom in her and experienced her there.

This sacred theater was a type of ritualizing where embodying and witnessing the story to be remembered actually drew the actors and audience into the mystical reality of it. The Daughters were writing their own history, telling their own story, and embodying Wisdom as they saw her, stimulating an ever-widening circle of acceptance and relatedness to a female-personified depiction of God.

While Sophia was experienced mostly during moments of joy, some Daughters related experiencing Sophia among the suffering. Many spoke of having encounters with Sophia with those who were dying through feeling a gentle, calming presence. "I had an experience of Sophia when my brother died. The family had decided to stop the respirator and as he was passing away, I had an image of Sophia being present there putting my brother in the hands of my deceased parents." One Daughter encountered Sophia Wisdom working in a nursing home where some of the elderly would have a grace about them even in their suffering as they approached death. As she pointed out, we often think of a wise woman or a wise man as someone older who has integrated a significant amount of life, exuding a balance and peaceful perspective that few have when they are young. For her, this exemplified the teaching "Wisdom dwells in experience."

Many of the sisters felt comfortable describing a world where they could have experiences not just of God, but also of those who had died, even calling upon them for help and assistance. A few mentioned Mother Marie Louise guiding them at certain moments, and sisters who had passed were never far away either.

One day while I was visiting the provincial house, the Daughters half-jokingly started calling out to Lucinda to help locate an item that was missing. When I asked who Lucinda was, I was told she was a Daughter who had passed on, but while she was alive she had a compulsive habit of putting things away so that only she knew where things were. Now, when things got lost, they still asked Lucinda for her help.

Unexpectedly, I too found myself participating in an extra-worldly exchange. During another visit to the provincial house, I was with one of the Daughters to tour the new archive storage facility when a phone call came in saying that a Daughter at the Marie Regina nursing center had just died. The Daughter made a note, and we proceeded with the tour. As we walked around, I noticed two boxes labeled "Dissertations and Theses." I was curious to find out what topics the Daughters had studied, and we opened one of the boxes. The first binder I pulled out was a master's thesis written by the sister who had just passed. The Daughter looked at me intensely. "This afternoon we will have to start working on her eulogy. I never knew she had earned a master's degree; I don't think any of us who will be planning the funeral knew. But she wanted us to know, and you had a part to play in it." Later I would learn that this Daughter had been the white-haired sister who had spoken at the United Methodist conference on behalf of Susan Cady and Hal Taussig. As I stood there with the sister's thesis in my hands, I was not just observing and recording accounts of these communications between worlds, but being placed inside them. My actions were seen by the Daughter as being directed by some unseen hand. I cannot say that I was aware of anything other than my own research motivations to look inside that box, but the thought that maybe two Daughters were communicating across the life/death divide and using me as the telephone line was a bit unnerving. If there were ever a moment when I wondered who I was in the mix of this research, it was that moment.

For many of the Daughters, this type of communication was normal. Sophia not only gave them a new perspective on life, but also called them into action. One Daughter credited a powerful experience of God-as-Sophia with moving her beyond her role as a nurse to become a social justice advocate:

> I was teaching nursing students who did a practicum at a government funded nursing home for the indigent. This place was the pits. It was located next to a chemical plant with fumes so strong that the patients were not allowed to go outside. It

> was nighttime and I walked onto the floor and smelled urine. It was horrible. My thoughts echoed the scripture where Jesus was on the cross crying out, "My God my God, why have you forsaken me?" Then I heard in a woman's voice, "I am here with them." I turned around thinking it was the night supervisor but no one was there. I looked in the rooms and found no nurses but saw the patients, many who had soiled themselves and had not been changed. Even worse, they were lying on plastic mattresses. There were no sheets. I was so upset. When I finally found the supervisor she said she had not been down the hall to speak to me. She also insisted that the patients were getting the government allocated care. When I asked why there were no sheets, she said it was because they were disappearing, so they decided not to put any out. I said "Why are you punishing the patients—they aren't taking them! Why not check the bags of staff as they leave?!" Later I spoke with the director of nursing but still no response. I felt this urge compelling me to do something. It was as if I had heard Sophia. So I contacted the local newspaper and they wrote an article about the poor care. As a result, medical interns were sent over to review the medical records. It turns out there had been sixteen recent deaths, and all had died of dehydration. How tragic. They had not been given water so they would not require changing! But in the end justice was served. Blue Cross/Blue Shield stopped paying for half of the beds until the nursing care was fixed. That's justice. That's Wisdom.

She admitted that she had been private about the experience of hearing God's voice, especially about the voice being female, because she did not want people to think she was crazy. But it was exactly the fact that she had heard a voice—and especially that the voice was female—that made her certain that Sophia was real. It gave her courage to act in bold ways to advocate for justice in patient care even if that challenged authority and disrupted her work relationships.

Some of the most interesting accounts of Wisdom Sophia experiences came from sisters who had initially resisted seeing Wisdom as "She." The Daughters had been an established community with a significant history together well before the feminist theology of Wisdom Sophia in the 1980s. Not all the sisters integrated these new understandings at the same time, or even at all. One such Daughter had her initial experience while walking the outdoor labyrinth at Wisdom House. The labyrinth was a circular stone pattern set in the ground for walking meditations. Labyrinths were popular in medieval Catholic cathedrals in Europe, and many Catholic retreat houses, including Wisdom House, added outdoor labyrinths to their properties in the 1990s. Unlike a maze, there is no getting lost, though the path meanders until the center is reached:

> I was on a guided retreat in Litchfield. During one of the talks, a phrase was used, "the womb of God." For some reason, it really grabbed me. Then an inner voice said, "Go down to the labyrinth." I wasn't into the labyrinth at that point and there was a grassy hill to climb down and I'm not steady on my feet. I found myself arguing with the voice because I didn't want to go. But the urging persisted and I found another way to the labyrinth by walking along the road. I was pleased because I really wanted to do it by myself and I wanted to do it prayerfully and both were possible. Then an amazing thing happened. When I got to the center of the labyrinth, I found myself in the womb of God. I was totally flabbergasted. I have no description for it, except to say that I was in the womb of God. It was beyond words, indescribable. It was a space of some sort, a spiritual space. I was being enveloped by this labyrinth circle, the placenta. The next early morning I sat on the back porch of the retreat house, praying with the sunrise. It was so gorgeous to see. Then all of a sudden words came to me, and I assure you I am no poet. I still remember, "And the sun danced with joy as I became aware of my rebirth and Wisdom wrapped me in her mantle of love." I will never forget the date. It was September 11, 2001, but it was early. It would not be until 9:00 a.m. before we learned about the planes hitting the World Trade Towers. It was a day of extremes. The "aah" of the womb of God and the "oh no" of September 11. I was torn by the two extremes.

I asked if there was significance for her that both events happened on the same day. "I did not see any direct connection because I had felt the urge to walk the labyrinth the day before but had not heeded it. What I did feel was a connection in a much broader way that God was forming me and I was being shaped by all of it. My relationship with God definitely increased that day." After this experience, she still had reservations about referring to Wisdom as female but now accepted that God could touch us in feminine ways.

As these Daughters shared their accounts with me, it was clear that these experiences had a profound impact on how they saw God and how they saw themselves in relation to God. Most had not spoken about these experiences with many people. Their reluctance seemed to come from a church culture where experiences of God were acceptable as long as you were modest and quiet about them. I wondered myself about sharing their experiences in my research and discussed this with the provincial. Her response was that everything they were experiencing, advocating, and celebrating had scriptural roots and could also be found in their founding saint's writings. The task from her point of view was how to bring this understanding to others inside and outside the church in a way that could be properly understood.

MARY, SOPHIA, AND THE RELIGIOUS MARKETPLACE

Having other ways to acquire wisdom helped the Daughters form new understandings of Sophia, but it also allowed the Daughters to refocus their devotion of Mary. Many felt that the church had put Mary on a pedestal, which ensured that no real woman could ever match the expectations; sisters in particular had suffered because of this unrealistic characterization of a holy woman. Mary was the theme for the ninth Wisdom Circle year starting in 2000. The Wisdom Circle material for the year began with an article by Catholic theologian Elizabeth Johnson titled "Mary of Nazareth: Friend of God and Prophet."[29] Elizabeth Johnson was a Catholic sister herself and a professor of theology at Fordham University. She was known for her book *She Who Is*, which explained how it was theologically and biblically possible within the Catholic tradition to image any aspect of the Trinitarian God as feminine. For many Catholic sisters, Johnson was their hero. Now Johnson was working on an updated theological and biblical understanding of Mary that directly addressed their pedestal concerns. The magazine layout highlighted a quote from the article in bold letters: "Relieved of the burden of being the ideal woman, Mary can simply be herself." Johnson would expand this in her 2006 book *Truly Our Sister: A Theology of Mary in the Communion of Saints*, which inspired many of the Daughters as well.

At the same time, there was a resurgence of interest in the pre–Vatican II Mary from a variety of sources. Catholic devotional Marian groups were growing, and conservative Catholics were praying rosaries at Right-to-Life rallies. Immigration into the United States from Mexico was also on the rise, bringing greater attention to Our Lady of Guadalupe. Even in the popular spirituality book market, there was a longing for a return of the mystical Mary. The book description of Charlene Spretnak's 2004 *Missing Mary: The Queen of Heaven and Her Re-Emergence in the Modern Church* asserts that "a deep loss ensues for women in particular when Mary's female embodiment of grace and mystical presence is denied and replaced with a strictly text-bound version of her as a Nazarene housewife."

These two contrasting images of Mary, as sister and as mystical mother, came into conflict during the Wisdom Colloquium hosted at Wisdom House in 2003. It started with the best of intentions. As a form of outreach, the Daughters of Wisdom had committed to hosting five annual Wisdom colloquia to bring greater understanding of Sophia Wisdom to the public. I attended the third colloquium, titled *A Call to Mysticism*. The speaker, Andrew Harvey, was a departure from the previous two colloquia led by Catholic sisters. He was primarily known for his popular books on spirituality and mysticism. He came to the attention of one of the Daughters through a national radio program. "I was listening to NPR while driving to an appointment, and Harvey was being interviewed. When he started talking about St. Louis de Montfort I almost drove off the side of the road! Who is this man talking about St. Louis de Montfort on NPR, and how can we find him?" As he told the Daughters, it was when his devotion to Mary took hold that he found the writings of their founding saint.

There was much anticipation for Andrew Harvey's talks. After all, he had a passionate conviction that St. Louis de Montfort was one of the greatest mystics in the Catholic tradition. This had many in the congregation very excited, and that excitement was reciprocated by Harvey. During the colloquium, he called for a marriage between social activism and mysticism. The marriage imagery was a launching point for the speaker to give his insights on "desire," one of the four ways Montfort delineated to acquire wisdom in *Love of Eternal Wisdom*. He linked the burning desire that longs for God with the longing to create a difference in the world.

Then the conference took an unexpected turn. It started when a Daughter asked, "What are your suggestions on how the Daughters could share Montfort's vision?" Harvey's response was for the Daughters to evangelize Mary as the full reigning Queen of Heaven. Clearly this was not what the Daughters wanted to hear, as the Daughters had come expecting to hear about Sophia.

For the rest of the weekend, Harvey talked about Mary, and not Mary-our-sister, but Mary divine. In fact, he went beyond current church teachings and advocated for Mary to be honored as co-redemptrix along with Jesus, a divine feminine complement for the divine masculine of Christ. This struck the Daughters as strange, given that the only Catholics they knew who were currently advocating this position were the most ultra-conservative Marian Catholics who also wanted the Latin mass back. Harvey advocated bringing back the very view of Mary that many Daughters were trying to get away from—Mary the miraculous, larger than life, the one who answers prayers and grants wishes, the one on the pedestal whom they were expected to emulate but could never expect to reach.

This exchange highlighted a difficulty the Daughters have continued to face as they reach beyond their province into the religious marketplace. Their founding saint is best known for his works on Mary and many, including Harvey, have been inspired by this pathway to God that has involved significant female imagery. For the Daughters, however, Mary could never be a divine complement because she was outside the Trinitarian godhead, highly regarded but always helpmate, portraying a human feminine that was always in service to a greater divine masculine. Meanwhile, those outside the tradition, or those who took it much more lightly, could embrace Mary as the preferred icon of a Christian feminine divine and have a rich tradition of images, prayer practices, and historical customs to draw upon without concerning themselves with the theological implications. As Harvey told the Daughters, "do not get hung up on the theology," but for the Daughters, that was not an option.

Perhaps this exchange was a contributing factor to inviting only Catholic speakers for the last two colloquia. The Daughters had a specific history, and they benefited from speakers who had lived as they had lived, as Catholics seeking a liberating progressive message within the contours of traditional Catholic theology. The fifth and last Wisdom colloquium in 2005 was titled "Wisdom and Globalization." The priest and sister leading the colloquium spoke of "God always on the birthing bed."[30] After the five public Wisdom colloquia, the Daughters decided to refocus their outreach efforts on those with whom they already had a connection: former Daughters, new vocations, and the international Daughters of Wisdom network.

EVANGELIZING WISDOM SOPHIA

In 1999, for the fiftieth anniversary of the US province, the province leadership organized a reunion weekend for all former and current Daughters of Wisdom called Chez Nous. It was held at Wisdom House, where they had experienced communal living together. "It was so good to see people who left but wanted to be with us and us with them. We did lots of things together, singing French songs and sharing meals."[31] Chez Nous II in 2004 took place as part of the province's centennial celebrations, with 150 in attendance. The closing ritual reflected this new understanding of Wisdom as the Tree of Life, and the group both reflected on its common roots in Wisdom and expressed "gratitude for Wisdom's continual blossoming."[32] The ritual ended with everyone writing blessings or petitions to be hung outside on trees around Wisdom House or put in baskets at the foot of a Montfort cross. The 2007 Chez Nous III continued to have strong attendance, with more than one hundred participating. While the bonds of friendship and mutual appreciation have grown between current and former sisters as a result of this program, the 2014 Chez Nous gathering might be the last because the participants are aging and finding it more difficult to travel.

Learning how to embrace and be in community despite differences has been a major lesson for the order and has been facilitated by the Wisdom Sophia teachings. As a Daughter explained, "That actual experience of being different yet holding it all together touches into who Wisdom is. She is diverse in her very self. Through generations, across cultures we have prayed for Wisdom to come. That connects to my experience of holding diversity together. It keeps us connected particularly to women who left the congregation. The bond is more than friends; it holds all who desired and prayed for Wisdom."

In 2003, the Daughters of Wisdom also accepted the permanent vows of their first new Daughter in twenty years. She was an unusual candidate but not atypical for the times. She had been a nurse employed by the Brooklyn diocese of the Catholic Church and worked with developmentally disabled children. When her husband left her after a twenty-seven-year marriage, she increased her church work at a parish run by Montfort priests. While there, she began spiritual direction with a Daughter of Wisdom and found the feminine presence of Wisdom alive in her heart, calling her to religious life.

At the age of fifty, with the support of her family, she wrote a formal letter asking for entrance to the Daughters, and her life dramatically changed. For the next few years she learned more about the Daughters, their spirituality, and mission while working in different locations and ministries. She served unemployed women in Connecticut, helped migrant farm workers in Florida, and looked after developmentally disabled patients on Long Island. For her international exposure, she lived in India for three months with local Daughters of Wisdom caring for street girls. At the age of fifty-seven, she gave up a house with swimming pool and took her final vows of poverty, chastity, and obedience surrounded by her mother, two married adult children, and four grandchildren. The *New York Times* profiled her in a December 2003 article titled "A Divorced Mother's New Vocation as Nun." The article noted that there were ten "sister moms" serving in New York State in 2003.[33] When we spoke, this Daughter said it was the Wisdom Sophia spirituality that drew her to join the order, even using mystical romance metaphors to describe the process:

> It started to feel like being in love, like I was being seduced. It made my toes curl. It wasn't that I wanted to be a nun so much—it was the spirituality that was getting me. It was Wisdom, Wisdom spirituality. I wasn't particularly looking for community, or community life. It was not easy at my age as there were different things to cope with. But I think I had a better appreciation of my vows because of it. I don't know if the others live their vows like I live my vows. But certainly I feel just as committed as anybody else and I believe that God meant for me to become a vowed religious at this stage of life.[34]

While the province has continued to advertise for vocations, the Daughters have had more success with their Daughters of Wisdom Associates program. Many Catholic orders now have programs in which laypeople can be formally affiliated with them. Associates do not take vows, but instead make "promises" to live out the charism of the order within the context of their lives. The Wisdom Associate program began in 1987, and by 2007 more than thirty associates were participating. The first international gathering of associates of the Daughters of Wisdom was held in France in 2003 to celebrate the 300th anniversary of the order. The associates defined their mission as "Together we love, live, proclaim Wisdom." In 2009, the Daughters formally passed over the directorship of the program to the lay associates themselves.

Perhaps the most successful arena for the US province to extend its understanding of Wisdom has been through the larger international Daughters of Wisdom network. By moving into international leadership, the US province and its work on Sophia Wisdom are being shared with Daughters around the world. A Daughter from the US province was elected superior general for the first time in the 1990s and served in Rome for twelve years. During part of this time, she was also president of the entire consortium of leaders of Catholic women religious, the top organizational position for a woman religious in the worldwide Catholic Church. Another Daughter from the US province designed and led a "Wisdom Year" in Rome for cohorts of approximately a dozen Daughters considered emerging leaders from Europe, Africa, the Americas, and Asia. A second Daughter from the US province has since replaced her in Rome to lead the program.

Most recently, another Daughter from the US province has been chairing an international task force charged to develop Wisdom spirituality resources for all formation directors of the Daughters of Wisdom worldwide. In 2008, the first module, titled "Wisdom Sets Her Table," was presented. When I spoke with the Daughter who chaired this initiative, she explained her background and perspective on the program:

> When the US province was discovering Sophia Wisdom, I was a missionary in Africa for twenty years, and would learn about this during my trips home. I was intrigued regarding female images of God in scripture but I had difficulty relating to the early Sophia work. The concerns of American Catholic women were different from the African women with whom I lived and worked. These women had so few rights and even getting families to allow them to go to school was a challenge. From the very beginning I wondered how this understanding of scripture could be inspirational for these women. So I began to teach the Wisdom messages by starting with images from the scripture, such as Wisdom setting her table. I taught the messages of hospitality, inclusivity, and generosity of God through having the women share about their experiences with special meals. Later, when I was asked to do this on an international level with Daughters from around the world speaking different languages, I would have them first act out without words their customs for hospitality and eating. The wisdom messages are wonderful because they are about everyday living

> and everyone has experiences that relate. There are so many parallels of Wisdom texts with the gospels that from the very beginning this connection of Old Testament Wisdom with the Christian understanding of God is irrefutable. As for female images of God, or even God as a tree, we have a mystical tradition where saints have written about experiencing God in a variety of ways. These include feminine images because God is beyond all of it and yet all we have to understand God with is what we know. So to teach this I have shown a variety of images. I might show images from nature, then a ballerina dancing, and then an icon of Jesus. This is not controversial. It is the teachings of the church.[35]

I found her comments about cross-cultural understanding of Wisdom interesting because in many ways, the American teachings of Sophia spoke to the American women's liberation movement, and this Daughter was seeking a way to address the concerns of women leading lives in very different cultural locations and not make the American perspective the universal one.

She then shared with me the Wisdom spirituality materials that her committee had developed. The program was titled "Religious Life in Wisdom's Way" and included six modules: Wisdom creates, Wisdom dwells among us, Wisdom sets her table, Wisdom speaks at the crossroads, Wisdom transforms and reconciles, and Through Mary Wisdom transforms. The materials included education as well as possible exercises to use with women in religious formation. One of the exercises for contemplation on the vow of poverty used a reflection technique taught during pre–Vatican II times:

> In a prayerful atmosphere, contemplate Christ in His poverty—Jesus as the poor One who invites you to follow in His footsteps. During prayer what gospel text and what facial expression of Jesus arise spontaneously in your heart and mind? Take time to dwell on the word and the facial expression that have arisen in you. (If the word is a scripture text, you may wish to find it in your Bible and pray from it. During your contemplation, what human faces come to mind spontaneously? Who are these people? How do you relate to them? What are your real relationships with them at the present time? How does discipleship of Christ in his

> poverty influence your relationship with the poor? How have individual poor people in your life helped you to follow Christ in His poverty? What connections do you see between these relationships and your vow of poverty?[36]

These questions may have been slightly altered from what was asked fifty years ago, but it was the instructions that came next that caught my eye: "Sharing in small groups and then in assembly." Before Vatican II, interior experiences were kept private and discussed only with a novice director or spiritual director, but now the sisters-in-training were being encouraged to discuss their interior experiences of God freely among themselves as well in formal group settings. Voicing and emplacing these experiences in community could affirm and demonstrate the range of images and experiences that their fellow sisters were having in prayer as well as provide possible feedback of the multiple ways these experiences could be interpreted and integrated, making spontaneous imagery in prayer one more way to explore their understanding, experience, and relationship with God. It seemed to me to be a healthy step forward for both personal spiritual formation and community development.

Back in the United States, the provincial and others became more and more convinced that "spirituality" should be a ministry for the Daughters to engage in with the wider public. Beginning in the mid-2000s, a core group of Daughters and staff began adapting international formation modules on Wisdom for lay audiences. In the past few years, these Wisdom programs have been delivered mostly at local parishes and retreat houses. "Fire in Our Hearts" is the program's name, and it comes from the title of an international chapter directive on Wisdom spirituality.

Wisdom Associates have been delivering the programs along with the Daughters of Wisdom to extend the program's outreach. Staffing ministry beyond the Daughters is becoming more and more of a necessity. From 2006 to 2013, more than twenty Daughters have passed away, and even with renewed interest in the order by younger women, the province will most likely continue to shrink in size. The vowed Daughters in the US province now number fewer than one hundred.

Even so, ministry and outreach of the Daughters of Wisdom continues to grow in new ways. Beginning in 2012, the Daughters of Wisdom expanded their Fire in their Hearts ministry to the Internet. Each reflection contains three sections with images. The first section is titled "Centering" and has simple flute music in the background. The second section is titled "Reflection" and contains words, both written and spoken, always beginning with a Bible passage on Wisdom. The third section ends with a short written prayer to close the reflection. One Daughter explains, "We hope to promote a grand circle of Wisdom spirituality. The new fireinourhearts.org website was conceived to actively reach out to Catholics and persons of all spiritual traditions extending an invitation to reflect on Wisdom as experienced in one specific tradition and to enter into dialogue with the wealth of other wisdom traditions."[37]

Most of the images in the reflections are of nature, but religious icons and other inspirational images appear as well. The reflection for April 28, 2013, contains an image of a woman dancing at the edge of the ocean. Nothing is defined for the viewer, so she could be Wisdom, or the one seeking God, or even the female speaker heard in the reflection. A prayer is written at the top of the image: "Loving Wisdom, You who are irresistible by your very nature, compel us to seek You as the SOURCE of all life within us. Fill us with your being so that we hunger no more for that which does not satisfy. Grant that we may share our experience of You with our sisters and brothers on the same journey towards wholeness. Amen."[38]

CONCLUSION

The exploration of female imagery of Wisdom has been important for the Daughters of Wisdom. Wisdom is in their namesake, and their founder wrote extensively about seeking wisdom. Because the Old Testament and St. Montfort's writings highlighted a feminine Wisdom, they began exploring Sophia Wisdom among themselves, within their ministries, and with the public at large. The Daughters of Wisdom now embrace their extended spiritual legacy, which has been associated with the feminine in Christianity for more than three hundred years.

The Daughters of Wisdom continue to live in highly gendered social and organizational spaces as an all-female religious order within an all-male church hierarchy. They follow a denomination that emphasizes gender complementarity, where women and men have different roles and inherent natures. All of this has contributed to making their exploration, understanding, and teaching about Sophia Wisdom a significant spiritual calling for the order.

The Daughters have been able to sustain their exploration of Wisdom Sophia in part because they have their own organization within the church. Being an approved Roman Catholic religious order has brought them a certain amount of autonomy, particularly since Vatican II. This autonomy, however, only goes so far. According to church law, when orders of Catholic women religious hold international governance meetings where leadership is elected and votes on strategic initiatives are taken, a priest must oversee the proceedings. In addition, Catholic women's orders are dependent on male priests to say Mass as well as to officiate at their funerals. This dynamic makes the Daughters reliant upon on the Montfort priests for essential functions, while the Montfort Missionaries rarely have to depend on others outside their order to fulfill these needs.

How the Daughters handle this is with a mixture of graciousness and resignation. At a Daughter's funeral I attended, a Montfort priest they all knew and liked said the mass. While the Daughters seemed to appreciate him, it was clear that he did not know the deceased Daughter as well as the provincial and the other Daughters in the room. For some reason, seeing these women who had dedicated their lives to the church and prayed upward of three hours a day not deemed fit to sacredly bury their own dead because they were women brought the injustice of the church's position into focus for me.

To their credit, the Daughters have dedicated themselves to a new vision for their order that has worked within the parameters set by the church by combining scripture study with church directives along with exploration of their founder's writings. While the other communities in this book first discovered Sophia theology and then took advantage of church protocol or directives to expand her use in worship, the Daughters of Wisdom were catapulted into these new discoveries by the church itself through Vatican II directives to rediscover their spiritual roots.

The Daughters often place agency on Wisdom Sophia herself for choosing the time to make herself known. As one Daughter expressed, "Through generations, across cultures we have prayed for Wisdom to come, 'O Sagesse, O Wisdom Come. Come and be with us.' I really believe she has finally done it in so many ways." The Daughters have been discovering their own voice and spiritual talents at the same time. Having interior visions and experiences of Sophia acknowledges both.

These visions affirmed a feminine face of God for the Daughters who experienced them. All took these images seriously as some type of extraordinary communication that they felt blessed to have had. Some believed their visions were externally generated from God and experienced the vision as Sophia intentionally reaching out to them. Others took a more Jungian approach, seeing their vision as a welling up of a feminine archetype within themselves yet connected to a universal truth.

Others believed their imaginations were involved in the visions but still accepted them as expressions of truth on some level.

Sometimes the visions helped Daughters make difficult decisions, such as deciding to stay in or join the order. The most recent Daughter joined the order in 1997 because of visions of Sophia that confirmed her spiritual call with the Daughters. Even some of those who did not initially agree with the new female images of God would come to accept them after having some affective experience later.

The Daughter's identification with mystics placed their personal prayer experiences within an accepted Catholic tradition. It has been more acceptable, however, to speak of Catholic mystical experiences from the past rather than contemporary occurrences. Before Vatican II, the Daughters were taught to keep their prayer experiences private and to only speak about them in confidence with a superior or priest who would give instructions on how to interpret and handle them. Yet the active interior life that many of the Daughters described has shown that no matter how much an institution may teach, preach, and try to mandate knowledge about God, interior experiences still have a prominent place in what believers deem to be true.

Today, the Daughters have found their own voice; no Daughter indicated that she needed a priest to interpret her prayer experiences. As one Daughter described, "It is a received language to express very intuitive experiences. Before this I did not trust these experiences, but now I trust that God has to be intuitive."[39] Even in the international formation of Daughters worldwide today, the sisters-in-training have been encouraged to share and discuss these experiences among themselves, normalizing their occurrences and placing them into larger conversations about spiritual formation.

In terms of the resource of personal prayer experience for strategic emplacement, this chapter provides us with a longitudinal examination of introducing new prayer imagery into a faith community. The Daughters of Wisdom have been exploring Wisdom Sophia for decades. A few Daughters were enthusiastic early adopters who already had Sophia-type experiences of God and quickly embraced Sophia theology and ritual as a result. Others were more skeptical. Many of these Daughters experienced Wisdom Sophia after they had received instruction and teachings, perhaps prepping them for the experiences they had, or at the very least giving them language and imagery to interpret the experiences that occurred. Some Daughters began to have new experiences and insights during prayer, and others had experiences outside of their prayer time.

The Daughters of Wisdom experiences reveal how religious understanding and interior experiences can be shaped through teaching, encouragement, and embodiment.

When asked about their prayer practices today, most Daughters say that their hour of contemplation in the morning has more to do with stillness and resting in God's love, without image, without message, just presence. Some do spiritual reading. Others take in nature, listening to the morning birds or watching the wind move through the trees. Sophia Wisdom has become their gateway for embracing both the mystery and immanence of God as well as coming to peace with their Catholic heritage.

Occasionally, a new image of Sophia appears. One Daughter described a vision from her most recent annual retreat that bridged her pre–Vatican II prayer experience with Sophia Wisdom today:

> The teaching that Wisdom comes in experience shows me that my small life experiences are really God experiences and they are holy. An image came at retreat last year. She was a crone. She brings me to a hut with a fire and hearth. She wears an iridescent green and brown cloak, shaped like the chapel cloaks from our convent days. I can hide in it. In these visions, Wisdom will come and put that cloak on me. It is a gentle and comfortable existence with her. I don't get a lot of conversation with her but a deep awareness, a heart to heart understanding. I'm in joy when I am there.[40]

Meanwhile, the Wisdom Circles have continued. In 2007, there were thirty Wisdom Circles with 185 participants in New York, Connecticut, Maine, Virginia, South Carolina, New Jersey, Florida, and Illinois, and the program continues today. The Wisdom Circles survive because the monthly gatherings bring Daughters together socially as well as spiritually. Most Daughters live in smaller groups or alone. The Wisdom Circles offer a way for the Daughters to gather with friends while still connecting with a province-wide initiative. This circle structure also allows for diversity of interpretation and expression during the meetings. As one sister admitted, "It still makes me uncomfortable to associate a feminine name for Jesus. I will change the Wisdom Circle materials as I am reading to say 'Jesus Incarnate Wisdom.' "[41]

In the end, the Daughters of Wisdom continue to live through a significant period of change in American Catholic women's religious history. The future of vowed Catholic religious life is in question, as is the role of women in the Catholic Church. The teachings of Wisdom Sophia offer inspiration, expressing the highest hopes for women on earth and the value of the feminine in heaven. Most Daughters cannot imagine being anything but Catholic. One sister described that being Catholic was "in her bones, as much as being Irish." Another Daughter concluded:

> I do think Catholicism has potential in its mysticism, its scriptural and social teaching traditions. Those three together I believe is the only hope for religious life. Protestant ministers have the same stories of sexual oppression. For all its warts, it is Catholic roots from which I grafted other plants. I grew up in the tradition and it is where I come home.[42]

Every Catholic woman religious has a personal prayer life of some kind, and every order has its own unique communal experience and interpretation of its founder's teachings. Like the Daughters of Wisdom, many orders are dedicated to singular themes such as charity, providence, and mercy that inform their spirituality. More histories of Catholic women's orders are needed. To include the interior worlds these women inhabit along with the ministries they undertake will illuminate the lives of Catholic women religious as well as offer insight into the religious impulse among women in general.

3

The Resource of Community

Motherhood of God and the Church of Scotland

> Although she is but one, she can do all things,
> and while remaining in herself, she renews all things;
> in every generation she passes into holy souls
> and makes them friends of God, and prophets.
>
> —Wisdom of Solomon 7:27

It was a misty spring day when I arrived in Edinburgh, Scotland. The area known as Old Town was a labyrinth of historic sites, pubs, and shops surrounding a medieval castle. The occasional bagpipe player could be heard playing for tourists. I eventually found my way to the Divinity School at the University of Edinburgh. In the entrance of the impressive neo-Gothic building was a large statue of John Knox, the sixteenth-century clergyman who led the Protestant Reformation in Scotland.

I came to the University of Edinburgh on sabbatical as a Visiting Fellow. I was looking forward to a relatively quiet time at one of the largest theology libraries in the United Kingdom. It did not take long, however, before my research took an unexpected turn. During my round of introductions, a professor asked if I knew of Anne Hepburn and the 1980s Church of Scotland controversy that had ensued over her prayer to Mother God. When he saw the surprise on my face, he walked over to his bookshelf and offered to lend me a book to read. The slim volume was titled *The Motherhood of God: A Report by a Study Group Appointed by the Woman's Guild and the Panel on Doctrine on the Invitation of the*

General Assembly of the Church of Scotland. The following week, I met the dynamic Mrs. Anne Hepburn, who continues to participate in events at the university. Over the next few months, I had numerous conversations with her and others in the Church of Scotland regarding the uneven legacy of female imagery of God in Church of Scotland worship.

The Church of Scotland is a national church with a congregational structure. Because Scotland is a relatively small country, local debates can easily escalate to a national level. Even so, the Motherhood of God controversy was ignited at an unlikely event. It all started with a prayer said at the 1982 annual meeting of the Church of Scotland Woman's Guild, an organization of churchwomen led by ministers' wives. The consternation over the prayer was so great that within one month it had become front-page news in Scottish newspapers, and it was eventually reported on by the BBC. The controversy would continue for years, and it would not abate even with a formal church inquiry and theological report.

In this chapter, we examine the critical role communities play in supporting or resisting strategic emplacement of female imagery in prayer and worship. We evaluate the importance of church-approved worship resources for arbitrating disputes, and we consider how communities retell the history of a worship controversy. Finally, we examine how female imagery of God is handled in Church of Scotland worship today.

BECOMING AN ASTERISK

The woman at the center of the controversy was born Anne Burton in 1925 in the southwest village of Dailly. She grew up with her blacksmith father after her mother died, and she was raised in the Church of Scotland. Burton was one of only two students from her primary class to attend high school, and she continued her studies in education at Glasgow University on government grants. When Burton graduated in 1945, she chose to teach at a small rural school as a way to give back to her country. After three years, she applied to and was accepted by the Women's Foreign Mission Committee of the Church of Scotland to train and serve for mission work overseas.

In 1950 Burton was sent to Nyasaland, now Malawi, where she was headmistress of a primary girl's school run by the mission. In Africa, her sense of social justice awakened. She knew that she was made principal of the school because she was white, and she saw how her local African friends were denied rights and opportunities because of racism. When the United Kingdom imposed Federation on territories that included the Rhodesias and Nyasaland in 1953, Burton sympathized with the local opposition, as did the Church of Scotland.

Burton's awareness of women's rights also developed through her missionary work. The school had a chapel, and Burton conducted worship functions that women rarely performed back home. As principal, she was expected to lead daily chapel service, choose the prayers and hymns, and deliver short sermons. It was during this time that she also married Hamish Hepburn, a fellow missionary who shared her love of the Nyasaland people and her sense of social justice.

After they married and she became Anne Hepburn, she had her first awareness about the importance of emplacement in written texts. She was shocked to discover that her name had been eliminated from the missionary list, while her husband's name now included an asterisk to indicate his married state. This incident became the moment she remembers awakening to her awareness of sexism, particularly around language. "I was furious! I had been a missionary in my own right, but when I married I became an asterisk! In the missionary records, I disappeared and Hamish's status was enhanced. My sense of injustice to the way women were being treated in the Church rose to the surface. Women were not ordained then, nor could they be elders. So I was very ready when I got back in Scotland and these issues were brought into the open."[1]

Over the next eight years, the Hepburns had three children, and Hamish worked as a district missionary. Anne trained local village women on a volunteer basis because it was against church rules for a minister's wife to be employed. In 1959, a state of emergency was declared by the predominantly white local protectorate government in response to the growing nationalist movement. Four years later, when the political tides had turned and Nyasaland had won its independence, the Hepburns were joyful and optimistic.

The elation, however, was short lived. The democratically elected leader soon began asserting himself as a dictator. Those who opposed him, including local friends of the Hepburns, either were killed or disappeared. In 1964, certain missionaries were told by the government to leave the country; the Hepburns were in Scotland on furlough, and they were informed that they would not be granted reentry. Eventually the decision was reversed, but they decided to remain in Scotland, as their presence in Malawi would pose a danger for any who worked with them. "All our friends were in exile already. It was the most difficult decision we ever made in our lives."[2]

In Scotland, the Hepburns settled in the small coastal town of Kirkcudbright in Bonnie Galloway, where Hamish became the minister of St. Mary's Church. In contrast to Nyasaland, Kirkcudbright was very staid; the previous minister had served the congregation for more than thirty years. A favorite phrase repeated by church members was *Its Aye Been*, "it always has been." As the minister's wife, Hepburn was expected to be president of the Woman's Guild. It was the traditional place where women served in the church, doing good works and raising money.

These traditions continued even as the Church of Scotland was reevaluating women's roles. The Church of Scotland changed its legislation in 1966 to allow the ordination of women as elders, followed by the ordination of women as Ministers of Word and Sacrament in 1968. The Church of Scotland was one of the first national churches to approve the ordination of women, but these currents of change had yet to touch the small town of Kirkcudbright in 1966.

The St. Mary's Woman's Guild was at first surprised when Hepburn suggested that the interim president remain to finish out her term. When Hepburn eventually did assume the presidency, she raised more eyebrows by leading the opening prayers herself instead of calling on her minister husband. Finally, she insisted that the presidency rotate so that other women could share in leadership. Meanwhile, Hepburn continued to speak to churches about the Church of Scotland's work overseas. Her visibility eventually led to her serving as national vice president of the Woman's Guild from 1972 to 1975.

Hepburn was also ordained as an elder in the Church of Scotland in 1974. In the role of an ordained elder, she assumed the "call and commitment to undertake, along with the minister, responsibility for the life of the congregation in all its aspects, including worship, mission, and service to the wider community."[3] As an elder, Hepburn served as a voting delegate at the General Assembly, the governing body of the Church of Scotland. She was also appointed to the Inter-church Relations Committee as well as the International Affairs Sub-Committee of Church and Nation.

It was during this time that Hepburn also became involved in the secular women's movement. Her first influence came from reading Mary Stott, who founded the Woman's Page in *The Guardian* newspaper, but it was the 1975 UN International Women's Year that propelled her into action. As she described her epiphany, "The three-fold aim of Equality, Development, and Peace so obviously equated with the Kingdom of

God issues of Justice, Fullness of Life, and Peace."[4] In 1974, the World Council of Churches (WCC) held a conference in Berlin for the UN initiative titled "Sexism in the Seventies." A questionnaire was sent to member churches, and Hepburn had the task of collating the responses for the Church of Scotland. She credits that project with awakening her awareness of feminist theology and inclusive language. "When a church committee I served on prepared a pamphlet titled 'The Faith of the Church,' I suggested that because of its exclusive language, the title should be, 'The Faith of the Men of the Church.' "[5]

THE PRAYER THAT SHOOK THE WOMAN'S GUILD

In 1981, Hepburn was elected national president of the Woman's Guild. At the same time, her eldest daughter, Catherine, was following in her father's footsteps to become an ordained Minister of Word and Sacrament. Hepburn was delighted with the advances women were making in the church, but advancing the rights of women through the Woman's Guild proved more difficult than she imagined. At her first executive meeting, she invited the pregnant Rev. Kathy Galloway to conduct the Communion Service even though some members were uncomfortable with a woman, particularly a pregnant women, leading worship. Undeterred, Hepburn used her leadership role as Guild president to advocate for greater acceptance of women being made in God's image. She gave many talks and workshops on inclusive language around Scotland during her tenure as president, not just within the Church of Scotland, but to other religious and secular organizations as well.

The greatest resistance to her advocacy, however, came from within the Woman's Guild itself. In 1982, one year into her presidency, Hepburn was preparing her opening remarks for the April annual meeting. She decided to use two prayers the Rev. Brian Wren had written and given to her. Wren would eventually pen one of the most popular books on inclusive language in the United Kingdom, *What Language Shall I Borrow?* While the first prayer was structured on the Holy Trinity and contained individual stanzas calling on "Almighty God, Our Father," "Lord Jesus," and "Holy Spirit," the second prayer began with "God our Mother." Hepburn felt the second prayer would resonate with the Woman's Guild because it contained the phrase "room to grow," which was the Guild's theme for the year:

> God Our Mother, You give birth to all life and love us to the uttermost. Your love surrounds us and feeds us. Within Your love we find our home, our joy, our freedom. You open the world to us and give us room to grow and change.
>
> As you love us so You love all Your children. Help us dear Mother God to catch something of Your love; Your delight in others' uniqueness, Your care for their well-being, Your grief at their suffering, Your patience and forgiveness, Your energy and hope, Your passion for reconciliation and peace throughout the world.
>
> We thank You, our God, that we have come to another Annual Meeting and we ask you to bless us in all that we do today; that this Meeting may be for each of us an opportunity to grow in grace and knowledge of our Lord and Saviour Jesus Christ to whom be the glory now and forever. Amen.[6]

As Hepburn read the prayer, some of the women were audibly upset. Later, the *Glasgow Herald* described the women's reaction to the prayer with a cooking metaphor. "There was a sausage sizzle at the Woman's Guild's annual meeting. Mrs. Anne Hepburn, the outspoken president started it in the opening prayer. 'God our Mother' she began. The sizzle of sharply intaken breath went round. She said it again. Sizzle. Then again. The fat was in the fire."[7] Despite this reaction, the meeting progressed as planned. In the weeks that followed, only two letters of complaint arrived at the Guild office, but Hepburn was aware that others were talking.

The first letter of complaint was written shortly after the event on Friday, May 3, 1982, and it offers us insight into these initial reactions. Even though the letter begins as a collective effort, "As Guild and YWG representatives, we . . . ," it is signed by only one person, a Mrs. Ann Allen, a minister's wife from Glasgow. Like Eric Umile from Chapter 1, Allen would become a major organizer and spokesperson for stopping female imagery of God as well as for challenging Hepburn; both themes are present in her first letter:

> While Mrs. Hepburn is entitled to her own spiritual and theological convictions, we wonder if the Guild Executive shares in the worship of this unknown deity "Mother God." As Christians within the Church of Scotland we know of

> only one God worthy of worship—the God and Father of our Lord Jesus Christ. As women who regard Jesus as the third Person of the Trinity we believe He had one mother—Mary—to whom as Protestants—we do not pray . . . To seek to address God as "Mother" we consider both nonsensical and blasphemous and we do trust that the Guild seeks to grow in neither of these directions! We trust the executive will take note of our disquiet.[8]

Allen's bold statement of faith unfortunately contains an error. Jesus is not the third Person in the Trinity but the second, as in "Father, Son, and Holy Spirit." Clearly, this was an unintended gaffe, but the mistake is illuminating because it suggests that Allen wrote the letter herself. Some have wondered if the Woman's Guild protests were guided by the men around them, but it is doubtful that Allen's minister husband would have made such a basic theological mistake. This point about authorship is not a trivial issue. Unlike all the other chapters, in which the biggest resistance to female imagery of God came from individual men or organizations headed by men, in the Church of Scotland it was a network of women in whom the original outrage and protest against female imagery of God was first expressed and organized.

Allen also misinterpreted the phrase "God Our Mother." Historically, Protestant reformers compared the Catholic veneration of Mary with cautionary tales from the Old Testament against Goddess worship. For Allen and her "collective," it was impossible to hear female language for God without equating this expression with "blasphemous" Roman Catholic worship. According to Hepburn, "The image of God as Mother did not seem to be within the frame of reference of these Christian mothers and daughters."[9]

The Woman's Guild annual meeting was held one month before the General Assembly when all official church committees report on their activities. The Woman's Guild had only been given committee status in 1975. Prior to that date, a man from another committee would report on the Woman's Guild, even though it was the largest women's organization in Scotland, carrying out large-scale service projects and raising significant amounts of money. Hepburn was only the third Woman's Guild president to present to the General Assembly. She expected that her report would be heard with little comment, as in previous years.

To her surprise, when Rev. James Weatherhead stood to deliver his report from the Business Committee, he noted his attendance at the

Woman's Guild annual meeting. He shared his concern over the reaction to Hepburn's prayer. He then proposed that the Woman's Guild form a study group in consultation with the Panel on Doctrine on the concept of "Motherhood of God" and to report its findings to the General Assembly.

Hepburn had to think quickly. Procedurally, it was up to her as the representative of the Woman's Guild to accept or decline this invitation. Hepburn trusted Weatherhead, and she felt it was an appropriate action given the amount of discussion and disquiet her prayer had caused. When she accepted, the General Assembly of the Church of Scotland unanimously passed the following motion, called a deliverance: "The General Assembly invite the Woman's Guild to appoint a small Study Group to consult with the Panel on Doctrine on the theological implications of the concept of Motherhood of God and report to the subsequent General Assembly."[10]

The following day, the *Glasgow Herald* endorsed the motion in its opinion column "Mighty Motherhood" but erroneously reported that the Woman's Guild had orchestrated the motion behind the scenes:

> By persuading the General Assembly to study the concept of the motherhood of God the Woman's Guild pulled off a feminist coup yesterday. To conservative churchmen the very idea may be startling and an unwelcome intrusion of sex politics into sacred things. No doubt the challenge to male dominance in ministry and ritual springs from the feminist desire for equality, which is a campaign for justice. Yet the Woman's Guild have raised a serious issue and one that goes deeper than linguistic trivialities and quibbles.[11]

Such media coverage inflamed the debate. From 1982 to May 1984, many letters were published in *The Scotsman*, *Glasgow Herald*, and the Church of Scotland magazine, *Life and Work*. A significant number of the letters were written by Woman's Guild members objecting to the study group being formed. "I am sure I am one of many members of the Woman's Guild who would ask to be dissociated from these deliberations."[12] "I know that many guildswomen will be very distressed if such a consultation to question the gender of our God goes ahead. Many of us feel that 'sexism' has really gone too far, when the gender of the Almighty is being questioned!"[13]

In terms of theological content, some letters to the editor affirmed the maleness of God. "From a distinctly Christian viewpoint, I can only ask why, when God desired to redeem humanity by sharing in human life, He became the man Jesus Christ—neither a woman, nor a hermaphrodite, but a man."[14] "I would have thought that Mother God was a contradiction in terms or a confusing of genders . . . The recent general assembly, by even agreeing to consider such an issue, has done a great disservice to the Church of Scotland."[15] "I am another Guild president who is in no doubt as to the gender of our God."[16]

Others felt Mother God was blasphemy, echoing Goddess worship and Roman Catholicism. "I find the concept of God being our mother near blasphemous and reminiscent of the Canaanite Asherah mother-goddess the Israelites were warned against—or the Hindu goddesses of today."[17] "Let them cease encouraging the Romanists in our camp to insinuate false doctrines into our Faith. Failure in this can only result in the Church of Scotland taking that road that leads to the worship of Asheroth, and so become more Roman than the Romans."[18] Not surprising, some found the Roman Catholicism reference offensive. ". . . It is important to recognize the status of Mary can play no part in understanding the theological nature of the Motherhood of God. Catholics, especially, may be disturbed at this representation of their beliefs."[19]

Still others were most concerned with preserving their current prayer practices. "To change the whole concept of God as heavenly Father to God our Mother seems to me and I'm sure to many others futile and ludicrous. Since we have all been brought up from cradle to grave to pray to God our Father, it would mean changing the whole pattern of our beliefs and worship, and seems pointless in the extreme."[20] "I hope I will be allowed to continue to pray to my 'Father'—as instructed not by the president of the Woman's Guild, or even by the Panel on Doctrine—but by the King and Head of the Church."[21] "My very great fear is that we shall not be content to stop with the motherhood of God concept but will carry it on to such ridiculous lengths. The hymns will change, our speech, our worship . . . what comes next, Scripture itself? God preserve us from such a change for, in my opinion, rather than helping us to be inclusive in our worship it only hinders it!"[22]

Those who endorsed calling God "Mother" tried to address these accusations. "No one in the Woman's Guild (of which I have been a member for 28 years) wishes to 'abandon the maleness of God.' What we wish to do is to remind ourselves that God cannot be bound by any human analogy—that God is beyond gender."[23] "Can any intelligent reader of Genesis 1:27, take it to mean that God created the human race half in His own image and half not? And yet some form of that belief seems to have bedeviled the Church from the second century onwards . . . Long ago Julian of Norwich called God Mother . . . Surely this would be one step towards the new kind of thinking which the Church and the world both need so badly."[24] "The crux is this: did God's becoming incarnate within a patriarchal human society mean that God prefers patriarchal culture for human society? . . . If the answer is no—and mine has to be No—then it behooves us to try to remove male distortions from 2,000 years of Holy Tradition."[25]

One letter even cited a historical precedent where the Motherhood of God was preached in a Church of Scotland sermon. "Thirty years ago, when I was a student attending Mayfield Church in Edinburgh, I heard a sermon by the great old evangelist, Dr. Robert Menzies, of Camphill. His theme was the Motherhood of God, his text the 66th chapter of Isaiah, verse 13: 'As one whom his mother comforteth, so will I comfort you . . . saith the Lord.' That is the Bible's own picture, clear and unmistakable. How can anyone, Jew or Christian, think of God in terms that are exclusively male?"[26]

Other letters expressed more pastoral concerns. "There are some homes in our land, where children have been so brutally battered by their fathers that it would be quite inappropriate to say to such, 'God is our father.' Much more appropriately could it be said, in some cases, that God is 'Mother.' In due course such a battered child might come to see God is rightly called Father as well as Mother, since He/She is ultimate measure of all love and care, on whom all parents should seek to model themselves, and after whom they should name themselves."[27]

The letters expressed a wide range of opinions and feelings on the matter, yet most were written in a civil tone. A notable exception was a poem titled "Womanhood and the Devil." Even more surprising was its appearance in the official church magazine, *Life and Work*, especially because the magazine stated that not all letters received on the subject were printed. The poem offers us a glimpse into the frustrations a certain segment of men were feeling about women in the 1980s. Its publication also reveals the peculiarity of the time when sexist tropes presented in a witty manner were deemed acceptable for a church magazine, even as the church was trying to address church language in a way that honored and included women. While the magazine did not endorse the poem, clearly the editor felt the letter was a voice in the conversation that warranted being heard; he even highlighted it by putting a box around its contents. Under the heading "Deadlier than the male?":

> In a supremely unenlightened moment, the General Assembly instructed the Panel on Doctrine and others, to consider the

> matter of "The Motherhood of God." To avoid a possible charge of sexual discrimination, the Panel should consider and report the related subject of "The Womanhood of the Devil." As outlined below, there appears to be strong evidence in favor of the latter hypothesis.
>
> Since Lucifer from Heaven fell
> And claimed to be the lord of Hell
> We visualize a handsome male
> Adorned with two horns and tail.
>
> But why? Since evil far and wide
> Stems clearly from the distaff side.
> Our father Adam made the plea
> Of "my Spare Rib hath tempted me."
>
> Eve's story of a speaking snake
> Is just a little hard to take,
> And but for her, we all would be
> Immortals, round an apple tree.
>
> The regicidal Thane of Fife
> Was motivated by his wife.
> Salome's mother's wicked hate
> Put Baptist john's head on a plate.
>
> The songs of sirens at their play
> Lured ancient mariners astray,
> And Samson's locks Delilah sheared
> To leave him feeble in his beard.
>
> When aged Faust to youth aspired
> (Because a young girl he desired),
> Upon the powers of evil cried,
> 'Twas MISTRESS SATAN who replied.[28]

Hepburn tried her best to set the facts straight, but the public debate had taken on a life of its own. "Over the next two years I took part in TV and radio discussions, and with Guild committees, trying to counter the misunderstandings and fantasies masquerading as facts, but to little avail."[29]

THE MOTHERHOOD OF GOD THEOLOGICAL REPORT

Meanwhile, the Motherhood of God study group began to meet. There were five members from the Woman's Guild, including Ann Allen, who wrote the first letter of complaint. There were also four members from the Panel on Doctrine. As the Woman's Guild national president, Hepburn was the convener of the study group, which met eight times over two years.

The final report was drafted by the Rev. Dr. Alan Lewis, secretary of the Panel on Doctrine and lecturer in systematic theology at New College. The two main chapters were "Reaffirming the Tradition: The Fatherhood of God," followed by "Complementing the Tradition: The Motherly Father." The report was unanimously approved by the committee and by the Panel on Doctrine. To encourage consensus, one significant accommodation had been made at the beginning of the study. The committee agreed not to issue worship guidelines, but rather to keep the study at the level of scripture and theology. In the final report, however, under a section titled "Provisional Assessment: Agreement and Controversy," the only remaining disagreement was on whether or not to speak this theological truth during worship:

> The preceding discussion sets out our agreed view that while never ever addressing God directly as "Mother," the biblical writings themselves fill out, add to, and complement our Lord's disclosure of God as our Heavenly Father, with a great range of hints and suggestions drawn from one aspect or another of female experience. This spectrum of female characteristics, activities, figures, and historical individuals, which we have reviewed, in no way retracts or replaces the fatherhood of God. Rather it serves to emphasize that this Father neither possesses male gender nor is of such a nature as to be humanly described only in conventionally masculine terms . . . And perhaps the shorthand we suggested earlier for all this is now seen to be well-attested by and fully in keeping with the biblical witness: God as "the motherly Father."
>
> . . . However we have to admit to disagreement among ourselves when the question is raised of going beyond such motherly *descriptions* of God the Father, to a motherly *address* of him . . . For some of us . . . since Scripture offers no precedent or authorization for addressing God as Mother, we

> are not free to invoke God thus either, but are constrained to approach him in the same terms as did our Lord.
>
> . . . There are others among us who see this distinction between describing and addressing much less clearly. For them it is a failing, not a virtue, when language of theology and that of doxology [formula of worship] are kept distinct . . . The Old Testament addresses God in the imagery of lifeless objects—"My fortress," "My shield," etc.; may we not do so in terms of human persons made in God's image and likeness? If we have had disclosed to us a Father who cares for us with an unsurpassable sort of love that summons up in Scripture itself metaphors of mother and infant, etc., are we not free to give voice and name to this love when we approach God and praise him for it? For those who take this view, to address God as Mother in such a spirit would be to do nothing inconsistent with what Christ and the Bible have done, but with gratitude and wonder follow the lead of the Bible, indeed of Jesus himself, in gathering feminine analogies, alongside others, into humanity's humble task of expressing the inexpressible and praising the One beyond all praising. This stands the principle controversy among us."[30]

The report was to be submitted to the General Assembly in May 1984, but Saint Andrew Press decided to publish the report independently a month before it was formally considered. The decision to publish the report in advance of the vote strategically emplaced the work in a larger public forum. The publication in paperback allowed anyone to read the committee's work, not just the voting members of the 1984 General Assembly. A short preface explained the decision. ". . . So intense was the reaction, both negative and positive, to Mrs. Hepburn's prayer, and so great has been the interest, both within Scotland and beyond its borders, in the setting up of a study group to examine the implications of what she said, that the Saint Andrew Press have judged the Report worthy of publication in independent form."[31]

The Saint Andrew publication of the report became available on the day of the 1984 Woman's Guild Annual Meeting, and Hepburn invited Lewis, the author of the report, to speak to the Guild at its Annual Meeting. Guildswomen usually listened politely to a male minister, especially an academic and a leader of the Panel on Doctrine, but not that day and not on that issue. During the meeting, Lewis was openly confronted by a core of highly dissatisfied, very vocal women who expressed their opposition despite not having read the report. The open conflict, however, resulted in hundreds of copies of the report being purchased in advance of the General Assembly meeting and making it even more newsworthy in the press. By the time the General Assembly convened, the BBC and other media outlets were on hand to cover Hepburn's presentation. For Hepburn, presenting at the 1984 General Assembly would be her last official act in her three-year term as national president of the Woman's Guild.

Because the BBC had broadcast the event, I was able to view a recording of the live proceedings. The historic General Assembly Hall is a large, square room that can accommodate more than one thousand people. Like a courtroom, one side has a large, raised platform with presiding chairs, desks, and microphones extending into the center of the room, edged with a bannister. The other three sides provide seating for voting members. A balcony on all four sides provides seating for nonvoting members and visitors. The most prestigious spectator seating is above where the Moderator sits and is reserved for the Queen or the Queen's representative. In the 1984 BBC coverage, the Queen's representative enters wearing a jacket, tie, and kilt as the Assembly stands. With a slight bow, the Lord High Commissioner greets the Moderator and Assembly. As he sits, all sit.

Six men of the church are on the platform below, all wearing robes. There is also a chair reserved for the committee representative who will be presenting their committee report. Hepburn is seated in the front row waiting to present. At the Moderator's direction, the Assembly sings Psalm 100, *All People That on Earth Do Dwell.* During the singing, the BBC camera pans the room. The Assembly Hall floor is mostly filled with white men, about half of whom are wearing some form of clerical garb, mostly clerical collars. There is a small percentage of women in attendance and even fewer people of color. A scripture passage is read, Acts 1:1–11, where Jesus appears to the apostles. The Moderator then concludes with a prayer that begins "Almighty and Ever Blessed God Our Father in Heaven."

The BBC announcer tells us that today's agenda is first the Business Committee, then the Woman's Guild report. When it is her turn, Hepburn stands and, with a slight bow to the Moderator, steps onto the platform and stands at the microphone. She delivers the Woman's Guild report covering issues of ecumenical outreach, evangelism, justice, and peace. She ends with the Motherhood of God Report and directs the assembly to page ninety-two of their Assembly handout so they can read the report for themselves. She stresses that despite misrepresentation, this report is a study of the scriptures and theology. She emphasizes that the report does not depart from God the Father, noting that the longest chapter in the report is on the Fatherhood of God. She emphasizes that the committee unanimously approved the report, even though differences remained. She notes that the main difference is whether Motherhood of God is descriptive or should be used as address in prayer.

During the question and answer period, things quickly heat up. The first question is posed by the minister husband of a Woman's Guild member, asking if Hepburn feels that the report vindicated her use of the Mother God prayer at the Guild meeting. Hepburn coolly responds that vindication does not seem to be relevant. The next questioner asks why Hepburn did not report on the debate about the report at the Woman's Guild annual meeting. Hepburn replies that there was no debate, as the report had only been published that morning and no one had read it. The third questioner asks, "Will the report tell us if the Divine Feminine is a vegetarian and does she wear a CND [Campaign for Nuclear Disarmament] badge?" The hall fills with laughter and the Moderator intervenes. "You asked the question. It is inappropriate and need not be answered."

A questioner continues to try to compel Hepburn to describe the Woman's Guild reactions. Hepburn responds, "They were unhappy with the setting up of the report, but cannot comment on the report because they had not read it." Another questioner asks her to describe the letters of complaint she received, and she answers that equal letters of complaint and support were received at the office. When a questioner states that 98 percent of the Woman's Guild was "enraged," Hepburn replies, "No vote was taken so that calculation of a percentage would be a wild guess." The BBC announcers intersperse commentary as the debate unfolds. "Usually the Woman's Guild reports are fairly contentious, but not this year . . . Mrs. Hepburn stoutly defends the report . . . The Guild is very much split on this issue . . . Mrs. Hepburn is getting a fairly rough reception from commissioners but coping fairly well . . ."

Then one BBC announcer comments on an unusual fact. He notes that even though the questions were about reactions from the Woman's Guild, only men were approaching the microphone. "All these men are lining up to take the support of the hostile elements of the Woman's Guild that they write this report off . . . It is interesting that no woman has spoken on the other side."

This absence of women is notable. The women of the opposition were not shy. They had written letters, openly challenged ministers, and had been interviewed by the press. Yet when it came to the General Assembly, not one of these guildswomen stood up to speak for herself. The women of the opposition wanted their voices heard but were constrained by the dictates of the traditional gender roles they were living and defending. For these women to have spoken at the General Assembly, they would have had to step across the gender divide and assume the new roles open to women in ordained leadership because only ordained elders and ministers could serve at the General Assembly. Because they were against women's ordination, these ministers' wives could not speak at the General Assembly, so their minister husbands had to speak for them instead.[32]

More insights about these women are revealed when Hepburn invites the author of the report, Rev. Alan Lewis, to respond to a question about who was interviewed for the report. He comes to the microphone and describes how the study group had consulted many men and women, including those who felt alienated from the church:

> At the Woman's Guild annual meeting, my comments met with disbelief and unmistakable derision. It was one of the saddest moments of my life. To hear a plea for help, a cry of anguish from people who feel excluded from the church being treated by derision by those who feel comfortable within the church. The problem is that many of those who feel this way about the church—its language, its forms, its orders—are not any longer functioning within the church because they don't belong to it. Therefore their voices are not heard as they should be in our courts.[33]

The BBC coverage fades out as Lewis is stating that the Motherhood of God has never been considered by the church before.

The debate was heated, but even bigger news occurred after the BBC turned off its cameras. The discussion had yet to engage the theological points of the report when a motion was made to depart from the issue *simpliciter*, meaning without debate. The political move was to stop the emplacement of any official document on the Motherhood of God or even any record of theological floor debate on the topic appearing in the annals of Church of Scotland governance. When this motion was discussed, anyone who tried to raise a point about the contents of the report was cut off because that would have amounted to debating the issue. One small accommodation was made to the motion to at least thank the participants of the Study Group for preparing the report, since the Assembly itself had commissioned it. The motion passed. The last official business was for the Moderator to thank Hepburn for her three years of service to the Woman's Guild, as her term was ending. The Assembly then let out early for its coffee break.

Hepburn and others were shocked by what had just happened. After two years of study with extensive coverage in the press, the General Assembly refused to discuss the issue. Hepburn was met by friends and family, who were visibly upset by what had just occurred. To see the report set aside without discussion and to see Hepburn treated so poorly by men in the Assembly was disconcerting.[34] Hepburn's daughter Catherine had been standing in the hallway when the Assembly let out. She described how certain men were leaving the hall with smug looks on their faces, clearly believing that they had successfully stopped the report.

Their actions, however, only heightened the controversy. Had there been some discussion of the report, the General Assembly might have appeared thoughtful and open instead of arrogant and sexist. A phalanx of reporters had come to the General Assembly to cover the Motherhood of God debate. Now they had a more sensational and accessible story about a woman being openly disrespected by male leaders of the Church of Scotland during its most prestigious church gathering.

The BBC was first in line for an interview with Hepburn. They had set up a makeshift studio with two chairs for Hepburn and a BBC commentator to discuss the proceedings. A portion of the interview aired on BBC TV. The BBC reporter asks, "How disturbed are you by what just happened?" Hepburn responds, "Well, there has been evidence that Scotland and the Church of Scotland has been out of touch with the worldwide church and I believe today confirmed it. But I do believe the tide is running." The reporter replies, "It didn't seem to be running in the Assembly Hall." The reporter then asks how Hepburn is going to convince people in the Church of Scotland about concepts they do not even want to discuss. "The report is published. The report is being read worldwide and people are reading it. You cannot convince people who do not want to be convinced, who don't want to be disturbed, who don't want to study and think."

The interview continues, "Why do you think there is so much hostility towards it, especially among your own Guild?" Hepburn places the blame on the guildswomen. "There are many answers to that. One is although people protest and say of course, when we call God Father we don't think of God as male . . . others quite unconsciously have projected maleness onto God. And for women that can be very comfortable. And I think they feel this is threatened." The interview ends with Hepburn being asked what message she has for women who are upset by what just happened. "The report is out. The matter will not go away. It is being studied, not only in Scotland but worldwide. Just go on and, well, not to leave the church, but to stay within it and try to bring some reasonable attitudes to it."

During this time, a broader culture clash was occurring within the Church of Scotland. Even though the ordination of women was approved in 1968, it was not until 1980 that the first female minister, the Rev. Margaret Forrester, was called by a congregation in Edinburgh. This occurred just two years before Hepburn said her prayer to Mother God in the same city. Both women and men were unsure of how women's ordination would impact traditional gendered roles for service in the church.

Prior to women's ordination, being a minister's wife and leading the Woman's Guild was the most visible way a Church of Scotland woman could serve the church in her own country. Some of these ministers' wives, including Hepburn, were excited about the new opportunities for women, but many ministers' wives were not. When Hepburn, as president of the Woman's Guild, prayed to Mother God, she disrupted the fragile fabric of a national church that was appointing women to ordained leadership in some churches while resisting it in others.

Ministers' wives held a tenuous position in these larger gender debates. They could not speak out against women's ordination because the church had approved it, so objecting to inclusive language became a way to vent frustration, particularly within the safe haven of the Woman's Guild. Hepburn's advocacy for women's equality was a threat to women who had come to believe that women were made by God to be in service to a men's leadership, both at home and in the church. The phrase "Mother God" disrupted this patriarchal view, as did Hepburn, an ordained elder and ardent feminist. By her actions, Hepburn had threatened the Woman's Guild, one of the last remaining public networks where the traditional minister's wife could be celebrated and revered.

In many ways, members of the Woman's Guild got their wish. The Motherhood of God theological report was neither discussed nor endorsed by the General Assembly. After the 1984 General Assembly, the new Guild leaders distanced themselves from the controversy. They elected a president to replace Hepburn who returned the organization to its more traditional role of volunteering and fundraising. Hepburn was invited only to events in which all past Guild presidents were invited; even then, her participation was minimized. According to Hepburn, "I was guillotined."[35]

Hepburn's treatment at the hands of the Woman's Guild and General Assembly did not stop her activism and service. Hepburn went on to become a Church of Scotland delegate to the British Council of Churches (BCC). She also participated in the WCC Ecumenical Decade Churches in Solidarity with Women 1988–1998. Inspired by Judy Chicago's iconic feminist art piece "The Dinner Party," she created a "Scottish Women of Faith Supper Party" for the closing event at Durham Cathedral. Hepburn also travelled to the United States and delivered keynote talks and workshops on inclusive language, women's rights, and Christian mission for the Presbyterian Health, Education and Welfare Association (PHEWA). In 1988, she led a worship wrap-up for a PHEWA conference in Washington, DC, titled "Reproductive Rights and Responsibilities" on the fifteenth anniversary of *Roe v. Wade* in support of a woman's right to choose.

In the 1990s, Hepburn shifted her efforts to secular institutions. She served as chairwoman of the Scottish Convention of Women (SCOW), a coalition of Scottish women's groups lobbying the new Scottish parliament on women's issues. She was also the Scottish representative to help design the Division of Women's Affairs for the newly created European Union. For Hepburn, praying to "God our Mother" was personally edifying, but it was just one facet of a much larger vision she had for women's equality in church and society.

HYMNALS AND HYMNODY

In the Motherhood of God theological report, all the committee members agreed that statements about God being motherly were biblically based and theologically sound. The one remaining disagreement among the committee members was not a theological point but a liturgical one. Many on the study committee, including Hepburn, believed addressing God with female language was appropriate given these scriptural references.

Those who were opposed, however, felt that only words that Jesus used to refer to God were appropriate as direct address in prayer and worship. Their argument was that because Jesus did not use these words as direct address, then churches should not be allowed to use them, either. The problem with this argument is that "Rock of Ages" and other well-loved hymns did not meet this criterion.

The fact that no Church of Scotland worship aids were scrutinized on this point shows that the opposition's claim was more tactical than ideological. Once they lost the theological argument that female imagery of God was biblical, the next level of protest was to claim that it should never be said out loud. Stopping the expression of female imagery of God in communal worship was the ultimate goal of those who opposed it. It was a protest against emplacement.

Communal worship defines and anchors denominational belief for the church community. What is considered acceptable language in church often comes from the language used in worship. Prayers and hymns are expressive and repeatable touchstones for what is considered "the tradition" of the church. From the perspective of ritual emplacement, hymns, psalms, and prayers continue to be repeated throughout a person's life, connecting personal experience with church teachings. These expressions of faith hold power with church members because they are memorized, expressed, and recalled in ways that theological reports are not.

Church-approved worship resources often become the arbiter for community disputes around ritual emplacement. Because the phrase "God our Mother" did not appear in the third edition of the Church of Scotland hymnal or any other official Church of Scotland worship resource at the time, it was considered suspect. Had the prayer read by Hepburn appeared in a Church of Scotland worship resource, it is doubtful that there would have been much controversy at all.

Church of Scotland worship resources have long reflected not just changing preferences for music styles and worship needs, but also theological and political concerns of the times. Initially the hymn itself was considered controversial. In keeping with the Calvinist reform of *sola scriptura*, John Knox and early Scottish reformers only sang the Bible texts of psalms.[36] Hymnody was thought to be too fanciful, and hymn writers were disparaged for expressing their personal experiences of God. Exclusive psalm singing also affirmed a distinct reform identity from other styles of church worship.[37] When a complete psalter from the English Westminster Assembly was presented for use, a Church of Scotland study group took years to "check" the translation. After making substantial changes, the revised work was named the *Scots Metrical Psalter of 1650*.[38]

When the Church of Scotland split during the Disruption of 1843, the main issue with the newly formed Free Church was kirk sessions (churches) wanting to choose their own ministers, but worship eventually became a defining feature as well. As time progressed, the Free Church of Scotland maintained older worship conventions, and by the early twentieth century it had prohibited hymn singing. By contrast, various Church of Scotland kirks in the latter half of the nineteenth century began adding pipe organs and singing hymns. The first *Church Hymnary* was produced in 1898 as a supplement to the psalter. Meanwhile, the Free Church of Scotland and the United Presbyterian Church of Scotland came together as the United Free Church of Scotland in 1900 and later reunified with the Church of Scotland in 1929. By this time, the Church of Scotland had a 1927 revised *Church Hymnary*, and hymns were widely accepted.

A remnant remained outside the 1900 union, however, claiming the title Free Church of Scotland for itself along with the prohibition against singing hymns. Locally known as the "Wee Frees," it continues today as one of the most conservative expressions of Presbyterianism in Scotland. Recently, however, there has been a change in its laws regarding hymnody. In 2010 the Free Church of Scotland lifted its 110-year ban on hymn singing, allowing individual kirk sessions to sing hymns and play musical instruments if they chose. While the church claimed it was not motivated by external factors, others felt the decision was made in order to attract conservative Church of Scotland members disgruntled with church discussions regarding homosexuality.[39]

During the Motherhood of God debate, the Church of Scotland was using *Church Hymnary*, third edition, commonly referred to as CH3. It was published in 1973, before issues of race, class, and gender became hot topics in church music. The introduction to the CH3 begins with a section about ecumenism. Titled "A Changed Context," it cites the different denominations that had been consulted in creating the CH3. In 1988, a separate *Songs of God's People* was produced as a supplement.

A fourth edition of *Church Hymnary* (CH4) was published in 2005, and it is the current hymnal in the Church of Scotland today. The introduction to the CH4 also begins with a section titled "A Changed Context," but instead of delineating church denominations, it focuses on cultural transformations of the third millennium. "Language and the society which articulates it have changed." The Internet and laser surgery are mentioned, as well as the improved rights and opportunities for women. The ordination of women is listed as one of many changes the Church has made to enrich congregational life.

While the CH4 is an inclusive language hymnal, in my first glance through the book it was not obvious. There are still many male hierarchical titles for God (Lord, King, Father), along with very few female pronouns. The two guiding principles used in creating the CH4 are described in a section titled "Language Issues." Inclusivity is one of two main concerns, but this concern is tempered by a desire to minimize disruption to the text:

> Language has changed in the last thirty years, and it was inevitable that issues of exclusivity and archaism had to be dealt with, as much with the twentieth-century texts as with older hymns. The committee decided against adopting a blanket policy, preferring to decide on each text according to its merits. Broadly speaking, where a text could be sensitively amended by the contemporizing of archaic language or by having an exclusive term replaced by an inclusive one, that was done. But where that was not possible, either the whole text was reworked or it was left intact.[40]

I had the opportunity to speak with a member of the CH4 hymn selection committee to understand how the inclusive language decisions were made. He concurred with my assessment that avoiding hierarchical language was not a goal for the CH4; terms like "Lord" remained mostly intact. When I asked other church members how they felt about royal language for God, most were not perturbed. They pointed out that the Church of Scotland is a national church, and the Queen has a place of honor in the General Assembly; Church of Scotland ministers serve as the Queen's chaplain at her country estate in Balmoral. In celebration of the Queen's Diamond Jubilee, the cover of the Church of Scotland magazine *Life and Work* was titled "The Spirituality of the Monarchy."[41] It is safe to say that royal hierarchical language has not been as much of an issue for Church of Scotland members as it might be for Presbyterians in other countries.

In preparing the CH4 hymnal, the General Assembly approved removing almost one-third of the CH3 hymns for the new edition. The removals had less to do with linguistic concerns than with lack of use in worship. This culling process made room for new hymns to be added that reflected new genres of music such as meditative songs, praise songs, and songs from non-European cultures. Emplacement in the hymnal would encourage use and would affirm that these new forms of music were acceptable within the tradition.

The CH4 includes female imagery of God; at least 6 of the 825 numbered psalms, hymns, short songs, doxologies, and amens include some female imagery for God. None of these hymns was present in the

CH3, and all have lyric copyrights after 1973, suggesting that they were written with inclusive language in mind. It is a small corpus of hymns given the size of the hymnal, but including female imagery at all is significant, as it weighs in on the Motherhood of God debate.

Today it can be said that the Church of Scotland accepts female imagery of God as an option for worship because of its emplacement in the latest hymnal approved by the General Assembly. Concentrating all the female imagery in just a few hymns, however, keeps the material segregated. The practical implication is that worship leaders who wish to include hymns with female imagery of God in their worship services now have denominationally approved resources to do so, while the book itself makes this imagery easy to avoid and ignore.

The hymnal does not provide titles for hymns, but it does index the first lines of each hymn. Of the six hymns that include female imagery of God, three hymns express this imagery in the first line, making them easy to find. One hymn that stands out for its declaratory female imagery of God is Hymn 117, which begins "Mothering God." There are two music settings, the first with the heading "Mother Julian," referring to Julian of Norwich, the fourteenth-century English mystic who referred to God as Mother in her writings. The second music setting has the title "Mothering God." The hymn is Trinitarian with three stanzas, each stanza referring to a person of the Trinity as Mother:

> Mothering God, you gave me birth
> in the bright morning of this world.
> Creator, source of every breath,
> you are my rain, my wind, my sun.
>
> Mothering Christ you took my form,
> Offering me your food of light,
> Grain of life, and grape of love,
> Your very body for my peace.
>
> Mothering Spirit, nurturing one,
> In arms of patience hold me close,
> So that in faith I root and grow,
> Until I flower, until I know.

Hymn 118 begins with "Womb of Life." The hymn also has a Trinitarian structure, with the first and third persons of the Trinity including female imagery. "Womb of life and source of being, home of every restless heart, in your arms the worlds awakened; you have loved us from the start. We, your children, gather round you at the table you prepare. Sharing stories, tears, and laughter, we are nurtured by your care." After the second stanza addresses "Word in flesh, our brother Jesus," the last stanza refers to the Holy Spirit as "Brooding Spirit . . . Labour with us, aid the birthing of the new world yet to be, free from status and division, free for love and unity."

Lastly, Hymn 593 begins with "She sits like a bird" and contains the most female pronouns for God, more than any other hymn in the hymnal. Significantly, it was co-written by Rev. John Bell, the convener of the CH4 hymnal committee. It was originally written for the Iona Community, an ecumenical Christian community founded by a Church of Scotland minister in the 1930s. Today, the Iona Community is known for its creative worship. "She sits like a bird, brooding on the waters . . . she sighs and she sings, mothering creation . . . She wings over earth, resting where she wishes . . . she nests in the womb . . . She dances in fire . . . she weans and inspires all whose hearts are open, nor can she be captured, silenced, or restrained. For she is the Spirit, one with God in essence, gifted by the Saviour in eternal love; and she is the key opening the scriptures, enemy of apathy and heavenly dove."

The CH4 hymnal contains three other hymns that include female imagery for God in their lyrics, but not in the first line. In hymn 592, the dove reference for the Holy Spirit is gendered female with one female pronoun. "Like the murmur of the dove's song, like the challenge of her flight, . . . Holy Spirit, come." Hymn 597 includes a second and third stanza where the Holy Spirit is described both as a mother and a father using essentialized gender characteristics. For the mother stanza, the pregnant female body becomes the metaphor for God. "Like a mother, you enfold me, hold my life within your own, feed me with your very body, form me of your flesh and bone." The next stanza celebrates traditional roles of fatherhood as its metaphor. "Like a father, you protect me, teach me the discerning eye, hoist me up upon your shoulder, let me see the world from high."

A different interpretation of gender is presented in Hymn 134. The author Brian Wren also wrote the Mother God prayer that Hepburn used in 1982. Originally written five years after the Motherhood of God controversy, the first line of the hymn states, "Bring many names, beautiful and good." There are two gendered stanzas to "mother God" and "father God," and they are significant because the imagery deliberately disrupts the gender essentialism found in the previous hymns. Here the strong mother God is working, while the warm father God hugs children. "Strong mother God, working night and day, planning all the wonders of creation, setting each equation, genius at play: Hail and Hosanna, strong mother God! Warm father God, hugging every child, feeling all the strains of human living, caring and forgiving till we're reconciled: Hail and Hosanna, warm father God!" By placing "masculine" characteristics on mother and "feminine" characteristics on father, familiar gendered language is maintained, but is employed in a mixed, or trans fashion.

In reviewing the hymnal, I was also interested in how the CH4 presented the Holy Spirit, because if a church wants to use a female reference for God, it is most likely to refer to the third person of the Trinity as female. As we have seen, however, female imagery for God in the CH4 is rarely used. The Holy Spirit section of the CH4 includes forty-six hymns. The majority of the hymns use nongendered imagery for the Holy Spirit, including fire, dove, wind, and tongues. The most obvious change from the CH3 is the overall reduction of pronouns. Only a few hymns to the Holy Spirit use gendered pronouns at all. Besides the few female references already listed above, the occasional male pronouns for the Holy Spirit appear mostly in older hymns, such as Hymn 581, "He whom the Lord foretold," and Hymn 582, "The coming of his Spirit."

The refrain of Hymn 133 states, "May the Church at prayer recall, that no single holy name, but the truth that feeds them all, is the God whom we proclaim." This perspective echoes the majority opinion of the Motherhood of God report. The Church of Scotland appears to have made only modest moves in its CH4 hymnal regarding female imagery for God, but the references that do appear are rich in imagery and significant in meaning.

REFLECTIONS FROM CURRENT CANDIDATES FOR MINISTRY

There is less controversy today about inclusive language than in the past. It may still be consciously attended to in liturgy, but the subject rarely draws headlines in church bulletins, sermons, or liturgy meetings anymore. Professors at the University of Edinburgh Divinity School have commented that few undergraduate students use inclusive language in their papers and few show concern, even when it is brought to their attention.

To get a better understanding of current attitudes about inclusive language in church and society, I conducted a group interview with Church of Scotland candidates for ministry who were studying at the University of Edinburgh. In addition to their academic study, these candidates were also working in ministry placements where they learned to prepare and lead worship. By graduation, they would have served at three five-month church placements to experience the variety of congregations, church ministries, and liturgical styles occurring in the Church of Scotland today.

As the candidates entered the room, it was easy to see how much had changed since the 1980s regarding gender and church work. More than half of the candidates were female, and almost everyone was studying to become an ordained minister of the Word and Sacrament. Reflecting changing attitudes regarding gender and work, the one candidate studying to become a deacon was male. The Deacon position had traditionally been called Deaconess and was traditionally held by women in the Church of Scotland; they were even sometimes referred to as "Protestant nuns."

Nine of the fourteen candidates attended the meeting, and they were a lively and collegial group. During our discussion, their thoughtful reflections were punctuated with good-natured joking with each other. They ranged in age from mid-twenties to early fifties. Six had grown up in the Church of Scotland, and three had converted from Anglican and Lutheran traditions.

All of the candidates were familiar with the term "inclusive language." When I asked them to provide examples, most gave examples for humankind rather than for God. "The psalm, 'Brother let me be your servant,' becomes 'Brother Sister let me serve you.' " "The scripture 'Blessed are all men who' becomes 'Blessed are all those who' or "Blessed are all that.' "[42]

The candidates were less concerned about gendered language for God because they felt the language issue was more complex. As one candidate explained, "I don't think gender is so much about God because God is so much bigger than what we can put into words anyway." When asked for examples, most said they would expect to hear terms like "Creator God," "Sustaining God," or "Redeeming God," rather than the feminization of God. "It is other language to explain properties of God. Less about pronouns, more about . . . awesomeness."

There was also a definite desire among the candidates to move beyond defining inclusive language solely in terms of gender. "It is not just a gendered context. It is the way we use language in a de-humanizing way." All the candidates felt strongly that inclusive language needed to be defined more broadly. They wanted to stay away from language that reinforced racism, classism, or any form of alienation. There was eagerness among the ministers-in-training to adjust language in worship so that all would feel included, particularly during service prayers and responses. "Recently we said we were 'standing before God.' Then someone in a wheel chair at the service mentioned that he would love to stand before God but could not. So now we say, 'We come before God.' "

There was some disagreement regarding whether inclusive translations provided clearer meaning or not. Some felt it did. "Inclusive language can help clarify. The problem with the word man or men is the lack of clarity. Are you speaking of humanity or are you talking about some bloke?" But others felt that inclusive language could conceal deeper meanings. For these candidates, instead of correcting the "flaw" in the text, they preferred the original word choice because it allowed the bias to be explored. I found it interesting that the example given contained a gender justice theme that was easier to illuminate by not adjusting the text. "We could be studying a passage about 'our son's' and the inclusive translation is 'our children' but that could obscure the meaning of unequal treatment of inheritance."

The one gendered name for God that did receive more discussion was the term Father. Some felt that it was important to be sensitive to people based on their personal histories with their fathers. "There are two sides to using Father. There is the male aspect, but there is also the positive or negative aspect that word has for people. It may have nothing to do with a male issue, it is just that they can't relate to God as Father because of their own father." This point was also raised in the Motherhood of God report.

Other candidates were reluctant to generalize reactions to "Father" language. "I don't have a father, but I never had a problem with calling God 'Father.' And my mum had an abusive father, and she doesn't have a problem with that either. So I think that a lot of people that have a good relationship with their fathers assume that people who don't will have a problem so they change it to mother language. Well, not all mothers are great either." "From the discussions I've had with people after services, people have far greater problems with how you talk about motherhood and mothering on Mothering Sunday than we ever have about images of God as a parent."

One strategy has been to move away from father and mother imagery for God in order to avoid these complications. As the candidates pointed out, however, other language presents problems too. "If you think in a concrete manner, then analogies to mother hens, rocks, or the concept of Sustaining God is possibly more difficult to understand than Father. I love language and poetry, but you need a certain level of literacy to understand the metaphorical language. So in trying to be inclusive, you are actually raising the literacy level you need to engage with God, which excludes other folk." Some extended these concerns to basic theology and Bible terms. "What does redemption mean to the bloke on the street? Once we use theological terms in church, does the congregation understand what we mean?"

Throughout the discussion, I found the candidates were most concerned with using language that did not alienate their congregations. These candidates wanted to make sure that inclusive language did not reach too far beyond the familiar. As one candidate put it, "How far can we go with things without actually imposing our thoughts and our ideas on other people?" I found this attitude interesting because the beginnings of the inclusive language movement intentionally challenged churches to be more conscious about the language they used. Anne Hepburn's prayer to "God our Mother" deliberately confronted the status quo.

It was also interesting that while the candidates hesitated to confront parishioners about their language choices, they had become aware of the importance of inclusive language themselves, often through abrupt, direct confrontation in the classroom. "Somebody challenged me in my first year here in a tutorial in front of the whole group on my use of language. And that ten minute outburst had a profound effect on my use of language. So there you are. I believe it was good. It made me think about the language I use that I never had to think about before." "I think we are all being taught in a context that says 'use inclusive language.' One professor who teaches here is very big on inclusive language. The first thing you get in the very first lecture is, 'Here is my handout on inclusive language. You will be marked down, if you are marked at all, if you do not use inclusive language. This is the way that we do things here. It is ill-mannered, it is rude, and it is not academic not to do so.' Once you get into the habit, it seems to penetrate everywhere because it is part of how you do things." Other candidates were challenged to use inclusive language in their ministry placements. "I got told off in my first placement for using Lord God in my prayers every week because that is just how I pray in my head. Now I seek what different words and phrases can we use."

Given their concerns, I asked the candidates if they felt inclusive language was important. Everyone said yes, because using new words about God expanded one's understanding and experience of God. "We shut that down when we just use Father. In my placement, I would be quite happy saying Father all the time but that's not what they do. And so I've had to explore in my language other ways of addressing God and other ways of speaking about God."

According to the candidates, there are still large portions of the Church of Scotland that do not use inclusive language, particularly in the evangelical wing of the church. "I'm going to throw something in here that might stir things up a bit more. In a fairly evangelical context, there hasn't been much attention to inclusive language." "That is the situation where I come from. There still isn't any consideration in any way that we should have inclusive language. I'm not saying that they were completely ignorant of it, because they did realize they were using exclusive language, but they looked at it entirely different. Many of these churches still will not appoint a female minister."

The connection between inclusive language and women's ordination has been made before. Inclusive language is just one front for fighting larger gender changes in church and society. Later I learned that entire presbyteries (regions) in Scotland still have yet to appoint a female minister or even a female elder almost four decades after women's ordination was approved. The Church of Scotland echoes similar themes from earlier chapters, where those churches resisting emplacement of women in ordained positions correlate highly with those resisting emplacement of female imagery for God in worship.

One major change compared with the era of the Motherhood of God debate is that local church communities today feel settled, free to worship as they wish without interference. Whether church members are for or against women's ordained leadership, they know which kirks and presbyteries to attend for worship as well as what language they will hear. Female ministers have told me they do not even bother applying for certain positions based on this knowledge.

While the candidates agreed that inclusive language is important, they also felt that there were situations when it was best to use the older, exclusive language when it came to pastoral concerns. They saw little reason to encourage infirm elderly to change. "I think there are some contexts where you go with what is known. I have regularly done services in nursing homes, ministering to people with dementia. You have to go with the old version. If you stick to what they know and understand, you at least are touching them in some way."

The candidates also described people who wanted more stability in their church language because of changes to their secular language. "There are certain nursery rhymes and fairy stories that can't be used because they are considered un-PC. I've come across certain people who will push against this by saying, 'They are not going to tamper with my Bible, with my hymns, the things that are spiritually important to me.' " The candidates appeared sympathetic to this sentiment. "Hymns and prayers are areas where people feel they can say no, because they are quite deep for them." Others explained it differently. "There have been changes in society, and the churches have actually been slow in adopting inclusive language. So I think within the church at the moment, there is very much a generation that has not bought into political correctness still."

There was less sympathy for younger people who did not embrace inclusive language. "I was astonished when I was tutoring last year and getting work back. Young educated women were happy to use utterly exclusive language because the new F word is feminism. 'I'm not a feminist! That's the worst thing you can possibly be.' That's been a fascinating thing for me because they are excluding half of humanity in the language they use."

I asked the candidates to describe instances when they saw church members most troubled by language changes. The examples had less to do with the meaning of the language and more to do with memorization. Many candidates mentioned seeing congregants confused or upset with changes to the Lord's Prayer. The word changes mentioned were relatively small: "Trespasses" to "Debts" and "Thou" to "You." Congregations, however, noticed these changes, and many were troubled because most people had recited the Lord's Prayer from memory since they were small children.

Adjustments to Christmas carols were also mentioned. The candidates discussed welcoming someone back who was raised in the church versus welcoming someone anew who has never been to church; as church attendance continues to decline overall in Scotland, both groups are increasingly represented at Christmas services. "You have people who only turn up at church for Christmas and when the Christmas carols have been changed, they feel a sense of alienation because what little they know by heart has been taken away from them. So how is that inclusive?" "You could also turn that around. For someone who has never been in church before, the old, male language could feel alienating and excluding."

The candidates acknowledged that the goal of making church language accessible, inclusive, and welcoming for everyone was a near impossible task. Perhaps for this reason, the majority of candidates were comfortable adjusting texts as they were read, and quite a few preferred it. "Often when people are reading they will insert the word themselves. So if Paul is saying, 'Brothers,' the reader may say 'Brothers and Sisters.' It becomes more natural when people add that inclusiveness into the reading." I tested them with a few other examples, and they responded quickly with alternatives. I was impressed with the candidates' ease and facility in making these language changes spontaneously.

The candidates also felt that the best way to approach inclusive language was to just do it, rather than draw attention to it. "If you make a song and dance out of it, saying 'Now we are going to use inclusive language,' you will get resistance. But if you don't, you just get on with it." Another candidate advised, "Just start the prayer, 'Mothering God.' You don't have to explain it. If you focus on Motherhood every week, people will have a problem with it. But if you scatter, sometimes using it and sometimes not, people will not notice." Others noted that when the language fits the message, there is more acceptance. "When I do the same sort of prayer in different weeks, I relate it to the topic of the service. Sometimes it will be Mothering, sometimes it will be Creator God, sometimes it will be Gracious God, whatever. The congregation doesn't question it because the image works with the context." If the goal was to normalize the practice, then the seminarians were accelerating the transition with their low-key approach. If the use of inclusive language emplacement was to change attitudes and perceptions of congregants, however, then the impact of this approach may be more open to question.

As the session drew to a close, I asked the candidates if any particular image of God was currently inspiring them and what word the image represented. Four candidates described images, and they reflected diverse ways people see God today. Two images had gender, and two did not. Jesus was one of the images, with arms open on the cross, communicating "embrace." A mother hen with chicks was another image, representing "gathering." The two nongendered images described were bread for "ecumenism" and rock for "strength."

I admired the candidates' willingness to struggle with complex issues around worship and inclusivity. They were not as polarized in their attitudes as Church of Scotland ministers had been in the past, but neither were they as concerned. One candidate summed it up with the following statement:

> Every language has problems, but there is an immaturity of kicking against it, forcing and shoehorning everybody into a different way of speaking because you think it is better. That can cause as many problems. Look. Somehow God has been capable of interacting with us when we haven't been using the right language, and is still capable of interacting with us when we change the language, so how can we model that? The language is always going to be provisional and is not as important as the relationship that is going on. God is far better at this than we are.

ECHOES OF THE MOTHERHOOD OF GOD

Today, most ministers who include female imagery of God in their services do so occasionally and without much discussion or debate. In 2000, the Moderator of the General Assembly was able to open a session with the prayer "O God, gentle, tender Father and strong, secure Mother" with no rebuke. A few years later, the General Assembly would approve the CH4 hymnal with similar language. In the end, emplacement of female imagery of God in Church of Scotland worship aids happened with little fanfare or debate.

There are still occasions, however, when the Motherhood of God controversy is remembered and retold, even in published liturgy. In 2010, Church of Scotland minister John Bell and Graham Maule, convener and member of the CH4s hymnal committee, authored a liturgy titled *God and Her Girls: A Celebration of the Giftedness of Forgotten Women.* It was created for BBC Radio and then performed in Iona, Glasgow, Canada, and the Christian Greenbelt Festival before publication.

The worship service features the naming of women in scripture and the singing of hymns with female imagery of God. In the middle of the *God and Her Girls* liturgy, the following account of the Motherhood of God controversy is read by the leader:

> The issues of women in the church and feminine language for God have long been vexatious topics. Different denominations have had debates on language and inclusion over the past thirty years, most of which have been fractious. In the early eighties, the Church of Scotland's General Assembly commissioned a report on how feminine images and language are used to describe God in the Bible. When the "Motherhood

> of God Report," as it was called, was eventually presented to the Assembly, it refused to discuss it. The Scotsman newspaper called it a "clear slap in the face." Although some members recognized the value of the report, the Assembly threw it out without debate. Why female language and images should have been so offensive to the predominantly male assembly, no one really knows. Today, we might expect the response to be different, although there may still be Christians who find the matter unsettling. Now, granted, feminine language is not on every page of the Bible, but because God has inspired and endorsed it, verses such as those we will hear from the Psalms, Proverbs, Isaiah, and Luke can't just be ignored.[43]

Following the historical account is the section "Words approved by God." The assembly sings scripture passages where God is described as mother (Isaiah 66:13), midwife (Isaiah 66:9), wisdom (Proverbs 8:1), table setter (Psalm 23:5), mother hen (Luke 13:34b), and mistress of household (Psalm 123:2).[44]

In the foreword, the authors explain the impetus for the liturgy and why the Motherhood of God controversy was included. "The roots of the liturgy—as indicated in the texts—are in the disdain once rashly demonstrated in the inability of a male-dominated church assembly to accept the fruits of a Bible Study about the nature of God. But other antagonisms have also hastened its appearance, including the perception still encountered in some churches that women of the Bible are either whores or virgins with little in between."[45]

I was challenged by the last statement because I was meeting very well-read and intellectually nuanced Christian ministers in Scotland. Even beyond the university, there was pride, rooted in the Reformation, in a rigorous commitment to scripture study. Was it true that some preachers continued to create shallow caricatures of women in the Bible based purely on sexuality? Then I remembered a visit to a small village in Scotland five years prior when I heard a sermon preached about "the prostitute Mary Magdalene." Afterward, I asked the minister how he knew that Mary Magdalene was a prostitute, because that characterization was more trope than fact. He referred to the seven demons cast from her and said that being a prostitute was the worst thing a woman could be. Apparently, that sermon was not an isolated case.

Luckily, other sermons correct these skewed perceptions. In 2012, on Mother's Day, the Very Reverend Finlay Macdonald preached at the historic St. Giles Cathedral on the Royal Mile in Edinburgh. Mothering

Sunday offered the opportunity to revisit issues around God and female language, and he used the church's own history to make the topic relevant and relatable:

> Thirty years ago, in the spring of 1982, the Church of Scotland found itself caught up in a controversy which rumbled on for the next couple of years. As these things do it ruffled feathers, divided opinion, and led to questions in the General Assembly . . . Thirty years on, and on this Mothering Sunday, what are we to make of that distant controversy and the issues raised by it? One, that there is a range of feminine imagery also in the Bible; two, that prominent and significant biblical characters include women and three, that, despite what many thought at the time, the imagery reflected in the "Dear Mother God" prayer was nothing new . . . The prayers which created such controversy in the Kirk thirty years ago were drawing on a rich, if somewhat forgotten tradition and reminding us, as it is good to be reminded on Mothering Sunday, of the God who gives us life and whose gracious love nurtures and guides us through all our days.[46]

In bringing up the report, he created an opportunity to preach and teach on its message. By focusing on three points that are relevant for Christians today, he made the teachings of the report current and visible.

Occasionally the report gets referenced by those who continue to oppose it. A book of daily reflections written by Selwyn Hughes was published in 2011 titled *Every Day with Jesus.* Day 324 is titled "A watershed issue," and Hepburn is mentioned by name. "When Anne Hepburn . . . used the expression "Dear Mother God" . . . so intense was the reaction . . . that a special committee was set up." He erroneously cites the Motherhood of God report as concluding that Father is the only correct term for God. "They concluded that though we should keep to the Scriptural term "father" when addressing God, we should think of him in terms of a Motherly Father." A second entry continues in Day 325 titled "Are we going too far?" ". . . the idea of addressing God as 'Mother' has not been an issue in the Church until recent times, but [with] the rise of feminism and political correctness the matter is being raised in almost every section of the church—the evangelical wing included . . . Is this going too far? Personally I believe it is. Unless we are careful, we will turn the God and Father of our Lord Jesus Christ into a goddess or female deity."[47]

The Motherhood of God controversy has become a cultural marker in the history of the Church of Scotland, and emplacement continues through recalling its history. The dramatic details, however, allow the story to be quoted and referenced in a variety of ways and with dramatically different conclusions. Hagiographies are developing in which the history is being reduced to fit more standard tropes of men against women or the perils of worshipping God with female imagery. At the same time, almost everyone agrees that the handling of the report was a low point in recent Church of Scotland history. Those who favor inclusive language point to the bad behavior of the 1984 General Assembly, while those who oppose inclusive language point to the folly in having it commissioned in the first place.

The Motherhood of God controversy also continues as a defining moment in the personal histories of those involved. At the age of eighty-six, Anne Hepburn published her personal memoir, *Memories of Malawi and Scotland*, in 2011. The section titled "Motherhood of God" is only five pages of more than one hundred pages about her life, but it is the period that is most remembered by others. The Rev. Alan Lewis passed away in 1994, but almost twenty years later friends still talk about his poor treatment at the 1982 Woman's Guild Annual Meeting. In 2012, an obituary appeared in *The Scotsman* for the Reverend Norman Macrae, and it mentioned his wife's participation in the study thirty years prior. "He also took enormous pride in—and gave much support to—Clare's continuing work, in particular her involvement in the influential study group set up by the General Assembly to examine the implications of 'the concept of the Motherhood of God.'"[48]

CONCLUSION

When Anne Hepburn prayed "God our Mother" at the 1982 Woman's Guild Annual Meeting, she had no idea of the controversy it would create or how much she would be identified with that prayer. Her leadership position allowed her to select and say the prayer in front of hundreds of women and men, but strategic emplacement of this new language and imagery of God in the Church of Scotland required a community of support and participation. The Motherhood of God controversy has allowed us to examine the essential resource of community to foster or impede change in prayer and worship.

The community that sought emplacement of female imagery of God was diffuse but effective. It included individuals in key positions across the church and did not need centralized coordination because of a network of personal relationships. The convener of the Business Committee, Rev. James Weatherhead, first proposed a Motherhood of God study at the 1982 General Assembly, thus creating a church-wide platform to engage the topic. Hepburn accepted the directive because she knew and trusted him, and the Woman's Guild central committee publicly supported Hepburn despite complaints. The Panel on Doctrine secretary, Rev. Alan Lewis, authored the report and defended the theology in front of the Woman's Guild and General Assembly. The publishers of Saint Andrew Press played a large role because they published the report and made it available to everyone when others wanted the report ignored. Years later, the Ch4 committee continued to advance the cause when it included hymns with female imagery of God in the latest Church of Scotland hymnal.

The community of those opposed to female imagery of God also had broad support. The vehemence against female imagery of God in the 1980s reflected a frustration with women's changing roles in church and society. The original opposition to Hepburn's prayer came from women, specifically ministers' wives. The Motherhood of God debate in the Church of Scotland empowered women's voices in unintended ways. These Woman's Guild ministers' wives voiced their protest by speaking up at meetings, writing letters, and engaging the press. Their activism, however, only went so far. By clinging to traditionally gendered church roles, these ministers' wives were not ordained themselves and therefore could not speak at the General Assembly; their husbands posed questions on their behalf instead.

As we saw in the Methodist chapter, once women's ordination was approved, it was no longer possible to openly object to women's ordination without appearing to be at odds with the church. Shifting the protest to female language for God allowed similar sentiments to be aired without appearing to be in schism with church decisions. Protests against the Motherhood of God also extended the reach of the opposition. Today, ministers in the Church of Scotland who dislike female imagery feel emboldened never to use it in worship, and ministers who do include female imagery of God prefer not to draw attention to the practice so as not to provoke questions or controversy. So while emplacement of female imagery has been successful in its inclusion in the latest hymnal, it has still been successfully dampened in practice by certain segments of the church.

There were other similarities with the *Wisdom's Feast* dispute in Chapter 1. Those opposed to female imagery of God first attacked the practice theologically, claiming that the imagery was non-Christian. In both cases, the original outrage linked the practice to Goddess worship, where an image of a deified female could only be an expression of heresy. In both cases, theological inquiries concluded that it was biblical to describe God using female characteristics. In the United Methodist example, the theological inquiry stopped the national debate. In the Church of Scotland, the debate continued, as a second argument was developing that acknowledged female characteristics of God, but claimed the characteristics should not be spoken. Rev. Selwyn Hughes published this argument as recently as 2011.

With time, the Motherhood of God controversy has slipped into history, but it also has been remembered and retold, sometimes as a hagiography of the original events. The 2010 liturgy *God and Her Girls* recalls a simplified story about men in power behaving badly toward women. This narrative passes lightly over the role of women who instigated the original outrage and who continued to oppose its exploration and performance. It also obscures the actions of men who were advocates for the new language. Other modern retellings have misquoted the facts. Contrary to Hughes's assertion in the 2011 devotional, the Motherhood of God report did not prohibit calling God "Mother."

Perhaps the greatest legacy of the Motherhood of God report on worship today has been the production of new worship aids. As we saw, the importance of church-approved worship resources for settling community disputes around ritual emplacement cannot be underestimated. If Hepburn's original Mother God prayer had appeared in a Church of Scotland worship resource, it is doubtful that there would have been much controversy. The compilers of the CH4 hymnal may be the unsung heroes of the debate. The current hymnal now contains six hymns with female imagery of God, including the hymn that begins "Mothering God." Twenty years later, the 2005 General Assembly finally approved the use of female imagery of God in Church of Scotland worship without discussion or controversy.

The contours of inclusive language in the Church of Scotland have some distinctive features when compared with the language used by other communities featured in this book. Worship leaders in the other chapters were interested in reducing hierarchical language along with male language for God to address their goal of inclusivity. By contrast, the Church of Scotland seemed less concerned with the terms "Lord" and "King" because of its history as a national church and its relationship to the monarchy.

Another striking feature for the Church of Scotland has been that even with feminine characteristics, the term "Father" often remains. In the Motherhood of God report, the main chapter on gender and God was titled "Complementing the Tradition: The Motherly Father." The prayer said at the 2000 General Assembly to a gentle Father and strong Mother also used this formula of maintaining a male/female binary, but inverting the essentialized characteristics usually associated with each.

A strong Mother is not out of character for a Scottish woman. One Church of Scotland minister complimented Anne Hepburn when describing her as a "a true Scot." In Scotland, a fighting spirit is respected in both women and men, as the Scottish people have a long history of being great warriors. Hepburn even described herself this way when she dedicated her memoir to her late husband Hamish, "The salt to my pepper."

Meanwhile, progress is being made on topics of gender in the church. Most presbyteries today have female ministers leading churches, and only a few presbyteries remain exclusively male led, yet all operate within the national Church of Scotland. In a similar vein, there are now hymns with female imagery in the CH4, yet there are congregations who will never sing them. Controversy surrounding women's leadership and inclusive language has settled down in part because church communities have been left alone for more than two decades to handle these issues as they see fit. Rightly or wrongly, a certain stasis exists. The controversy today has now shifted to homosexuality as the Church of Scotland wrestles with allowing openly gay ministers to serve the church.

The Woman's Guild has also changed. The name is now the Guild, and men are allowed to join. It remains one of the largest voluntary organizations in Scotland, and fundraising is at an all-time high. The Guild also now actively promotes contemporary social justice campaigns to support women, and it has taken a lead role in Scotland to help stop domestic violence and human trafficking.

Today, there is also a balance of men and women training to be ministers, and they have less polarized views around inclusive language. The candidates' understanding of inclusivity has expanded beyond gender to include class, race, and disabilities. Updating archaic language also fits within this broad definition of inclusiveness. These ministers-in-training are also less concerned about the exclusivity of the printed word, as they have developed oral skills to add inclusivity to their speaking of written texts during worship.

Younger ministers today are less likely to make waves, as the Church of Scotland is focused on making the church more welcoming rather than challenging for its members. Creating community is more important than ever, and having community support for the language used and the message preached remains a central concern. Meanwhile, Hepburn is now in her late eighties, and she proudly carries a bag with the famous phrase "Well-behaved women rarely make history." For the Church of Scotland, she is a reminder of this truth.

4

The Resource of Evangelization

Lutheran Herchurch

> Does not wisdom call, and does not understanding raise her voice? On the heights, beside the way, at the crossroads she takes her stand; beside the gates in front of the town, at the entrance of the portals she cries out.
>
> —Proverbs 8:1–3

The road to the Twin Peaks neighborhood of San Francisco wound up and up, revealing a spectacular view of the surrounding area. Famous bridges and iconic skyscrapers dotted the urban landscape. The church had a traditional look, with a large steeple that could be seen from miles away. It faced six lanes of traffic, a major artery into the city with a strip mall across the street. As I got closer, I could see three large banners with less-than-conventional messages: "God welcomes all to Her table," "www.herchurch.org," and "Goddess Rosary, Wednesday 7:30."

I was looking forward to meeting this Lutheran community. The congregation only began including female imagery of God in their liturgies in 2003. I wondered how feminist theology worked for them in worship, especially because gender and sexual orientation in San Francisco were often seen as more fluid than the binary claims underpinning much of the ritualizing found in the other communities featured in this book.

I also knew that the pastor was a generation younger than the other religious leaders I had interviewed. Why would someone of her generation begin to embrace feminist theology in such a public way at this time? I wondered if something about this church would reveal where feminism and Christianity might be headed. They also used the words "Goddess" and "God/dess" in their liturgies. Could the polarizing discourse of God versus Goddess also be giving way to something new?

One thing was certain—this church was committed to evangelization. In all four communities profiled in this book, the resource of evangelization provided the momentum and courage to take risks in the strategic emplacement of female imagery of God in worship. Only this congregation, however, had a formal mission statement to promote Christian feminism. The church advertised its mission with a developed Web site, Internet-based rosary ministry, Faith and Feminism conferences, and YouTube videos. Evangelizing was important to the community's survival, both financial and spiritual. In this chapter, we learn about the events that spurred the church to embrace Christian feminism as its mission. We consider how evangelization became a key resource for sustaining emplacement of female imagery of God in its worship. We explore the major evangelizing initiatives of the church and review how the religious marketplace has responded to its efforts.

I had arranged to meet Pastor Stacy Boorn before her Wednesday evening rosary. In the vestibule of the church, there was a small lending library with an impressive array of Christian feminist authors, including Elizabeth Schüssler Fiorenza, Rosemary Radford Ruether, Elaine Pagels, and Karen King. Above the books was a sign, "Goddess Rosaries for Sale," with rosary prayer beads made of semiprecious stones including amethyst, rose quartz, malachite and tiger's eye on display. Each had a gold or silver charm of a spiral or Goddess figure at the end. Even before I entered the worship space, feminist theology was emplaced in the signage on the exterior of the building and by the selection of books in the foyer.

As I entered the main sanctuary, all the lights were dim except for the altar, which was lit with candles. A contemplative CD of a woman softly chanting was playing. The altar displayed a mix of traditional and contemporary religious art and ritual objects, both Christian and non-Christian. The all-clear altar table, draped in red fabric, had been moved to the right side, and it held Tibetan singing bowls, bells, drums, and incense. On the back wall hung three medieval icons of a man, a woman, and three figures sitting at a table. Overhead was a large, simple wooden cross painted light green. On the left side of the altar was the ambo, or preaching podium, and mounted on the front was a contemporary painting of what appeared to be a Goddess with her arms outstretched toward the congregation.

Pastor Boorn was alone setting up chairs for the meditation, and she welcomed me warmly as I arrived. She was petite, perhaps five foot two, with a cherubic face, large round glasses and a head full of blond curly hair that made her look perennially young. She was wearing the traditional dress of a Lutheran minister of black trousers, black shirt, and white Roman collar, but with a multicolored blouse on top. When I commented on the blouse, Boorn explained that it was a gift from an older member of the congregation who had recently passed away. The woman's story provided an introduction to the transformation the church was currently undergoing.

The member had been an older Swedish woman much loved by the congregation. In her later years, the church community had become her only family. Upon her death, she bequeathed her remaining savings to the church. The gift was modest, less than ten thousand dollars, yet the church leadership council wanted to help others as well as support the church with her gift. In keeping with their Christian feminist mission, they voted to underwrite one year of schooling for the only female seminarian studying in a Lutheran seminary in Ethiopia. The remainder was used to remove the pews in the church and to install a new bamboo wood floor that made the space more flexible for worship and more intimate for the small congregation. Chairs had arrived that week, and the new seating was to be used for the first time on Sunday.[1]

The interior and exterior of the church emplaced the message that the church was forging a new kind of religious community. At the same time, I was struck by how normal it all seemed. I realized that much of this had to do with Boorn herself. She appeared to be without guile, presenting her commitment to feminism, Christianity, and church worship with a joy and matter-of-factness that was disarming. I was not the only one to notice her charismatic style. Later, when I interviewed members of the church, all agreed that her ability to work within the Evangelical Lutheran Congregational Association (ELCA) structure as well as to engage a wider non-church public was the key to the success of this unique church.

As far as Boorn was concerned, a distorted view of women was a sin. God in baptism liberated believers from sin, death, and all that produced evil. The church included significant amounts of feminine imagery in its worship because Sunday worship was the call to practice this liberating, God-given promise. She wrote the following explanation for the church Web site:

> We gather for worship each Sunday because we are happiest when the center of life is not ourselves, but the Holy One. It is God/dess who created this world and all its blessings. It is the Ever Living One who has forgiven us, restored us, and blessed us with new life through the saving act of Jesus' death and resurrection. And it is God/dess who enables us to turn from lives of self-absorption to live in partnership with God/dess for the sake of the neighbor. At least every Sunday we need to be reminded of the focus and purpose of life, and we are grateful that the Spirit of the Living One blesses us through our sharing of the Word of Grace and the Holy Communion Meal. We are sent into the world to be bearers of that divine word that can raise the dead to new life.[2]

THE CALL TO MINISTRY AND MISSION

During our conversations, I learned more about Boorn's personal history. She had grown up Lutheran in the conservative Missouri Synod in upstate New York. Her parents owned a photography shop, and she loved her religion. "As a little girl, I loved the Lutheran hymns. I would take my hymnal into the bath and sing my heart out!"[3] At the time, she thought that pastors were female because their robes looked like long skirts, and she wanted to be a pastor, too. At church, her parents were told that she would outgrow this phase, as the Missouri Synod did not and still does not ordain women. Meanwhile, her parents continued to nurture her Lutheran faith. Her father's high school graduation gift to Boorn was a collectable 1933 German coin commemorating the 450th anniversary of Martin Luther's birth.

In the 1980s, Boorn was in her early twenties when her call to ministry resurfaced. While the Missouri synod still did not ordain women, she was aware of a more progressive branch, the ELCA, which did allow female pastors. She attended the Pacific Lutheran Theological Seminary in Berkeley, California. Boorn was ordained a Lutheran minister in the Sierra Pacific Synod of the ELCA in 1987, just two years after *Wisdom's Feast* was published.

For twelve years, she pastored a growing Laotian congregation in Richland, California, where immigrant rights and liberation theology became her focus. It was there that she developed her skills for connecting mission, theology, and community through emplacement. In her experience, ritual had a significant part to play. The sign for the church was bilingual, and the worship service incorporated Laotian elements along with sermons focusing on liberation theology. Eventually, she encouraged a member of the congregation to become ordained himself so he could go on to become the pastor.

Feminism was not a big concern for her then, but looking back she saw how her gender presented certain dilemmas for the congregation. At Laotian parties, where men and women traditionally sat separately, she would be expected to drink with the men because she was their religious leader, and she would also have to spend time with the women as well. She remembered one church banquet where the tables were set up in a square, men on one side, women on the other, with her seated right in the middle.

In 1998, Boorn began looking for another position. There was an opportunity at an aging Swedish congregation in San Francisco where the pastor was retiring after twenty-four years. Ebenezer Lutheran had a long history in San Francisco dating back to the Gold Rush. It was established in 1882 to serve Swedish immigrants. Membership swelled after World War II, and Ebenezer moved to the edge of the city for more land and a new building. In 1956, the current church was built with a large meeting hall and kitchen in the church basement for social functions. Over the next fifty years, immigration from Sweden slowly declined, and subsequent generations were less identified with their Swedish roots. If Ebenezer did not change its course, it was at risk of closing.

Four interim pastors were interviewed, and the church leadership council chose Boorn, the only woman to apply. They understood that a new purpose for the church had to be identified and developed. Some said it was Boorn's education and background in developing mission that made her the winning candidate. When I asked the older women of the congregation about Boorn's arrival in November 1998, they described how quickly she changed the culture to be more open and friendly. She would bring those sitting by themselves to sit with others. She instructed the congregation on how to make all visitors feel welcome and comfortable. She also created new opportunities for existing members to get to know each other better through senior outings on which she drove the church van.[4]

Yet not all were pleased with the changes. Some members were upset when Boorn had the large black cross painted light green to represent a move away from a focus on sin to a focus on resurrection. Others were uncomfortable when Boorn began welcoming the LGBT community at the church. Some even tried to get Boorn to say she was gay, which would have been grounds for dismissal, as no openly gay pastors were allowed to serve in the ELCA at that time.

When I asked Boorn about this treatment, she told me that as a single pastor, she was expected to remain celibate until marriage. She acknowledged that some members may have been offended that she connected Ebenezer to a consortium of "open and affirming" ELCA churches so that gays and lesbians would know they would be welcomed at the church.[5] Conflicts at Ebenezer echoed struggles about theology and gay rights happening within the ELCA at the time, but that did not lessen the divisive local impact. A couple of members of the congregation recalled how embarrassed they were when a liberal pastor from out of state attended worship one Sunday and a retired conservative pastor followed him into the parking lot afterward, shouting at him to never come back.[6]

Two years into her tenure, Boorn stood before the Ebenezer congregation during Sunday worship to perform a baptism. It was a welcome sign of new life for the aging community of faith. The parents brought their infant forward to the altar to be sacramentally committed to Christianity. Boorn poured water on the infant's head and baptized her in the name of the Trinitarian Christian God. Boorn had met with the parents beforehand, and they liked the idea of baptizing their child in the name of "God who is both Mother and Father, Jesus the Christ, and the Holy Spirit."

Boorn had been interested in opening up the language of the liturgy for a while. The previous pastor had ignored directives to change to inclusive language, and Ebenezer was well behind the times. Besides, Boorn had learned from her previous church how life giving alternative words and images of God could be for expanding a congregation's conception of God, and she saw this as one small step to help Ebenezer move forward. After the service, some of the older members of the congregation told Boorn that they did not care for the term "Mother" when referring to God. She noted their concern, but she felt justified, as it had been a modest move and prearranged with the parents.

A couple of weeks later at the leadership council meeting, she was shocked to find only one agenda item—to fire her over the God-as-Mother reference. She realized this was the last meeting for certain members to take action before rotating off the council, but the timing seemed particularly cruel because it was December and right before Christmas. While technically they had the power to fire her, Boorn convinced them to wait for a full membership vote. Boorn viewed the controversy more as a power struggle over who would control the church, but female language for God galvanized those opposed to her leadership, and it became the issue that was used to force people to take sides. In the weeks leading up to the vote, slanderous letters questioning Boorn's character and pastoral leadership were mailed to all in the congregation and even shared with other Lutheran churches, creating heightened controversy and resulting in the bishop coming to oversee the vote.

The campaign waged against Boorn was reminiscent of the treatment Susan Cady received, as discussed in Chapter 1. There were slanderous letters written, along with gossip about her single status and sexual orientation. After the vote, Boorn managed to retain her position as pastor, but she won only by a slight majority. It did not quell the controversy over female language for God, and the debates continued for two more years, even though the ELCA had approved its use. Eventually, those who opposed Boorn's leadership left.

The leadership team that remained started to see its purpose in light of the hard-fought battles that had taken place. It had become clear to many in the remaining Ebenezer congregation how deeply rooted sexism and patriarchy were in Christianity. As a result, Christian feminism became the new mission for the church.

Because the church drama had erupted around ritual, the new feminist purpose included emplacement with a strong liturgical component. Under Boorn's leadership, Sunday services at Ebenezer slowly transformed; prayers and hymns were adapted with inclusive language, and more female imagery was displayed in the worship space. Sermons began focusing on justice issues affecting women. Rosemary Radford Ruether's term "God/dess" appeared in worship aids to express both the male and female sides of God, along with asterisks explaining their use. Boorn also used sermons and Bible studies to explain how this feminist language fit within the Christian and Lutheran tradition. After pursuing social justice at her previous church around class and ethnicity, Boorn was now evangelizing out of her own mistreatment as a female minister. Christian feminism as mission was a powerful combination that connected social justice around gender with personal identity and worship expression.

Growing a Church in the New Religious Marketplace

The challenge to Boorn's leadership had taken a toll on an already struggling congregation. Ebenezer's membership dropped to a low of only a couple dozen members; it was the older women who kept the church financially afloat. This church was where they had been married, had their children baptized, and buried their husbands. The building and location were important to the older women, and they could not imagine leaving. They could also see that Pastor Boorn genuinely cared about them.[7]

Ebenezer was one of ten churches in the San Francisco Conference of the ELCA. The decline in membership that had brought Boorn to Ebenezer was part of a larger trend. Mainline Protestantism as a whole had been shrinking across the nation, but it was particularly acute in San Francisco, in part because of the high cost of living. Younger members would often leave when they wanted to own a home and start a family. Those who remained in the city were often older, and the practicing Lutheran population continued to shrink as the group aged and passed away.

Like other communities featured in this book, denominational directives opened up opportunities for pursuing female imagery in worship. A consulting group had been invited to make a proposal on how the San Francisco ELCA Conference could survive. The recommendation was that instead of having ten churches, the conference should view itself as one large congregation, with each church specializing in a particular mission. The proximity of the churches to each other alleviated the expectation and expense of individual churches to provide a full spectrum of services. Instead, each church could focus on what it did best. Boorn's choice of feminism as a mission was accepted because it was unique, defined, and different from the other church ministries in the San Francisco Conference.[8]

The challenge was to ensure that the congregation could be financially self-sufficient. The church property posed both problems and opportunities. The problem was that the church building was in need of repairs, and it was expensive to operate. It was also much larger than what the current congregation needed. However, the opportunity was that real estate in San Francisco was quite valuable, both to sell and to rent. Some of the San Francisco congregations decided to sell their church properties and bank the millions of dollars they earned in order to operate as "churches without walls," opting to meet in rented space for worship and using free spaces such as coffee shops for ministry meetings.

Other churches retained ownership of their buildings but rented out space to generate revenue. Ebenezer chose this path. A Montessori school operated during the week in the basement, and a South Korean Christian church rented an office and used the sanctuary on Sunday afternoons. Boorn was now doing all the church secretary work herself to save money. Ebenezer's big break came from its location at the top of Twin Peaks, allowing it to rent its steeple to AT&T, Verizon, and Sprint for cell phone towers. Once it was brought to my attention, I could see an area in the parking lot that was fenced off for the additional telecommunication equipment. When I looked up, I could see three straight antennas on the top of the steeple next to the cross. The cell phone rental agreements carried the majority of the modest annual church budget.[9] The hope was that the member base would grow before the fifty-year-old property needed a major repair or renovation.

EVANGELIZING ON A SHOESTRING

The church had two pressing needs. The first was a need to attract more people. The church leadership realized that if it could communicate with those driving in the six lanes of traffic speeding by the church every morning and evening, they could reach a lot of people. A large banner was an obvious choice because it was relatively inexpensive, temporary, and could be hung right on the church edifice with little effort.

The second was a need to explain the new direction of the church. Boorn began brainstorming ideas, but another pastor thought that Boorn's phrases sounded too theological. Her colleague recommended using words that people could easily grasp. In the end, a five by twenty foot banner was made that read, "Everyone welcome at this table. Worship 10:30. God loves all Her children."

When the banner went up, it immediately generated attention. There were phone calls, both positive and negative, and they highlighted the difficulties the church faced in attracting new members. On the one hand, positive calls came mostly from local residents who were delighted that a church in their neighborhood would communicate such a progressive message, but they were not churchgoers and would not be attending the service. On the other hand, negative calls came mostly from practicing Christians who were highly offended by anything connecting God and femaleness. Boorn was surprised that most of these calls came not from men, but from older women. "I just remained pleasant and let them talk. There was no point in arguing."[10] One call that stood out for Boorn was from of a woman who said a female pastor at her church once proclaimed during worship, "God loves all Her children." She was quickly informed that if she wanted to keep her job, she would stop. And she did.

This type of pushback also appeared in the Methodist case, where female language for God was silenced using heavy-handed techniques, including threats of firings. One way to object to female pastoral leadership has been to prevent pastors from speaking certain feminist theological truths. The reactions to the banner seemed to crystallize the marketplace opportunities and challenges for this new feminist direction.

Church leadership wanted to reach out to those who had been alienated by their experiences of patriarchy in church. The problem was that those who wanted to see Christianity change were not particularly interested in joining an organized religion. In response, Boorn began hosting events at the parsonage, a house the church owned a couple of blocks away where the pastor lived. This less "churchy" setting made an attractive first step for friends of church members who were interested in the mission but were not so interested in the church. Boorn started a group called First Fridays, where she hosted a potluck supper with a feminist spirituality topic for discussion. Over time, a core group developed; some attended Sunday worship and others only attended First Fridays.

The nickname "herchurch" came from the first banner. It was only when people started to refer to Ebenezer as the "her church" that the community decided to embrace the name. It was also decided not to capitalize herchurch in order to emphasize a radically egalitarian point of view. When the community decided to rename the Web site, another large two-by-twenty-foot banner went up with the Web address www.herchurch.org. The leadership team was learning about reaching people in the new religious marketplace. Instead of expecting the advertising to get people through the door, as signs on church properties had done for centuries, the goal of the banner advertising was primarily to motivate a look at the herchurch Web site, allowing the curious to inquire with little effort. It also gave the church a much larger space to explain itself. A more robust communication platform to express its vision was useful because herchurch was challenging preconceptions of church, feminism, Christianity, and God all at the same time.

The nickname herchurch along with a strong Web site was a winning combination. It appealed to a younger audience. Most of the newcomers I met at the church had viewed the Web site before their first visit. By engaging new technologies to communicate the new name of its Christian feminist mission, herchurch had managed in a few short years to "brand" itself, creating a unique and distinct identity in the religious marketplace.

The Web site was dedicated to boldly evangelizing Christian feminism. It stated that herchurch participated in a "Lutheran feminist movement that exists to celebrate feminine dimensions of the sacred as expressed in worship, learning, mutual care, and acts of justice."[11] To that end, the art on the Web site included only female figures of the divine. At the same time, herchurch maintained a more traditional stance regarding worship and Christian beliefs. The description of the worship on the Web site still focused on Jesus's death and resurrection as well as the benefits of attending weekly Sunday worship.

REMEMBERING THE GODDESS

Boorn described how the initial foray into using Goddess language and imagery was not originally a move to connect Christianity with more ancient pre-Christian times. In fact, it was just the opposite. She had wanted to help her community evolve, using female language and female images to expand people's images of God. She wanted to reinforce that God had female as well as male characteristics, and she wanted to reflect the scriptural message that both women and men were made in God's image.

I was surprised to learn that Boorn had started using Goddess language without knowing the neo-Goddess perspective put forth by Marija Gambutas, Carol Christ, and others. This outlook possibly reflected Boorn's generational difference from the older worship leaders profiled in this book. It also revealed her exclusive use of Christian sources for her initial religious feminist research because there were many Goddess publications readily available. In fact, one of the most famous Goddess authors, Starhawk, even lived in the area.

Then Boorn met a woman who would become one of the anchor members of herchurch. She introduced Boorn to a different way of framing the use of female images, not just as something cutting-edge and new, but actually something very ancient. "I remember my first conversation with her. I said that patriarchy had been with us forever. She said that was not true, and that patriarchy was only five thousand years old. Here I had been thinking that we were using female images for God only as a way to move forward, but it was actually restoring a much more ancient practice."[12]

After that conversation, Boorn started reading Carol Christ's *Rebirth of the Goddess*, and she decided to use the book for the Sunday morning class she offered after worship. The group was inspired by the book, and they came to discover through the Internet that Christ led Goddess pilgrimages on the Greek island of Crete, where a Minoan culture had celebrated the Goddess from 2700 to 1450 BCE. Five female members of herchurch, including Boorn, signed up for the trip one year in advance.

Inspired by this imagery, herchurch developed a Goddess Rosary. Boorn had been getting together monthly with female Lutheran pastors who wanted to support each other in their pastoral pursuits. At one meeting, a colleague had given Boorn a gift of an Anglican rosary in which she had replaced the cross on the end with a Goddess symbol. The Anglican rosary was a modification of the more familiar Catholic rosary, and other denominations, mostly Protestant, had begun using the rosary, too, calling them "Christian prayer beads" or "ecumenical prayer beads."[13] Back at herchurch, Boorn began making Goddess rosaries herself with another church member. Soon, herchurch members started praying the Goddess Rosary with the prayers that were already being used in the herchurch Sunday worship:

Our Mother (by Miriam Therese Winter)

> Our Mother who is within us, we celebrate your many names. Your wisdom come, your will be done, unfolding from the depths within us. Each day you give us all that we need. You remind us of our limits and we let go. You support us in our power and we act with courage. For you are the dwelling place within us, the empowerment around us, and the celebration among us. Now and forever. Amen.

Hail Goddess (adapted from Carol Christ)

> Hail Goddess, full of grace, Blessed are You and blessed is the fruit of your womb. For you are the mother of us all. Hear/ Heal us now and in all our needs/ dreams. O blessed be, O blessed be, Amen.[14]

Boorn opened the church sanctuary during the week for members who wanted to pray the rosary together. Those who came appreciated quiet time during the week to be contemplative. They experimented with alternating group recitation of prayers with unstructured time when they prayed and meditated individually. Some would sit quietly, while others moved around the worship space in an improvisational manner.

Soon, another banner went up: "Goddess Rosary Wednesdays 7:30 PM." An instruction card was created for newcomers: "The Goddess Rosary is spoken as a community at 7:10, 7:30, and 7:50 PM. During and at other times please feel free to use the prayer stations of candles, singing bowls and bells, incense and tree of life icon, anointing oils, and water." Participants said that they enjoyed the freedom to move and express themselves as they prayed and that this deepened their relationship with the divine in ways they had never experienced before. For some, it became the highlight of their week.

A Goddess Rosary prayer ministry soon formed, with a special page on the herchurch Web site. The Internet ministry allowed the church to connect with those outside San Francisco. For $35, those who were interested were invited to submit a prayer request, and Boorn and the rosary team would read and pray over the request while making a rosary with semiprecious stones such as rose quartz, tiger's eye, and amethyst. Boorn admitted that it was not priced to make the church a lot of money, nor could the team handle making more than a few rosaries per week. Still, it allowed outreach and provided a way to pray for others. In the first three years, herchurch made rosaries for a couple hundred prayer requests. The prayers requests were for people who were homebound, those struggling with illness or other misfortune, as well as those who were inspired by the herchurch ministry but lacked a local place of worship to meet that need. Emplacement of the church mission was growing through creating material objects that could be mailed anywhere.

By the time the date approached for the Goddess pilgrimage to Crete, Boorn was on to new projects and no longer felt a need to go. She went along with the four other members of the congregation because she had already paid for the trip. Because she went with few expectations, she was surprised by her response to seeing emplacement of female imagery from an earlier time. "To see the physical places, and to see the Goddess figurines in the museum was profound. To be with both Christian and non-Christian people from around the globe who were asking the same questions, made the ancient connection very real and very physical. That trip helped me see that herchurch was not just about moving forward, but also about connecting with a piece of history that could inspire us today."[15] Boorn brought Goddess rosaries as gifts for everyone on the pilgrimage, and they were well received, particularly because they included prayers from Carol Christ, the pilgrimage leader.

Boorn was a professional photographer, and she returned to San Francisco with evocative images of nature and the local women of Crete. Having just experienced the power of emplacement of female imagery herself in Crete, Boorn turned the annex space of the church into a photography gallery, where a cooperative for female photographers could share their view of beauty and the world. The name, "A Woman's Eye Gallery," would be another way to extend the mission of herchurch and attract the public to its ministry through art.

RITUALIZING A FEMINIST MISSION AT SUNDAY SERVICE

Boorn's experience of almost losing her employment over one "mother" reference for the divine convinced her that feminist theology in general needed more emplacement in Christian ritual. She wanted to go beyond just using gender-neutral terms for God, because gender-neutral terms did not radically change the look or feel of the worship; nor did gender-neutral terms propel the congregation to consider the implications of language and image of God in their greater world. It was not enough to intellectually know that God was beyond gender. The word "God" might help those who were bothered by male language, but it did not directly challenge those who liked to think of God as exclusively "Him." For Boorn, using distinctively female language and female imagery was an intentionally disruptive move.

Boorn also felt that feminine divine imagery could produce a profound shift in how women viewed themselves and how men viewed women. For her, ritual was an important aspect of changing societal norms. She believed that if people could see the divine imaged as female in worship and refer to the divine with female words, then the full gender spectrum and mystery of God could be embraced. She also hoped that these images would encourage men and women to treat each other equally on earth. Words for God used in herchurch worship included Mother-Father God, God/Goddess, Christ-Sophia, Sophia, Holy Other, and Holy One.

Boorn began experimenting with the readings used during the Lutheran liturgy as well. She wanted women's voices represented, yet all the scriptures had been written by men. She began adding writings by holy women to the rituals, including women mystics and female poets. Boorn also added women's names to the lists of disciples in the Gospel readings based on feminist studies that claimed women had been disciples but were unacknowledged in the scriptures. Boorn smiled as she recalled overhearing one of the older women in the congregation telling a friend about "the men and women apostles who followed Jesus."[16]

Boorn also offered alternative translations for key words that described the women of the Bible to expand the possibilities of their roles in the minds of the congregation without being dogmatic. I attended a Good Friday service where Boorn offered a different view of Mary Magdalene in this manner. Boorn was reading the empty tomb account in John 20:6 to the congregation. "Jesus said to her, 'Mary!' She turned and said to him in Hebrew 'Rabbouni!' which means teacher." Boorn then paused, looked up from the text, and added, "or spouse," offering an alternative translation before returning back to reading the text.[17]

Boorn kept Jesus in his male personage, having him advocate as a male for more equal and progressive attitudes about women. Jesus was the positive role model for how women should be respected, honored, supported, and treated. To make her point during a sermon, sometimes Boorn would state, "Jesus was a feminist."[18] When we discussed this statement, Boorn acknowledged that Jesus was not a feminist in the way we think of feminism today. She also acknowledged that feminism was a modern term, but she was deeply convinced that Jesus's teachings and attitudes elevated the status and roles for women. She also believed that if Jesus were conducting his ministry today, he would indeed be a feminist in every sense of the word. Her approach echoed more traditional Christian preaching that makes Jesus alive today by imagining Jesus in current times facing modern dilemmas. The popular 1990s Christian campaign "What Would Jesus Do?" encouraged people to imagine Jesus in their contemporary circumstance. For Boorn, Jesus would be a modern feminist.

The liturgies at herchurch also celebrated women more generally. When I attended worship on All Saints Day, Boorn preached on the great women in secular and sacred history whose accomplishments had been overlooked. She held up as her book of saints *The Dinner Party*, about feminist artist Judy Chicago's famous art piece celebrating famous women in history. At the end of her sermon, she invited the congregation to take handfuls of white rose petals and sprinkle them all over the altar while they remembered the wonderful women in their lives. She ended the service with a rousing rendition of "Oh When the Saints Come Marching In."[19]

Boorn celebrated older women in the congregation with croning ceremonies, a tradition from the Goddess movement for honoring older women, or crones. For the first year, a seventy-year-old retired architect and grandmother was chosen to be honored. In the middle of the Sunday service, she sat in a chair facing the congregation, surrounded by her spouse and children and grandchildren. Boorn and the grandchildren blessed her with chrism oil, and she was given a silk purple scarf in acknowledgement of her life experience and wisdom. The ceremony was well received, and it became an annual event. The croning ceremony has now been integrated into the liturgical calendar during the second Sunday of Easter. It echoes the liturgical season of celebrating resurrection and new life, and the ceremony has become quite popular. Because of increased demand, Boorn has had to consider how to continue honoring specific women while also opening the ceremony to allow other women to join in the blessing as well.[20]

FRUITS OF EVANGELIZATION: NEW MEMBERSHIP

With the growing community, it was now possible to see whom herchurch was attracting as visitors and members. The group was predominantly female, but not exclusively so. There were men joining, both heterosexual and gay; some were related to women in the community as husbands, fathers, and sons. Not all new members were Lutheran, but most came from some form of Christianity. Many were disaffected from church for a variety of reasons, and herchurch provided a place to reconcile and heal past hurts.[21] The largest group of new members consisted of women who felt Christianity was too male centered. They felt inspired to be worshipping as Christians with female imagery that validated their female form in images of the divine. Others joined herchurch more for their daughters, wanting them to grow up with positive images of themselves as full reflections of the divine.[22]

When I asked Boorn about the benefits she saw at the church as a result of worshipping with female imagery of God, she concentrated on two main issues: community participation and community acceptance. She noticed that the older Swedish women of the congregation had begun to speak up and express their views more, particularly after the croning ceremonies were added to the liturgical year. She also believed that the congregation's voting for a transgendered member to participate on the leadership team indicated that the congregation's gendered perceptions of God were expanding.

I also asked Boorn how she was serving the boys who only saw female images of God. Boorn saw herchurch as a small corrective for the large patriarchal liturgical imbalance. She noted that the boys at herchurch were still seeing and hearing much about the male side of God in the wider society. Boorn agreed that gender parity in images of God was optimal, but that Christianity was far from expressing that reality. Until then, she recognized a need to display predominantly female images in at least one worship setting because the overwhelming majority of churches expressed exclusively male images of God.

The Faith and Feminism Conference

In 2007, the congregation wanted to do something special for their pastor in recognition of her twentieth anniversary of ordination, which also coincided with her fiftieth birthday. The church leadership council told Boorn they wanted to give her a special gift and asked her what she would like. Her answer surprised many of them. Instead of a personal gift, she wanted a public conference. She could think of no better way to celebrate her twenty-year milestone in her pastorate than to push forward the mission of Christian feminism, something to which she saw herself dedicating the remainder of her pastoring years.[23]

Boorn's request daunted the leadership team. A conference was a stretch for such a small congregation. There were only one hundred names on the church roster, and only a handful of those members were dedicated enough to plan and execute a conference. Boorn still believed that they could pull it off. As she pointed out, the church already had a Web site for advertising, and she had contacts within the ELCA. She also thought a conference would be good for herchurch congregational development. Just like the Goddess rosary and First Friday ministries, the conference might appeal to another group of people who might become more regular members. In Boorn's mind, emplacement of innovative evangelization and outreach continued to be the strategy to make herchurch viable and successful.

The herchurch Faith and Feminism conference weekend was set for November 2–4, 2007. The conference was titled "Wisdom's Urgent Cry: A Faith and Feminism/Womanist/Mujerista Conference." The event gave herchurch an opportunity to assess its position in the religious marketplace and to see its place among the many "feminisms," including womanist and mujerista theologies.

I was invited to observe the pre-conference session, where about two dozen female church leaders sat in a circle to discuss the conference topic within the context of their work. Approximately two-thirds were Lutheran, and almost all were ELCA ordained. Most were ministers, and a couple were Lutheran theologians. Most said they appreciated the opportunity to have a forum together because they usually pursued their feminist theological interests alone. I found their answers different from those of the Daughters of Wisdom, none of whom spoke of this level of isolation. I was also surprised because many Protestant-ordained women from the 1970s and 1980s, such as Susan Cady (Chapter 1), had formed support networks for this very reason.

Women's clergy support groups were not as common as they were in the past, but this group clearly appreciated being invited into something already formed by Boorn and herchurch. Many of Boorn's colleagues in ministry had private bookshelves lined with feminist theology, even if they performed rituals that did not express it. The conference allowed them to get their personal needs met without having to risk the political capital associated with being known as a leader of such an initiative. The decline in ELCA membership meant it was more difficult to obtain and keep a pastor position; thus, the Lutheran religious marketplace further restricted innovative and potentially controversial actions by these women in their public roles. A few older women in the circle, some retired from their pastorate, commented that younger women entering Lutheran seminary were not as interested in issues of inclusive language or feminist causes.[24] But, as one younger Lutheran minister explained to me on break during the conference, "As a woman, I am already a symbol of inclusive change. In some ways, it is easier for male clergy to champion inclusive language today. I have a male colleague and inclusive language is his main issue. Great for him, because it makes him look more broad minded; but if I were to do it, I would appear radical."[25]

During these discussions, I could see how the history of ordained female clergy was actually a local history. Regardless of when the denomination permitted females to be ordained, only when the first woman served as pastor of a particular church did the local community of faith wrestle with the decision. The ramifications of the glass ceiling being broken were lived out church by church, whether it was Rev. Susan Cady arriving at Emmanuel United Methodist Church in 1987 or Pastor Stacy Boorn arriving at Ebenezer in 1998; both women faced similar church dynamics. As a consequence, the cross-generational dialogue at the pre-conference session offered strategies and tactics that were relevant for all who attended.

During the discussion, one elderly clergywoman stood out in her articulation of how she dealt with being a feminist within a patriarchal church structure for more than thirty years. She admitted that when she became a feminist in the 1970s, she had participated in the women's movement for only two years before she had to leave the National Organization of Women (NOW) and other organizations because it made her too angry. Even reading Luther's writings about women made her angry. She decided that she could not address these issues directly in her professional work or they would consume her. She decided to "chew at edges" of the issues instead in order to be constructive and keep her sanity; others concurred.[26]

The wisdom being expressed around the pre-conference circle was a centrist progressive view. The women discussed how to survive and be constructive agents for change within their denominations. Some spoke of staying connected through personal relationships with colleagues. Others commented that it was essential to keep perspective and a sense of humor. Many spoke of being conscious of maintaining a welcoming stance in order to have opportunities for dialogue with others about difficult subjects, as well as the need to realistically scale back expectations. One pastor commented that if issues were resolved in a satisfactory manner 60 or 70 percent of the time, there was progress.

Hearing other ELCA clergywomen share their views showed me how leading edge Boorn and herchurch were with regard to feminist activism and sacred ritual, and the pre-conference session also revealed the role herchurch was serving within the broader Lutheran denomination. The participants appreciated herchurch for facilitating conversations and providing support in dealing effectively with patriarchy in church situations. They also got to see a ritual space where feminist concerns were openly addressed in the church art and liturgy.

After the pre-conference afternoon session, herchurch catered a dinner for the participants downstairs in the church hall. Meanwhile, other conference attendees began arriving upstairs, and all received packets that included a Goddess rosary. The conference fee was kept to twenty-five dollars to encourage participation, and approximately seventy-five participants came.[27] One disappointment for Boorn was that even with their conference fees waived, no seminarians from the local Lutheran seminary attended.

The format of the conference included three keynote talks, two panels, and a few small group discussions. Each section of the program began and ended with some form of ritual, be it singing an inclusive language hymn, watching and participating in sacred chant and dance, or praying the Goddess rosary. On Sunday morning, the conference attendees were invited to worship with the regular Sunday herchurch community. All were invited to participate in the Eucharist, and those who enjoyed singing could join the choir for a day. During the service, a brass quintet from the San Francisco Lesbian/Gay Freedom Band performed a special musical tribute to the weekend by combining Shubert's "Ave Maria" with "Maria" from *West Side Story*.

The sessions during the conference revealed differences between the invited presenters and herchurch members. During one session, a speaker from out of state began describing a binary of male and female gender, then stated with certitude that a "divine feminine" was the needed corrective for society's troubles. I wondered how her messages were being received, and I soon got my answer during the question and answer period that followed. "You are in San Francisco, a town with fluid gender and sexuality. As you explore the feminine aspects of God, do you explore bisexual, transgender? How does your work on dismantling patriarchy in the church through feminine images help with this? Gender is on a continuum. Have your thoughts and imagery moved in this direction?" The speaker responded hesitantly, noting that she was not sure that the church fathers intended limitation with the Trinity, but rather expansion, and finally offered, "So a variety of images?" As for sexuality, she deflected the question, saying, "I am not into body part theology."[28] Even with a binary view of gender, her answer was different from that of the Daughters of Wisdom, who embraced sexual metaphors for cultivating "desire" in passionate mystical ways.

When the other speakers presented, instead of making bridges with herchurch, their messages seemed more directed at why the herchurch rituals did *not* address their concerns. The mujerista speaker started her talk by saying she was not sure how the mujerista angle related to the herchurch offering. She explained that for Latina women, Jesus was an important friend, brother, and companion in the midst of oppression, and Mary was not weak, but a strong, empowered woman who "incarnates not just our gender but as a mulatta, our race."[29] The womanist panelist mentioned to me before her talk that her Christian experience was in Pentecostal settings, and she found the worship at herchurch "a bit staid."[30]

These comments revealed how difficult it is to create a new type of worship that will appeal to both the identity and worship style preference of a wide range of people, even when there is theological agreement. The first point of identity was expressed when the mujerista speaker said that imaging her community's race was as important as gender. She also identified with Jesus, who was wrongly judged by those in power.

The womanist speaker also identified with Jesus, who was captured and mistreated, as she reminded the audience of the problematic history of Christianity being used to justify slavery.

Equally important was the second point raised by the womanist speaker's comment on worship style. I heard other guests in the audience also say they had trouble singing so many hymns. At the same time, there were many who relished singing these traditional hymns with updated woman-positive lyrics. Boorn, in particular, was visibly moved during these worship moments. These comments about worship were not theological, but about aesthetics and personal preferences. There were opinions about the building as well. Some came to the herchurch in spite of its traditional church architecture, while others found ritualizing female imagery in a traditional church building particularly uplifting and transformational. These differences became topics of conversation with many of the visitors participating in worship during the conference.

The panelist representing queer theology also had concerns. She cautioned against moves in inclusive language Bibles to erase the queer stories such as the wedding in Hosea where the king marries his sons. She noted in the New Standard Revised Version (NSRV) Bible translation that "sons" had been replaced with "daughters" on the assumption that the women had been erased from the texts. She liked the ambiguity and challenge that the original translation provided. She encouraged the group to lift up feminist concerns without erasing other groups.[31]

After these comments, I sat in a small group discussion with a transgendered member of the herchurch community. While she did not completely agree with the queer theologian, she believed the speaker "probably identified more male" as a way to explain why she wanted Bible passages to remain where the king married his sons.[32] She described how she first came to herchurch to hear her friends in the San Francisco Lesbian/Gay Freedom Band who were performing there. On that visit, she noticed the books in the lobby and was impressed with the offerings, including *The Goddess in the Gospels* and works by Elaine Pagels, because these books had inspired her own faith journey. She described herself as "transitioning female" and said she liked herchurch because she found female God images life giving.

At herchurch, many members of the community were personally living out and seeking a home for their faith lives where their sexual orientation and gender identification would be accepted. Boorn, more than any other worship leader in this study, often used the term "Holy Other" as a name for God in worship. Many in the congregation identified with "other" because they were female, homosexual, bisexual, or transgendered. Just as the other cases privileged femaleness as the central missing component of God that brought them a sense of wholeness, herchurch needed something broader, and Holy Other encompassed all the ways community members perceived being "othered" around gender and sexual issues.

At the same time, the subtext in the mujerista and womanist speakers' comments was that the herchurch rituals and messages inspired a Christian community that was predominantly white and middle class. Despite these differences, Boorn was optimistic when she spoke to the group at the end of the conference. She acknowledged that a variety of opinions had been shared, but the fact that dialogue among feminists revealed such varying ways of seeing things and interpreting symbols meant that conversations were taking place and that progress was being made. While I agreed with her assessment, I could not help but notice how little coalition building about ritual issues among these groups had taken place.

Was it possible that herchurch had yet to find its voice within this broader coalition? In some ways, the feminist perspective was the older conversation. Had the predominantly white, middle-class herchurch inadvertently touched on the historical wounds that had led to the splits? Was it even appropriate to claim feminism as the meta-title for this larger movement? Boorn must have reflected on these questions as well, because later she changed the Web site from indicating that herchurch participated in the "Lutheran feminist movement" to the "Christian-Lutheran Feminist/Womanist/Mujerista Movements."

To her credit, in her closing comments Boorn stayed true to her voice and experience. She noted that for the first twenty years of her pastorate, 90 percent of her theological study had been written by white, middle-class men, so she pledged that for the next twenty years she would listen to 90 percent women.[33] She also announced that the church had committed to purchasing a large painting by the conference artist, titled *Heart of God*, as a lasting transformation of the herchurch ritual space. The three medieval icons at the back of the altar were taken down, and in their place now hung a female face framed by a veil of roses looking down lovingly upon the altar. While the large cross still remained, the other symbols for God were now all exclusively female images.

Boorn and the herchurch conference team were pleased with the conference, and they felt people were surprised by the quality of the program, handouts, and hospitality. As Boorn had hoped, after the conference there was an increase in herchurch activity. Regular worship grew to approximately fifty people every Sunday, and participation at First Friday gatherings also increased.

YouTube and a Different Type of Dialogue

During the conference, a photographer from the photo gallery cooperative shot a five-minute video titled "A Faith Journey" and uploaded it onto YouTube. It included an introduction by Boorn with footage from the conference weekend showing participants in conversation, choir rehearsal, and Sunday worship. There were no close-ups of the art of God/dess, but Boorn's explanation was explicit. "There is a new congregation emerging—people who are attracted to being together in the Divine Feminine . . . We are a Lutheran church, but we are also a feminist Lutheran church, which is not always easy to find. And that's the core of our spirituality, not a peripheral group that meets down the hallway; it's all that we are." As for a church dedicated to feminism, Boorn's explanation focused on emplacement. "There are a lot of pockets of feminism. There are women who have a lot of political clout in the feminist movement, and there are some in the spiritual realm, and there's a lot in the academic realm, and they often converge and talk with one another. But as far as it goes for people who are seeking a daily or weekly communion to do a kind of faith journey—to be in touch with spirit, the Holy One in whatever ways they call her or by whatever practices, it is not always as available."[34]

Posting the video on the Internet was an intentional move to publicize the church; within a year, the video had been viewed more than 2,700 times. The power of the Internet and YouTube allowed herchurch to get its message out for relatively little cost. What a difference this was from the options available in the 1980s to Cady and Taussig when they published *Wisdom's Feast.* Their publishing options required money for mailings or interest from newspapers or book editors to disseminate their work.

In contrast, herchurch had access to communication technologies that were less expensive to use and allowed greater self-expression. The photographer donated her time, and she used a digital camera that fit in the palm of her hand. She edited the video on her computer and posted the video on YouTube free of charge. The comment section on the site also allowed members of the congregation to craft their own messages and express them directly to a larger audience with little editing or filters.

This exposure brought both wanted and unwanted attention. By sharing a video of their worship space, ritual, and theology on YouTube, herchurch put itself in a situation to be openly critiqued because anyone could view the video and post comments for all to see. In the first year that the video was available on YouTube, forty-seven comments were posted that ranged from enthusiastic support to harsh condemnation. Taken as a whole, the commentary reflected the dialogues and debates provoked by herchurch both within and outside the church.

The harshest critiques came from those upset by herchurch identifying itself as Lutheran. "Please do not claim to be Lutheran. You mock all things of our faith!!!" "This is an abomination. There is nothing Christian about ignoring God's Word and creating a pagan goddess worship religion. You are not Lutheran and it is offensive that you claim you are. Nothing in Scripture or our Confessions supports what you are doing. This is paganism. Ms Boorn I call you to repentance. To the Congregation at HerChurch, repent and leave now Romans 16:17." "Jesus Christ the ONLY SON OF GOD is in and with us in the practice of holy communion. I am glad that I am a member of a true Lutheran confessional congregation. I will pray for you and your congregation that you will someday come to know the true Lutheran faith and Christian faith. In His service and glory. Again please do not claim to be Lutheran!"

Some negative comments blamed the ELCA. "Because it is a member of the ELCA Synod, that is why they allow it. The synod leaders themselves do not have any idea what they are doing. Why should they make the congregations under them any more accountable. I know of another 'Lutheran' church in Chicago that is also called Ebenezer and they worship and commune with gays. Talk about against Gods word." "You are exactly the reason I am a member of the Missouri Synod. The ELCA allows its parish ministers too much freedom to change wording and the pattern of worship to draw the masses. It is all about numbers not about the worship. The other reason is that they ordain women." "Disturbing. This place is not at all Christian. One wonders why the church authorities allow this kind of nonsense." "Fake Church."[35]

In response, the postings that supported the efforts of herchurch took issue with the legitimacy of anyone claiming sole authority to define what was Christian as well as what was God. "I applaud this church for their mission. And I love their Web site and Goddess Rosary. I encourage those who want to wag fingers to focus on their own faith journey instead of judging others. Your attitude is why people leave. You aren't

God/Goddess. Stop acting like you speak for it. Kudos to HerChurch!" "Amazing faith journey—faith in action. It is a relief to see people (both men and women) worshipping in a feminist context. What a joyful celebration of life! Blessings to you all!"[36]

But even within the postings that supported Christian feminism, some questioned the need to use female names for God. These responses also reflected the limitations of the word "God/dess" because when written, it reflected both genders, but when spoken, it sounded like only female gender. "I respect the church's mission in trying to reach out to others who have turned away from the faith because of patriarchal misogyny. However, I question whether or not herchurch is giving off a perception of the same exclusion. I've never been there so I cannot speak on it. I can just respond to what I saw and heard on the video." "I understand the need to see the feminine qualities of God, but I don't get why goddess is the term used? Why is goddess any more or less inclusive than God?"

Other herchurch supporters responded. "From what I understand they are not trying to 'exclude.' But the masculine has been used to such an extent far too long. It is time to include feminine terms. It's silly to say that this church because they use a lot of feminine terms is doing the same thing that the Patriarchal system was doing before. I think the feminine aspects of the Divine need to be acknowledged. There needs to be a place for people who are tired of the patriarchal language and system that has hurt them." "As a member of Ebenezer, I can attest that we refer to the Divine in both genders. There is an emphasis on using female language to address the Divine, because we are trying to get in touch with the feminine aspects of God, since that has been largely left out of our Christian heritage. Of course, God/dess is beyond gender, but since our language is gender based, we are trying to expand our understanding. Knowing female and male aspects of God/dess allows us a larger grasp of the Divine."[37]

When I discussed the video with the leadership of herchurch, they did not know if the video on YouTube generated more interest in their Web site or more participation in Sunday worship. They were aware, however, that many members of the herchurch community were proud to be represented in this electronic public square.[38] They also noted that the debates in the postings were happening in Lutheran circles more generally, particularly over what was claimed as "Lutheran." Despite the heated rhetoric online, herchurch would soon be caught up in larger political debates that extended well beyond its church denomination.

THE SECOND CONFERENCE: THE GODDESS AND PROPOSITION 8

From June until November 2008, the state of California legalized same-sex marriage. During this time, herchurch officiated seven same-sex marriages for its membership. In November, forces against same-sex marriage, including conservative Christian churches inside and outside the state, sponsored a state ballot initiative known as Proposition 8 to constitutionally define marriage as between a man and a woman.

I attended the second Faith and Feminism conference on November 7, 2008, just three days after the nation elected Barack Obama to be president of the United States. I assumed that the politically liberal members at herchurch would be joyful, so I was surprised by the subdued mood when I arrived. Then I remembered that Proposition 8 had also passed. The musician for the opening night session arrived late because she had been performing at a protest march in front of city hall. When the president of the herchurch leadership council stood up to welcome the conference attendees, she included the following in her opening remarks:

> I want to share with you some issues I am going through these days. A lot of members of our congregation have gotten married in the past few months. Steve and Jim, Judith and Eileen, Norma and Judy, Jonathan and Brent, Kathy and Carol, Nicole and Michelle, myself and Andrea. In fact there have been as many as 18,000 gay and lesbian marriages taking place since the California Supreme Court ruled that same-sex couples could marry. That has stopped for now since Prop 8 passed. For me, the issue of inclusion is one of the most central issues facing the church today. Thanks goodness we no longer burn heretics at the stake, but the effects of the burning days are with us still. The church has not had a great history of inclusion or respect for other religions, or even other interpretations of Christianity. And these barriers can cut deeply. My mother was a conservative Christian who never accepted my life choices. We had a very strained relationship until the day she died. I left the church in my teens and didn't look back until I stumbled upon herchurch in my early 50s. Had I been in an inclusive religious setting I would not have felt exiled for 30 years. Yet I don't think that

> is what Christ had in mind. He was criticized for hanging out with tax collectors and sinners. He talked to women he didn't even know. Yet that was part of what made his message universal. Anyone could join his movement. Anyone . . . We all deserve love and acceptance. I pray that Christians move to be more and more inclusive. I think Jesus, Mohammad, Buddha, and the Goddess would like that.[39]

Her reflection encapsulated both the need for, and the fragility of, an accepting Christian community that could claim a vision for a more tolerant society around sexual orientation. Her sorrow was palpable. It was fellow Christians who negated her marriage and used her own religion to denounce her. Transforming the world was the herchurch vision, but at that moment it was more a safe harbor of consolation for those being buffeted by larger political storms.

Despite the subdued mood, I noticed how herchurch members had grown in their eloquence and confidence. When I first came to herchurch, many explained their rituals and initiatives as "because Pastor decided."[40] Boorn agreed that it was ironic that she had been so autocratic in the beginning for a mission about equality, but she said that when she was first taking the church in a new direction, the congregation was understandably tentative. Even those who were excited about the changes looked to her for direction. I could see that the dynamics were changing as the core team took on more leadership roles at the conference and expressed themselves in confident new ways. The speech given by the herchurch council president was just one example.

The focus of the second Faith and Feminism conference was the Goddess. Carol Christ, who led the Crete pilgrimage, was the keynote speaker. The leadership team knew this would attract a contingent of women and some men to the conference who would come only to hear Carol speak and quite possibly have issues with Christianity. They hoped that some of them, especially those with Christian backgrounds, might get interested in joining herchurch once they experienced their community and worship.

The pre-conference session had far fewer Lutheran ministers, and two women introduced themselves as Isis priestesses. One participant even spent a fair amount of time promoting her own Goddess activities, directing us to a table in the foyer with information on her own Goddess pilgrimage, despite the presence of the much more famous keynote speaker with her much more famous Goddess pilgrimage. The commercialism and competition was also heightened when another woman set up her paintings across the back of the worship space without permission and made announcements about selling her art and DVDs during the conference question and answer sessions. I was left with the sense that these Goddess women were not as interested in learning about dialogue with herchurch as they were about finding new audiences to which to present their ideas and wares. Other participants privately voiced their objection to the commercialism, and some felt the sacredness of the worship space was not being honored.[41]

These actions also drove home the point of how difficult it was to get alternative religious viewpoints heard. In an interesting twist, herchurch appeared mainstream at this conference, as opposed to the previous year, when it appeared to represent the fringe. Broadening the conversation to include Goddess groups also reversed the roles of religion and art. At the first conference, Christianity was the unifier while the debate was how best to image and relate to God. At this second conference, the unifier was sacred female imagery but with a range of interpretations and theologies.

Carol Christ managed to engage both Christian and Goddess audiences and offered thoughts and insights for both groups. She said she felt connected to all feminists, including Christian and Jewish feminists, around issues of gender injustice. She cited statistics about the continuing inequality of pay and housework between men and women. She noted that the Internet has facilitated an explosion of pornography viewed mostly by men with a concurrent dramatic increase in cosmetic surgery among women. She saw a need for celebrating the female body in a healthy way as well as worshipping an image of a Goddess as an independent power so men could see positive images of women and women could envision themselves without looking for male approval.[42]

Christ felt using the term "Goddess" and the pronoun "She" was needed to break the image of God as a male lord and ruler. It bothered her that the trend today has been toward gender-neutral language, which from her perspective removes the offense for some women but does not change men. For her, if men cannot accept full interchangeability, then why allow the term "God," which in the minds of many still only represents the male? Why do women accept it?

Even with her critiques, however, Christ still believed the wider community could change because God/dess was a God/dess of love. This vision was shared by those in the room. During the conference, participants were invited to reflect on what "She" was calling them to do, to write this on a piece of paper, and to place the prayers in a basket on the altar. A member of the herchurch leadership team later typed the responses into an anonymous list and shared them with me. There were fifty-one responses, and they provided a glimpse into the hopes, desires, and prayer life of the conference participants.

All of the messages spoke of a relationship with a distinct deity that was personal, intimate, and nurturing. More than half of the responses described a call of self-transformation to love, peace, and healing. Some wanted help to overcome personal flaws such as anger. A third found encouragement for making new life choices, whether looking for new work or adopting a child. Many spoke of engaging or recommitting themselves to initiatives to help the earth or justice causes affecting women, such as domestic violence. This call also included making the "Divine Feminine" more known in the world, some being explicit about doing this work in either Christian or Goddess settings.

As a result of the second conference, Boorn began differentiating herchurch from other Lutheran feminisms using the term God/dess. I asked her how this was different from describing the church as Sophia oriented. She said that while Sophia continued to be a significant way the congregation referred to God using Judeo-Christian scripture, she felt that God/dess was a recognition of and connection with the historical roots before Judaism and Christianity. Because God was ever present and everlasting, she preferred the broader God/dess term, which allowed it to recapture, redevelop, and reconstruct images and language of God that expressed Christianity with this larger truth.[43]

The congregation of herchurch has continued to evangelize the wider Lutheran Church on the need to engage feminist theological exploration through emplacing ritual within a local church community. The Web site has added links to other Lutheran social justice causes that connect to its mission of feminism, such as fair trade chocolate for Valentine's Day through the Lutheran World Resources. The annual Faith and Feminism conferences have also grown in reputation and stature. In 2010, Ada Maria Isasi-Diaz, a leading voice in the construction of mujerista theology, was a keynote speaker. Interest and participation in the conferences have grown as well, and herchurch has been able to raise the registration fees to help cover its costs.

Boorn and the leadership team continue to work on how best to communicate the ministry of herchurch. In 2012, the conference was renamed herconference, retaining the lower case convention of herchurch to emphasize community over hierarchy. The word *feminism* from the original title now appears in the subtitle along with womanist and mujerista; minjung was added in recognition of the 2012 keynote speaker, Chung Hyung Kyung, who spoke on South Korean liberation theology. The word *faith* from the original title now appears in a tagline that succinctly sums up the herchurch vision, "where faith traditions and Goddess meet."

Conclusion

The work of herchurch is bold and shows how critical the resource of evangelization is as a resource for the strategic emplacement of female imagery of God in worship. When the herchurch ministry began, Boorn concluded that the best way forward was not through small incremental change, but through a prophetic expression of all that was missing in Christian worship around female gender. According to the herchurch leadership team, only with explicit female-gendered language and art will Christians' imaginal realm be altered. From Boorn's point of view, "[w]hile the literalizing of the male God brought on patriarchy, some literalizing of the female is important for half of the planet to image their own divinity."[44]

The ministry of herchurch shows that there is still a need for some Christians to worship at a church that is focused on gender equality and empowerment. Ritualizing this message with female imagery keeps the message central to the community's life. Emplacement of female imagery has meant modifying rituals and performing a different view of church, God, tradition, and society. It has allowed for sermons, congregational projects, Bible studies, and social outreach to be focused on feminism and encourages celebration of this message in communal worship.

Evangelization of this ritual emplacement has involved opening the church doors to connect with the local community. Those who resisted this change wanted the church to gird against these social changes. Today, the progressive LGBT-friendly ethos of San Francisco has been welcomed into the church sanctuary as the community of faith embraces an image of God as Holy Other.

There has always been a strong pastoral dimension to herchurch. Many herchurch members have experienced rejection from family, society, and church. The alternative images of God at herchurch inspire those who have been marginalized in a variety of ways, as do the intergenerational relationships. Younger LGBT members, possibly estranged from their families, now find a home at herchurch and have been welcomed by older Swedish women who could be their grandmothers. At the same time, the croning ritual has helped these older women find their voice and purpose within this new parish family.

The benefit of Christian feminism as an evangelizing message is that it directs both the social justice and the ritual innovation of the parish, tying them together in dynamic, synergistic expressions of outreach. When a church fully commits to evangelizing its mission, a momentum can be created that is essential for emplacement. Every decision and action of the herchurch community has been another step toward even more concrete emplacement of female imagery in worship and message.

This commitment to evangelize was demonstrated when the church needed painting. While it was not Boorn's first choice, the leadership team chose the colors purple and periwinkle, colors they felt were "spiritual" as well as communicated that they were not a typical church.[45] Clearly, the days of "Pastor" making all decisions has passed and the lay leadership is taking more responsibility. As a result of the painting decision, herchurch is now known also by another nickname, the "purple church." The leadership team has also commissioned a huge mural for the church tower so that female images of God will appear on the exterior walls of the church and be seen for miles.

The church's evangelization on the Web has garnered attention outside San Francisco, too, but Boorn is not interested in growing an "Internet church."[46] Instead, she wishes that every major town in America had its own herchurch where women and men could be fed by Christian feminist worship and where they could find a local community to transform not just themselves, but also the face of Christianity. She hopes this movement grows internationally to deconstruct what she sees as a root cause of patriarchy—the image of God as exclusively male.[47]

Boorn says she will gladly balance the gendered imagery in herchurch when greater Christendom has done so as well. As the YouTube commentary showed, this predictably has bothered some Christians, particularly conservative Lutherans. Liberal allies who accept "God" as a nongendered term have also been challenged by herchurch. While few Christian congregations may consider expressing exclusively female imagery in worship, herchurch still challenges them to question their own ritual choices around gender and God and to ask if what they are doing is enough regarding gendered imagery of God.

The story of herchurch shows the value of documenting the histories of groups that are best positioned, because of their geography, political milieu, and denominational progressiveness, to be on the forefront of new social and religious movements. They show both the pitfalls and creative workarounds that make new ritual expressions possible. They become the histories that raise the bar and show a vision of worship and church that both challenges and inspires others. Boorn and herchurch have embraced this role, accepting that their worship community in San Francisco has both the opportunity and possibly the obligation to use the freedom of their location to engage leading-edge gender issues in church and society.

Conclusion

> Wisdom teaches her children and gives help to those who seek her. Whoever loves her loves life, and those who seek her from early morning are filled with joy. Whoever holds her fast inherits glory.
>
> —Sirach 4:11–13

In the wake of the 1960s women's movement, many Christians began exploring female imagery of God in the Bible. Today, Christian worship resources express female imagery in a variety of ways: from hymns to scripture readings to published sermons and art. When using these resources, church congregations generally include female imagery along with more standard worship conventions. Unlike what many critics predicted, most congregations that use female imagery of God do not deny the centrality of traditional imagery of Jesus and God the Father. Instead, their goal is to expand and enhance parishioners' conceptions of the mystery of God.

In this book, we have explored Christian communities that use female imagery in their ministries to examine core questions about God, gender, and church. I sought out communities of established Christian denominations that were led by ordained or vowed leadership in order to investigate the tensions between innovation and tradition in mainstream worship. These Catholic, Lutheran, Methodist, and Presbyterian congregations invited us behind the scenes, and they revealed how challenging yet rewarding this type of worship can be. This research has offered insights into three central issues: how gender is understood in Christian worship; how patriarchy continues to operate in churches today; and how individuals and communities have used the resources of leadership, personal prayer experience, community, and evangelization to strategically emplace female imagery in their worship despite resistance from both inside and outside their churches.

GENDER AND GOD

Imagery of God with female gender brought many of the participants in these church communities closer to their Christian faith. Ritualizing female imagery of God in community affirmed that females as well as males were expressions of God. Women were encouraged to see themselves in God's image, and men were prompted to explore and honor their feminine side. Those who were exploring and affirming their gender and sexual identity in new ways appreciated new Christian imagery that decentered the religious images and messages from their childhood. Overall, new images of God facilitated new relationships with God, reigniting faith.

How these communities interpreted the femaleness of God revealed varying assumptions about gender, equality, biological sex, and sexual orientation. As we saw throughout this book, the uniqueness in their gender claims was connected to the language and theological understandings of their churches as well as to the particular pressures each community was seeking to overcome. Because the congregations felt compelled to explain why a female image of God was significant to them, they had to articulate their understandings of gender.

Each community focused on a different view of gender. These four interpretations reflected the gendered power issues being negotiated within their particular denominations as well as their social contexts. Strategic emplacement of prayers and worship services made these understandings explicit.

Rev. Susan Cady's message reflected a wing of the women's movement that focused on opening up all-male power networks to women. This activism drew upon a philosophical ideal of an autonomous rational subject but asserted that it should include women. A simpler expression of this view might be "women are people too." The message was that being female should not preclude access to any profession or public role. Much of the justification for women's ordination included this logic. This advocacy did not question the need for hierarchy within churches but asserted that women as well as men should hold these ordained positions of power.

Cady was comfortable putting a female face on what some might consider masculine character traits. She was the only religious leader in the study to highlight scripture quotes of Sophia entering battle, slaying the Egyptians, and showing her might as she meted out justice. She communicated the strength of a single female who could inspire and lead her people in times of peace and in times of conflict.

Cady's vision reinforced this view when she saw an independent Sophia who contained the entire church within herself, unconcerned with how others saw her. This ideal was also communicated when Cady and Taussig called her by one name, Sophia. Unlike the other communities we met, her name in *Wisdom's Feast* was not attached to other names, such as Wisdom Sophia or Christ Sophia; nor was she referred to with the relational titles of "Holy Other" or "Mother."

The Daughters of Wisdom took a different turn. As an all-female religious order operating within an all-male clerical hierarchy, the Daughters continue to live in highly gendered social spaces and church environments. The Daughters' focus on God as both male and female drew upon the Catholic understanding of gender complementarity, where males and females are seen as having complementary natural gifts. The difference in the Daughters' telling was that both males and females are needed to lead the church. They interpreted the problems in the Catholic Church as resulting from an all-male hierarchy having forgotten the feminine side of God. The Daughters of Wisdom believed that the church could be healed of many of its ills by embracing Wisdom Sophia.

Extending this complementarity view of gender, the Daughters also believed that women better understood this feminine side of God. They believed that governance of the church would improve by including women in church leadership. For the Daughters, God first appeared female in Sophia before incarnating as the male Jesus. Because Wisdom was another name for Jesus in their founder's writings, Wisdom Sophia provided a name for the Daughters that was both male and female.

The Church of Scotland preferred the relational term "Mother." As we saw, Anne Hepburn prayed to "God our Mother," and the theological report was titled "Motherhood of God." Yet even with the term "Mother," the Church of Scotland kept Father imagery at the center of its discourse, more than any of the other profiled communities. In the 1984 Church of Scotland theological report, the chapter discussing the feminine side of God was titled "Complementing the Tradition: The Motherly Father." When the Moderator of the 2000 General Assembly included female imagery in his prayer, he followed a similar formula with

"O God, gentle, tender Father and strong, secure Mother." The Church of Scotland was the most intent on using female imagery to expand conceptions of God without refuting the traditional male image. This strategy was in keeping with its responsibility as a national church to accommodate a range of perspectives and practices while maintaining its traditions. The latest Church of Scotland hymnal reinforced this view by including a handful of hymns with female imagery scattered among the more pervasive, traditional Father-God lyrics.

Finally, Rev. Stacy Boorn and the herchurch leadership team were a generation younger than the others profiled in the book, and their views of God and gender no longer embraced the gender essentialism of male and female expressed by the other communities. They saw gender more as performance, with masculine and feminine characteristics acted out along a continuum rather than a gender binary. They also accepted that biological sex characteristics might not match an individual's gender identity, and they did not hold heterosexuality to be normative. Because God as male was the convention, herchurch presented a female image to disrupt assumptions around God regarding body, sex, and gender in the most provocative way possible. To this end, herchurch prominently displayed female imagery in art on the altar.

The congregation of herchurch also decentered a fixed image of God with a variety of names: from the single Sophia and Goddess to the hyphenated Christ-Sophia as well as God/dess and the performative Holy Other. Because referring to "God who is both Mother and Father" kicked off the maelstrom at Ebenezer, Boorn found that "literalizing" female images in people's minds with a title such as Goddess intentionally provoked a reaction and at the same time neutralized previous discourses that had made a deified female something that was distinctly non-Christian and unholy.

While there were clear differences in these dominant gender messages, the communities also gave credence to other types of gender claims as well. Cady spoke not only about Sophia entering battle, but also about the feminine side of God that empathized with women's pain, as well as the gentle mothering of God. The Daughters of Wisdom acknowledged that men could develop their feminine side, even though the Daughters' complementarian view was that women were needed in the hierarchy for a feminine perspective. At herchurch, while the female imagery was meant to be performative and disruptive, in fact many females joined the congregation because they liked seeing their female identity expressed in church art. Finally, the Church of Scotland hymnal used female imagery to communicate mostly feminine characteristics, even though the theological explanation of the Motherly Father was more complex.

The experiences of these communities show how messy applying gender theory and feminist theology can be when engaged in the terrain of lived experience. Sometimes these mixed messages would surface after long explanations of what female imagery could do in the world, particularly when emphasizing the benefits of the essentialized feminine characteristics of compassion, inclusion, and forgiveness. When I asked if privileging femaleness was excluding maleness, most respondents said no. Many responded that God-as-female was inclusive of all, even though this explanation was identical to what their critics claimed for keeping God exclusively male. This muddling was bound to occur as community members tried to make sense of the twists and turns in their individual and communal faith journeys. Boorn was the most strategic in her explanation that herchurch intentionally used exclusively female images as a small counterbalance to the overwhelming use of male images seen in Christian worship today.

It was striking that rarely did any of these worship communities focus on gender queering as a reason for exploring Sophia or the female side of God, even though there were ample opportunities. The Daughters of Wisdom had their founder's writings, which described a female Sophia Wisdom incarnating as the male Jesus, but instead of queering explanations, they provided complementarity explanations that God was gender balanced. The gender-bending complications for this progression might have been one reason why the priest who provided the first translation of their founder's writings into English used exclusively masculine pronouns for the Sophia texts. The Church of Scotland used the term "Motherly Father" while also maintaining a perspective that gender had two forms, male and female. Boorn was the best positioned to explore the queering of gender because of the population she served, yet she kept her messages more general when referencing the "Holy Other."

In all four communities, the primary justice issue they sought to address with female imagery was gender equality. Most of those who advocated for female imagery of God in worship reflected the attitudes and worship style preferences of their white and middle-class congregations; their personal stories were mostly about gender injustice without race and class distinctions. In their characterizations of Sophia from the Bible, Sophia held status in the community, as kings listened to her wisdom, and her value was placed higher than silver and gold. The most marginalized image of Sophia was of her standing at the gates, exhorting the people to return to God's instruction. Even this image, however, placed her in the elevated prophetic role of being God's mouthpiece among the people.

Others have been inspired by the Sophia texts in different ways, although how much these other interpretations have appeared in church worship rituals is open to question. Taussig's students in the Methodist chapter were inspired by the queering figure of a female Sophia who incarnates as the male Jesus. Others have written poems and prayers about Sophia from a variety of perspectives, including the poem "What Shall We Call Her?," featured on the Web site for the Womanist Institute. "I am told the stories of the brightness in her eyes that painted visions of the moon through her tender touch, and the purple cloth she pressed tightly between her fingertips. I am struck by the tenacity they tell me she had and the will she held on to. She was once young like me resisting the madness the world had to offer. She was a brown skin girl that was made in the image of the divine with the imprints of her ancestors on her skin. I could sense her fearlessness, but I felt her pain . . . Wisdom birthed me, Wisdom birthed us. Wisdom is her name."[1]

It is difficult to create new worship with imagery that will speak to a wide diversity of people, not just because of theological themes, but also because of different personal preferences regarding sacred music, ritual, and art. The womanist, mujerista and queer theologians invited to speak at the initial Faith and Feminism conference did not connect to the herchurch message or worship style with the same enthusiasm and connection as the hosting community. As we saw, the queer speaker preferred Bible texts that showed more ambiguity about gender and sexual orientation. The mujerista speaker stressed the importance of imaging Mother Mary as a strong role model for the Latino worship community. Both the mujerista and womanist speakers emphasized the inspiration of Jesus for their communities as an ally who had faced injustice himself.

Critics against female imagery of God in worship also advocated for the centrality of Jesus, but for different reasons. While the womanist and mujerista speakers noted their worship preferences without making the Sophia imagery wrong, the critics simply used the image of Jesus as a litmus test for orthodoxy; a female image of God was interpreted as heresy. Cady and Taussig were critiqued for not engaging more of the historical male Jesus in their work *Wisdom's Feast*. The Daughters of Wisdom were chided for making too much of the female representation of Wisdom as the precursor to Jesus. Both Hepburn and Boorn were criticized for presenting deified female imagery as Christian.

Boorn was also criticized for saying "Jesus was a feminist" because feminism is a modern concept, not an ancient one. It is important to remember, however, that many Christian worship leaders struggle with how to present the historical Jesus and the resurrected everlasting Christ. To refer to Jesus only in his past historical context loses the power of speaking of Christ being alive today, yet to speak only of the resurrected, non-bodied Christ can be too esoteric for many. The solution for most Christian preachers is to speak of Jesus alive today in his historical biological maleness from the past, dealing with contemporary issues and using contemporary language and concepts. This slippage of time, biological embodiment, and personae may not be noticed until something as dramatic as an image of Jesus as a feminist is introduced. It is important for us to remember that certain critiques against the preaching in these communities could be levied at standard preaching about Jesus heard every Sunday.

CHURCH PATRIARCHY TODAY

The experiences of these communities have allowed us to look closely at how patriarchy continues to operate in Christian churches today. Controversies around worship are particularly effective ways for conservative coalition building in churches wishing to stem the tide of liberal reform. These cases show that insisting on patriarchal language and imagery is a first line of defense for churches that do not want women's ordination, and it is a second line of defense for churches resisting women's ordination when it is allowed. By engaging the body, mind, and feelings, worship is evocative by design, both personally and communally. It should come as no surprise that many in this study, both those for and against female imagery of God in worship, hold strong convictions about it.

The types of actions used against the communities profiled in this book have included official decrees, theological objections, ritual complaints, letter-writing campaigns, retaliatory firings, excommunication threats, and personal slander. The religious resources used to support these efforts have included church law, "tradition," theology, and ritual guidelines as well as the more generic hiring and firing power, money, media outlets, and informal rumor networks. Each case had its own mix, depending on its denomination and sociocultural context.

Church law continues to be the most overt and formal way to perpetuate patriarchy in certain denominations. Not allowing certain populations to lead worship or to deliver sermons ensures that perspectives that emerge from these groups will not be as visible to the wider church faithful. While the Daughters of Wisdom ritualized Sophia in prayers and blessings, they never officiated at a Catholic mass because women are prohibited by church law to serve as priests. In addition, because ordination is a requirement for most top positions in the Catholic Church, patriarchy is further reified, as only men are appointed and only men make most church decisions.

Church law can also perpetuate patriarchy by silencing dissenters and punishing transgressors. The Church of Scotland General Assembly used the legal voting process not to receive the Motherhood of God report as a way to silence its findings and its advocates. Points of formal protocol were used to silence those who tried to start a discussion.

Church law can be created to deflect attention away from the justice issue as well. Four years after declaring that women's ordination would not be allowed, the all-male Catholic hierarchy took a further step in 1998 to forbid discussion on the topic. This ruling made even casual conversation about women's ordination dangerous with the heavy-handed threat of excommunication. As a patriarchal strategy, this type of directive allowed the Church to characterize those who publicly disagreed with the ordination decision to be rule breakers, rather than address the larger underlying issue of gender justice.

Women in church leadership and the men who supported them were also targeted using the church legal system. Hepburn and Lewis were openly challenged at the Church of Scotland General Assembly. Bishop Susan Morrison was compelled to respond to heresy charges against Cady and Taussig because the formal church legal process had been engaged. Morrison herself endured a petition from a male subordinate who challenged her leadership when she did not censure Cady. Even when complaints were dismissed or overruled, the church's legal process created stress and cast doubt on the pastoral leadership of those targeted. The petitions and theological inquiry into their writings had a similar effect.

The most prevalent patriarchal strategy against gender justice in worship has been to claim "tradition." As Chapter 4 on the Lutheran congregation of herchurch reveals, even when the Evangelical Lutheran Congregational Association gave a directive to use inclusive language in worship, some pastors and parishioners justified their resistance based on tradition. In Chapter 1 on United Methodism, the Jesus Christ is Lord Committee objected to *Wisdom's Feast* on similar grounds. Many letters objecting to the Motherhood of God printed in Scottish newspapers had tradition as their justification as well.

Those who were claiming tradition were also insisting on the exclusive use of male royal hierarchical language for God. Words such as Lord, King, and Ruler reinforced patriarchal stratification. When these profiled communities advocated for expansion beyond all-male language and imagery, they were charged with blaspheming God. During these conflicts, the worst sinners were the ritually aberrant for using gender-inclusive language.

It is worth noting that many of those advocating to preserve patriarchal language in worship have claimed to be preserving ritual tradition for tradition's sake despite the fact that traditions constantly change and evolve.[2] It is worth noting that all four denominations in this book officially modified their Sunday worship in recent decades. The Catholic Roman Rite was radically changed in 1969 to include a new *Ordo Lectionum Missae*. Both the United Methodist Church and the Evangelical Lutheran Church of America officially adopted the Common Lectionary in 1983 and Revised Common Lectionary in 1994, when more Wisdom literature was added to the selected readings. All the featured denominations officially approved new hymnals during this time.

It may be more accurate to say that what is really being challenged when tradition is claimed is *who* gets to define the tradition. The call to tradition provides an acceptable way to leverage older patriarchal attitudes in more contested modern settings. Those who claim tradition are privileging ways of thinking and operating from the past. Because women have not had a voice in making church decisions until recent times, claiming tradition becomes a particularly effective way of cutting down women's perspectives on church matters. Many female worship leaders and biblical scholars prefer not to work on gender issues directly in their professional roles, even if they have strong interest in them privately. As we heard the female Lutheran pastors discuss before the first Faith and Feminism forum, it is easier for male colleagues to take the lead on gender inclusivity in worship because it appears more objective and less personally motivated.

Theology has been another location for patriarchal pushback. Critics brought up theological themes of atonement and sacrifice to undercut the empowerment message of liberating theologies. They chided those who advocated for Sophia theology as being too prideful for not emphasizing these themes. When advocates for female imagery began to express and assert themselves within church contexts, they were charged with not being humble, not accepting their broken natures, and not foregrounding their primary identities as sinners in need of Christ's sacrifice and salvation on the cross. Their critics, however, rarely admitted brokenness or sinning with any level of personal specificity, either.

These theological debates often served to divert attention from how real men were treating real women, both socially and within the church. Critics of these communities rarely acknowledged the imbalances and injustices in church and society that female imagery of God was meant to address. Occasionally, there was some acknowledgement of how the contributions of women and femaleness had been discounted in society, but with little reflection on how churches contributed to normalizing or sanctifying this behavior.

In addition to legal, liturgical, and theology challenges, these cases revealed a willingness among critics to use whatever positional power, ecclesial leverage, and funding pressure was available to silence offenders. Parishioners tried to fire pastors, and disapproving bishops exercised power in punitive ways. Financial boycotts of offending parishes were organized, and conservative media outlets sought to sway public opinion.

Despite these efforts, if a worship leader continued to express female imagery in prayer and ritual, she or he could be personally maligned through rumors and character attacks that were repeated in editorial columns, news stories, and letter-writing campaigns. The boldness of these pushback efforts reflected the de facto privilege that the opposition assumed it possessed. Both Cady and Boorn bore the brunt of their personal attacks as single women. In both cases, their detractors speculated as to why they were not married. This slanderous commentary included questioning not only their attitudes toward men but their sexual orientation as well. The maligning of Hepburn was equally as virulent, but perhaps because she was married the discourse never veered into sexual speculation. All were characterized as angry, heretical women, which echoed ancient tropes used for millennia to sideline women who dared to make their voices heard.

Reflections on Four Resources of Strategic Emplacement

Strategic emplacement of female imagery in liturgy, readings, sermons, art, and music moved the debate from an intellectual discourse to embodied expressions. It emboldened those who were inspired by feminist theology as they danced and sang for joy at finally expressing a view of church and God that felt cohesive and affirming. Others for whom this did not fit their sense of self or church were also emotional in their protests. The struggles that ensued were both highly personal and political. When the rhetoric was at its height, the stakes were no less than a cosmological and sociological showdown about self and God.

The leaders and their congregations demonstrated steadfastness to their cause with a strategic perspective on their ritual emplacement efforts. Their acts of creating new Christian prayer and worship highlighted certain themes within their larger church traditions as well as positioned new voices in the ritual act. Their rituals provided ways for these communities to get their story told and to express their religious understandings in meaningful ways.

The challenges these communities faced with their rituals were different. For the Daughters of Wisdom, it was an all-male hierarchy with the injustice of women not being included in top decision making in the Catholic Church. Cady's challenge began not with the ecclesial structure, but with her congregants and colleagues who disagreed with the United Methodist decision to allow women's ordination. Hepburn was maligned by ministers' wives who were protecting their place of honor within an older church social structure. The challenge to Boorn's leadership came from parishioners who were resisting her outreach to the progressive, gay-friendly environment of San Francisco.

Despite their differences, the resources that all four communities employed in order to sustain their worship expression were surprisingly similar. This finding suggests that other Christian communities interested in including more female imagery in their Christian worship may be able to apply the lessons learned here, even if the particulars of their worship situations are different. Let us now consider what this study reveals about each of the four strategic emplacement resources employed by the profiled communities: leadership, personal prayer experience, community, and evangelization.

1. LEADERSHIP

Ritualizing female imagery within traditional Christian settings required worship leaders with passion, political savvy, creativity, and organizational skills. It required leaders with a love and commitment to the denomination as well as a deep empathy for gender justice issues in order to remain committed in the face of challenges and threats. All of the female religious leaders we profiled had personally experienced sexism in their ministry work from their congregations, colleagues, and/or superiors. The male religious leaders who supported these efforts had personally witnessed this form of discrimination taking place. Imaging God-as-female challenged sexism, as it brought attention to the sacred worth of femaleness and provoked people to examine their gendered assumptions of God and people. Female images of God in worship highlighted and privileged female embodiment and feminine characteristics. These rituals helped faith believers expand their concept of who was fit to be their spiritual leader.

As these cases reveal, it was necessary for the leader to have the positional power to direct prayer and ritual. Only when co-pastors Cady and Taussig brought their witness and authority into worship was the whole congregation engaged in considering new images of God. Without Boorn as pastor, it is unlikely that Ebenezer would have become herchurch. The Daughters of Wisdom leadership team put learning about Wisdom Sophia into the U.S. province strategic plan, which directed the whole community to experiment with Sophia prayer. Finally, Hepburn's position as president of the Woman's Guild gave her the public forum to pray to God our Mother in front of almost one thousand women and men at its annual meeting.

In addition to directing prayer, these positions of leadership also legitimated any ritualizing that occurred. Ordination and vows served a credentialing function and provided a stamp of approval. These church leaders now had the official power to shape, mold, and influence what others practiced and believed. Positions of leadership offered these agents of change a public personae, platform, and audience. These leaders used their positional power to express a female-centered experience of God, making it identifiable and visible to many for the first time.

The official church leadership positions gave endorsement to the ritual practices as coming from the tradition or at least being in harmony with it. Their positions may not have held significant power within the larger structure of their denominations, but in the eyes of practitioners of that faith, ordination or vows conferred an institutional identity and power that those individuals carried and represented wherever they went. Their positional power gave them legitimacy with others. For many, seeing Protestant ministers or Catholic sisters advocate for female imagery of God became signs of hope.

These charismatic leaders also demonstrated courage and boldness of vision to use official church directives to explore female imagery of

God in worship. The Daughters of Wisdom used the Vatican II directive to recover the original charism of their order through studying Wisdom in their founder's writings. Cady and Taussig used the additional Wisdom readings in the updated United Methodist lectionary to preach on Sophia theology to their congregation. Hepburn accepted the Church of Scotland General Assembly directive to form a study group and prepare a theological report on the Motherhood of God. Boorn embraced the charge to reinvigorate a dying ELCA parish by introducing feminism as its new mission. Taken together, all of the cases exhibited examples of church leaders who were able to recognize church-directed opportunities within their denominations for exploring female imagery of God in worship.

These leaders exhibited political savvy by navigating their worship expression around the current hot buttons of the day within their churches. They were also adept at cultivating allies. These allies either officially gave an organizational stamp of approval for the practice or informally protected them by not carrying out requested chastisements.

The leaders were as much appreciative stewards of their church traditions as they were advocates for reform, and this is why they were successful. They were well versed in referencing denomination-specific theological resources to explain their efforts. They understood church politics, and they knew how their churches operated from the inside. They justified their prayers and rituals using the language and theology of their denominations and presented worship innovation within the opportunities and constraints of both the church they loved and the people they loved to serve.

2. Personal Prayer Experience

The sharing of personal prayer experiences was the second strategic resource employed by all four communities. Community members shared personal stories to explain why female imagery of God in Christian worship was life giving for them. The value as a strategic resource was that members who did not initially accept female imagery of God in worship often supported it after they learned about the personal prayer experiences of others.

Many women shared that it was life giving to pray with an image of God that reflected their bodies, and that highlighted divinity, power, and beauty of femaleness. The biblical Sophia reflected an image they already had or wanted to have regarding this divinity, power, and beauty of femaleness. For the men in the study who preferred a female image of God, it was often a reflection of something they were cultivating or honoring within themselves or to show solidarity in worship with women they knew. Male and female members who were exploring their gender identity and sexual orientation also appreciated worshipping with alternatives to strictly male images of God.

Testimonies in these communities also came from people who experienced God in prayer through hearing a female voice or seeing a female body. Some individuals described a motherly love or comforting immanent presence best described as "feminine." There were people in the study who had already experienced God as female even before they learned about feminist theology or heard inclusive language. These members had mostly kept these prayer experiences private until there was a way to relate them to Christian scripture. The experiences shared were always recounted as profound and deep for those who experienced God this way. These personal "God stories" served to invite the larger community to at least consider that female imagery was valuable for others.

Personal prayer experiences provided otherworldly endorsement to support the scriptural and theological explanations and justifications for praying with female images of God. They suggested that God could and should be imaged and honored as female. By sharing these experiences with the larger community, female imagery of God in worship seemed less invented and more divinely inspired. For the wider community, the sharing of a past experience was particularly powerful for endorsing the ritual practice because it suggested a truth about God that predated the worship expression. It helped others feel more natural praying with female imagery of God.

In addition, once congregations started praying with female images, some community members began to have their own personal prayer experiences. A herchurch member joined the church after praying the Goddess rosary because she experienced the femaleness of God there. Rev. Susan Cady said she saw Sophia as a luminous female figure once she began exploring Sophia scripture. These stories invited other community members to be open to an experience while praying and worshipping with female imagery. These testimonies not only helped to affirm the theology, but also invited exploration for others to experience the truth of it.

Some of the most persuasive sharings came from those who were initially doubtful that God could ever be experienced as female. The Daughter who walked the labyrinth and felt enveloped in the "womb of God" was an example of a community member who at first was skeptical and did not relate to the ritualizing of Wisdom Sophia. Often, these community members would interpret their experiences in ways that showed a greater openness to female imagery but still allowed them to keep their preferred prayer images intact. This particular Daughter was clear that Wisdom would always be Jesus for her and never Sophia, but she could now accept that God could be experienced as female.

Participants would sometimes explain their preference for a male or female image of God based on their family systems. A good relationship with a mother or a bad relationship with a father would be a reason given for preferring a female image of God. Those who did not feel a personal need to pray with a female image of God sometimes gave the explanation that they had a good relationship with their father, so the father-God images did not bother them. These explanations gave the community a way to speak about the diversity of opinions regarding female imagery of God as prayer preferences rather than doctrinal certainties.

Stories of childhood abuse were by far the most heart wrenching. For some, being traumatized by male authority figures as children made imaging God with male gender particularly difficult. A female image was affirmative for them because it helped them heal and stay in a relationship with God. Female imagery was also a way to claim a different view of God while staying within their religious tradition, since the abusers, particularly family members, often practiced the same faith. While the seminarians in the Church of Scotland warned against assuming the ritual preferences of others based on their personal histories, if people wanted to see alternative images of God, then female imagery in worship was often cathartic and life giving.

When Susan Cady's feminist spirituality group ritualized their first Sophia Triduum, they connected the violence Jesus endured with violence against women. During the scourging, they repeated verbal abuse that women have endured: "You're just a woman. You're a bitch. You are nothing." Then, at the crucifixion, when invited to draw their own images, every woman included rape in her imagery and shared a personal story of knowing someone who had been raped.

There was also a connection with this theme at herchurch. During one of the Faith and Feminism conferences I attended, I participated with a small group making art. As we were working on our individual art pieces, each woman introduced herself to the group. When someone mentioned volunteering with an organization that operated a rape crisis line, everyone stopped what she was doing to affirm the speaker for the important work she was doing. The women's reactions over every other good deed mentioned caught my attention. I asked the group if they saw a connection between praying with female symbols for God and the preponderance of violence against women, and they all said yes. The artist leading the session, who made a name for herself painting female divine images, said, "It is what drives my work."

Later in the conference, Carol Christ echoed similar themes in her talk "Why Women Still Need the Goddess." She cited statistics of violence against and trafficking of women and children. She gave these as reasons for the continuing need for deified female imagery, not only to help people heal who have been victimized by violence, but also to help change the mind-set of those who feel justified in violating and subjugating others in this manner.

This issue touches both men and women. In 2007, a male Christian evangelical writer authored a best-selling novel titled *The Shack: Where Tragedy Confronts Eternity*. In his fictionalized story of meeting God after a terrible tragedy, God the Creator is an African American female, the Holy Spirit is an Asian female gardener, and Sophia appears as a Latina; only Jesus is male. The novel became a blockbuster hit, particularly among Christian evangelicals, staying number one on the *New York Times* best-seller list for thirty-three weeks.

The author claims that the book was not autobiographical, but his personal biography has similar themes. In his article "Why I Wrote the Shack," he describes the sexual violence he endured as a boy, first by a tribe where his parents were Christian missionaries and later at a Christian mission school. After eleven years of counseling and at the urging of his wife, he wrote the book for his children to try to explain how he felt God helped him heal from the ordeal.[3] In the novel, how much gendering God as female might have been influenced by his childhood trauma is open to question, but his use of female imagery to portray a loving, accessible God is clear.

For some men and women who are struggling with their faith, female imagery provides a potent counterimage to the images and lessons about God they were taught as children. Imaging God as female gives them a way to remain in their religion while making a clear break with past understandings. As we saw, personal prayer experiences, both the spontaneous God experiences as well as the self-generated prayer images, resulted in a willingness and excitement to ritualize female images of God.

Even so, there were those who still questioned whether this female imagery was Christian because of long-standing rhetoric that an image of a deified female must be pagan and heretical. Sadly, even with biblical references, this ancient trope against female imagery of God still holds sway in the imagination of many Christians. Some of the negative reactions to these communities were so visceral, highly emotional, and heavy-handed that they appeared to transcend the specifics of the worship and to reinscribe the historical slander.

Perhaps for this reason, all four communities felt that it was very important for Christians to see a diversity of God images to support the variety of ways people personally experienced God. As we saw, when people prayed, the images produced in people's minds could easily be more free form than traditional church art. Including female imagery in worship was one way to both inspire and challenge the faithful to expand and deepen into this mystery.

3. COMMUNITY SUPPORT

The third resource for strategic emplacement of female imagery of God in worship is community. In all four cases, there was a motivated core community that was as passionately committed as its leaders to create new forms of worship with female imagery of God. Innovating worship takes more effort and creativity to produce than a typical service, and community members often augmented a leader's efforts as well as assisted in performing the new ritual acts.

In all four communities, there were congregational members creating significant components of the new worship expression. Individual Daughters of Wisdom authored original music and lyrics for Wisdom Sophia songs that were sung at group gatherings. Other Daughters developed simple Wisdom rituals and commentary for their Wisdom Circles and Wisdom colloquia. The Sophia study group helped Cady develop and perform the Sophia Easter week services. At herchurch, community members created new ministries for dance and other arts to enliven the new worship. In the Church of Scotland, new hymns and liturgies were created by the local community to address emerging pastoral needs.

Having community members enthusiastically participate during worship also helped to normalize the practice. Despite what the leader wanted, the community had the power to promote or dismiss the new ritual practice by its level of participation, and committed community members could influence the outcome. They provided a key legitimating function to help the wider community accept the changes. Active and enthusiastic participation during the worship also encouraged further development of the ritual practice.

The social bonds in the community, whether friendship, familial, or social, increased the amount of tolerance shown for the new worship expression and for accepting those with differing opinions. These bonds among community members also provided an informal means through which casual conversation could address objections or resistance before they rose to more formalized debate and reaction. At herchurch, the gregarious dance minister often sat with the older women over coffee after worship, and they shared their opinions with her in ways they rarely did with the pastor. These informal communication channels allowed everyone to save face, as misunderstandings, confusions, and objections about the worship could be raised and addressed early without open confrontation.

As a result, supporting the new imagery was a way to enhance and deepen community bonds as well. The older Daughters of Wisdom never felt a need to change from their more traditional prayer forms, but they did not object to the Wisdom Sophia initiatives because they understood how important these initiatives were for the younger sisters. In the Protestant cases, ministers and seminarians alike were more likely to include female imagery in worship once they understood its importance for members of their congregations.

Female imagery of God also created opportunities for women in the community to speak out. In these communities, the faith experiences of women became regular topics of conversation as community members reflected on where their femaleness had been honored as well as slighted. Several women had experienced the maleness of Jesus being used to justify restricting their leadership and gifts. For some, these hurtful messages were experienced in church, while for others they were repeated in their marriages and careers. To affirm that God was as much female as male was a counternarrative that was both inspirational and emboldening. Even younger women who had not encountered as much overt sexism found worshipping with female images refreshing, as it balanced all the "maleness" in their lives.

Congregational participation with the new worship imagery was also a bonding experience because it gave the group a unique image. Once female imagery of God was highlighted in worship, it gave the community a distinct communal identity that could be seen, spoken, and understood by both those inside and outside the church. The distinctive worship helped individuals who felt alienated by the dominant discourse of their denominations find these communities within the institution. The fact that herchurch attracted some parents who wanted their daughters to see themselves fully in the image of God also pointed to this theme of female empowerment through religious ritual. For the Daughters of Wisdom, it was something that attracted others to join them as sisters or associates.

The visibility also brought new challenges. The time needed to educate one's audience put this worship innovation at risk when others received it as a sound bite, particularly those who were predisposed to object to the practice. This was the case for the United Methodist parishioner who found a picture of his pastor conducting Sophia worship in his local city newspaper, or when conservative Lutherans caught the herchurch video on YouTube, or when Church of Scotland membership read about the Motherhood of God debate for the first time in the newspaper or church magazine. By becoming more distinctive and more public, many of these communities became targets for the discontent others felt about the liberalizing aspects they saw within these denominations.

Not everyone who stayed with these communities did so in order to worship with female imagery. The oldest members in the Daughters of Wisdom had committed themselves to the order long before Sophia Wisdom became part of the community's identity and practice. At herchurch, some community members remained because of their personal connections to the church building where they had married, baptized their children, and buried their husbands. Some young families were joining herchurch mostly because it was in their neighborhood and they were meeting other local families, not because they necessarily sought out this particular form of worship.

One aspect of successfully sustaining female imagery in worship was the extent to which those who were not enthusiastic about the practice were still embraced as community members. At herchurch, the older Swedish women who refused to say certain prayers with the new language nonetheless were still honored as wise grandmothers of the church, seated in the front row, and acknowledged in congregational celebrations. The Daughters of Wisdom had a similar attitude toward their older members, whom they always honored as mentors, teachers, and former leaders of the congregation.

4. EVANGELIZATION

The fourth, and final, resource of strategic emplacement found in all the communities was a commitment to evangelization. All the communities felt that God was calling them to represent a new face of Christianity to a wider audience. The call to evangelize brought the community courage in the face of resistance, and the pushback these communities experienced was strong. If these communities had approached their ritualizing as an experiment rather than a sacred mandate, they may well have stopped their activities prematurely.

Evangelization was particularly important to focus the communities on explaining the new worship practice to visitors and others in the denomination. It was important for these communities to publicize, teach, and express that female imagery was both scriptural and theologically allowable. To view this educational work as a call by God made it a priority.

As a resource, evangelization has become increasingly necessary for churches in general. There was a time when church membership was a shorthand for identifying with a cluster of identities: familial, social, economic, national, racial, ethnic, and geographic as well as religious. Church participation today is now less predictable and less stable over a person's lifetime, creating greater need for churches to commit to outreach efforts in order to attract new membership.

Nonetheless, it is important to note that the worship leaders and key community members of all four communities came from these core identity clusters. Being seen as insiders helped the worship leaders with the admittedly hard work of evangelizing the new ritual practices. All were born and raised in the denominations they were now leading. Hepburn and most of the key advocates in the Motherhood of God debate were from Scottish families who had worshipped in the Church of Scotland for generations. Boorn was a Swedish Lutheran, the largest traditional ethnic group of Lutherans after German. Methodists helped to establish the town in Ohio where Cady grew up. Most of the Daughters of Wisdom came from French, Irish, and Italian Catholic families from the New York City area where many Catholics lived.

These multiple identity connections to their denominations were carried into how the message was evangelized and to whom. For the Daughters of Wisdom, their Wisdom colloquia and Wisdom Circles garnered mostly Catholic participation. The Sophia outreach that Cady and Taussig conducted away from their churches attracted broader participation, but the work they did with Sophia worship at their own parishes served and attracted Methodists. The Motherhood of God discussions engaged mostly Church of Scotland members. While herchurch did significant outreach in San Francisco, it still attracted predominantly Lutherans to financially support the church and serve on its leadership team.

Evangelizing female imagery of God also enabled alliance building with other churches and traditions to help overcome local resistance. The Catholic sisters benefited from their ordained Methodist allies who worked out the biblical references and theology within their preaching and worship communities and shared these insights with the sisters. The Daughters of Wisdom returned the favor when they testified in United Methodist circles to the three-hundred-year-old Wisdom heritage of their order, giving a traditional caché to what some saw as contemporary pastiche. At herchurch, Boorn found that connecting female imagery to an ancient Goddess heritage deepened the message. In Hepburn's case, the prayer that created the original controversy in the Church of Scotland was given to her by Brian Wren, a famous hymn writer ordained in Britain's United Reform Church.

Communication technologies also helped with outreach. Cady and Taussig were able to touch a wider audience through publishing books. *Wisdom's Feast* offered possible sermons, small group exercises, and study guides to teach others about Sophia. The Daughters of Wisdom communicated with a larger audience by publicizing events on its Web site, which attracted people from great distances. Newspapers and television coverage heightened the awareness of and controversy surrounding the Motherhood of God report in the Church of Scotland. New technologies extended the reach of herchurch, which allowed the broadcast of its message through its Web site, YouTube videos, and Internet rosary ministry.

The call to evangelize female imagery of God brings the courage to act regardless of obstacles. The call to evangelize emboldens local communities to create Christian prayers and worship that speak to their greatest needs and longings. The call to evangelize inspires sacred artists and worship leaders to produce new images and messages that communities of faith find inspiring, hopeful, and holy.

It is also worth noting that our four communities reflect the hybridity many liberal Christians pursue in their faith lives today, particularly women. Many Christians do not directly challenge what their churches present, but expand their experience and understanding of God through books, films, workshops, and other means instead. This study suggests that there are more women and men who want to see more female imagery of God in Christian worship than is currently being offered.

While the four resources of leadership, personal prayer experience, community, and evangelization have been essential for the strategic emplacement of female imagery in Christian worship, female imagery in worship has bolstered recognition and acceptance of these four resources as well. As these cases have shown, female imagery of God symbolically legitimates women in church leadership and provides identity for feminist Christian communities. It also affirms personal prayer experiences of female images as God experiences, particularly Christian God experiences. Finally, female imagery makes it easier to evangelize and celebrate the value of women and "the feminine," both in church and in society.

Whether or not these four resources are needed for strategic emplacement of ritual more broadly remains to be seen, especially for institutionally mandated changes. For grassroots worship innovation to be successful, however, I would argue that the more visible the change, the greater the effort and courage needed to be an agent for that change. The advocates involved in these local efforts believed that the changes in worship were based not just on personal preferences, but also on larger God-truths they personally experienced. Believing God is on your side may be the most essential resource of all.

Strategic Emplacement and Ritual Studies

Debate in religious circles often is waged rhetorically using scripture and church law without acknowledging the underlying conflicts between individuals and power alliances. A study such as this, which examines contested rituals and their aftershocks, makes visible what otherwise would be internal church feuds. Strategic emplacement examines how these rituals take place, with an emphasis on the behind-the-scenes actions that can both assist and prevent these rituals from being performed. Studying strategic emplacement can illuminate struggles within religious contexts that might otherwise remain obscure. This type of analysis has particular application for studying the lived religion of all liberation theologies that seek to broaden the voices, perspectives, and messages within a particular religious tradition and community.

Strategic emplacement foregrounds the question of place within theories of ritual action. A major contribution of ritualization and action-oriented ritual theories has been to see ritual in unexpected ways, places, and expressions. Strategic emplacement contributes to this inquiry by specifically asking how the placement of the ritual is contributing to the larger goal of the ritual action. Performing feminist Christian rituals outside of formal church space has nourished many in their faith lives. If a larger goal, however, is to transform the existing church rituals performed in churches every Sunday, then ceremonies performed off-site or down the hall might be relieving pressure from within the larger congregation to transform its main worship practice. Attention to emplacement brings focus to this dynamic.

Additionally, strategic emplacement examines the interplay between theology and practice. It examines the interaction of ideas and rituals within organizational and physical contexts. When ritual theorist Jonathan Z. Smith used the term emplacement in his work *To Take Place*, he began with physical place, extending it to liturgical space and finally to mental constructs. This study shows that emplacement can work in the other direction as well, beginning with the theological insight that becomes expressed in ritual and is eventually anchored in a particular denomination and physical worship location. It also shows that this process is not strictly linear, as we saw a fair amount of interplay in how performance and interpretation evolve.

Some scholars have objected to Smith for extending the category of place to cover other distinct categories of ritual.[4] For our purposes, however, strategic emplacement foregrounds the politicized act of placing rather than defining what the category of place should contain. Smith's linkage of place, action, and thought offers a wide lens for examining the strategy of emplacement. This distinction is important for a range of contemporary theologies seeking to update existing church teachings, worship, and traditions. Theological ideas alone will not revolutionize the practice of faith, and theories of ritual that connect them can open this larger view.

Final Thoughts

Arguably, the largest Christian worship controversy over the last forty years has been regarding women, specifically how much and to what extent Christian worship could or should be modified to accommodate and recognize the needs, worth, contributions, participation, and aspirations of women in church traditions, teachings, and rituals. While the largest debates have been about women's leadership and ordination, some churches still restrict female bodies from their most sacred spaces. Christians may be taught that all humans are made in God's image, but never hearing or seeing female imagery of God in Christian art, hymns, selected scripture, sermons, or prayers helps to normalize the unequal treatment of women both in Christian settings and in society more generally.

There was a time when the exclusive use of male imagery of God in Christian worship might have been considered an oversight, but not today. For churches in countries where the politics of gender and language is widely known, continuing to use only male imagery and language for God, especially when female imagery exists in the Bible, is a decision consciously made. It is significant that worship leaders who oppose female imagery of God rarely show how they are helping girls as well as boys to see themselves in God's image through the rituals they perform. It is also telling that churches that do not ordain women or appoint women ministers are often the churches with the strictest adherence to male-only images and language for God.

When female imagery of God in churches becomes too dangerous to express or even discuss, then these churches are communicating that femaleness in God's image is wrong. They are sending mixed messages to women to see themselves as being made in God's image but never to *actually* see themselves in God's image. It would be naive to think that sexism is not involved in sustaining these liturgical standards based on "tradition," especially in Christianities with a Trinitarian view and multiple female biblical passages for reference.

While a proliferation of female images of God will probably not be the answer for most Christian churches, some female imagery could go a long way toward healing this patriarchal tilt. Normalizing the practice of female imagery and not making it controversial would help. The worship communities profiled in this book have demonstrated ways to introduce and integrate occasional female imagery of God into more standard Christian rituals. These communities challenge other churches to reach beyond nongendered solutions to balance the preponderance of male imagery in their liturgies. Worshipping with female imagery encourages more Christian expression of embodiment and incarnation by including femaleness in this understanding. Our profiled communities have offered persuasive cases for why a Christianity that embraces full equality of females benefits from ritualizing gender inclusivity of God, and they show how more balanced gendered imagery of God in worship would go a long way toward this goal.

Perhaps the greatest contribution these Christian communities offer is their role as experimental worship labs. These congregations have been willing to analyze and experiment with approaches to preaching, liturgy, ritual, study, and community making as well as God imaging over extended periods of time. They offer expertise, worship aids, education, and inspiration for other Christian worship communities. The model of herchurch as a specialized parish with a strong experimental worship component offers an exciting model for developing a denomination's congregational life.

I was asked during this research if I thought emplacement of female imagery of God in Christianity has been successful. Certainly, the development and use of female imagery of God in contemporary Christian ritual has had a complicated history over a short period of time. It started out boldly in the 1970s and 1980s, only to experience a backlash in the 1990s by those who were upset and afraid of women's ordination and leadership. Because many questioned whether this worship expression would survive the attacks, the fact that it is expressed at all in established Christian denominations today is impressive. At the same time, Christian worship communities that foreground female imagery of God as a justice issue are rare, and even inclusive language continues to be controversial in many quarters.

Still, it is encouraging that many Christians want to hear and see more female imagery of God in Christian settings than is currently being offered. These communities have shown that many more Christians can accept female imagery of God in worship with proper education at the congregational level. As the Christian evangelical novel *The Shack* demonstrates, female imagery of God does not have to be a cause for dissent between conservative and progressive Christians. Ongoing support at the denominational level can help to normalize this expression in worship.

The communities themselves believe they are making positive impact. The Daughters have been pleased that multiple Wisdom Circles have continued for almost two decades and that Wisdom Sophia has been an inspiration for those joining the order. As for herchurch, even with the upkeep of a large building, the community has managed to keep its doors open while pursuing feminism as its mission. Sunday worship attendance has shown a slow but steady growth, and the Faith and Feminism conferences as well as other projects have attracted international attention and participation. The Church of Scotland has had success as well. By approving female imagery of God in its latest hymnal, the church has made this type of expression one of many ways to relate, describe, and explore the mystery of God.

While Cady and Taussig believe that Sophia theology was sidelined in the 1990s before it had a chance to fully develop, they see potential for the movement to develop further among theologians and worship communities. Taussig has continued publishing scriptural studies on the Wisdom texts. He sees renewed interest in Wisdom as a queering image, appearing female as Sophia and then incarnating as the male Jesus. If so, Sophia might be one of the few Bible figures to stay relevant as conversations around gender theory and God imagery continue to evolve.

More studies are needed to identify, document, and analyze the range of ways Christian communities celebrate God with female imagery; some communities operate within established church institutions and many do not. Early readers of this volume have mentioned other groups, and I see this as a hopeful reaction to the book if it stimulates more interest and research. The more these worship communities are identified and documented, the more evidence and encouragement there will be for churches to include a broad range of liberating theologies in Christian ritual. Analyzing how female imagery is handled in mujerista, womanist, queer, and other feminist contexts is particularly important and could shed light and understanding on the similarities and differences in these movements. Embodiment and incarnation are essential Christian themes, and documenting how female images of God are imagined and represented in different churches adds important sensory and artistic insight to these theological discussions.

Creating a known network of these communities can increase the sharing of resources as well. More published liturgies, hymns, sermons, and prayers that include female imagery are needed to support new liturgical efforts. Knowing what has worked with other congregations and having examples to draw from can assist in the inspired yet time-consuming process of creating new worship. Communal worship ceremonies can reinforce societal standards or stimulate change. Creating new ritual expressions is important because worship plays a role in what believers consider to be normal and reasonable about their church and society.

The subject of feminism and religion requires understanding and contributions from many disciplines, and more interdisciplinary work is called for among scholars of women's studies, religious studies, biblical studies, and theology. In particular, more research is needed on how imagery informs religious understanding, both how it functions for the individual as well as how it serves and is shaped by the larger community. The potential implication of this work extends well beyond the academy, as many young women and men continue to wrestle with reconciling their religious or spiritual personal experiences with their religious upbringing and social activism.

This need was brought into focus for me when I watched feminist activist Gloria Steinem deliver two lectures on college campuses in 2007. At both events, students asked her about religion during the question and answer period. In the first talk, Steinem was asked, "Can a feminist believe in God?" She replied, "Yes, if God believes in the feminist," and the room erupted in applause.[5] In the second question and answer session, Steinem focused her comments on the image of God, rejecting a remote and judging Father-God in favor of a more immanent spirituality.[6] While her solution only partially aligns with the Christian communities in this study, there is agreement about the problems and limitations of the traditional Father-God image. Steinem's book *Revolution from Within: A Book of Self-Esteem* delved into these more reflective, internal issues, and there have been other voices advocating for feminism to combine spirituality with social justice.[7]

In Christian contexts, ritualizing female imagery of God is one way for individuals, communities, and denominations to address this need. The director of programming at a large Christian retreat center serving thousands of participants every year concurs. "Christian women have been reading feminist theology for decades now. What I see in our retreats is a need for women to embody these messages, to ground them in themselves. There is a need to ritualize these understandings, not just read about them."[8]

It is time to revisit Christian worship conventions around gender. Gender theory continues to break new ground, offering new analytical tools for biblical hermeneutics. Feminist theology is seeing a resurgence among younger scholars who are offering fresh new insights on the subject. Christian institutions continue to engage and explore church teachings on gender and leadership. There are denominations still debating women's ordination or episcopate, and other denominations are discussing LGBT acceptance and church leadership.

There is also a renewed global focus on the status of women, bringing attention and hope to improving the lives of women worldwide. Mainstream organizations around the globe, including the Church of Scotland Guild, now advocate against domestic violence and human trafficking. In 2009, the book *Half the Sky: Turning Oppression into Opportunity for Women Worldwide* correlated women's empowerment with economic prosperity and spurred a worldwide social movement of the same name. In 2010, the member states of the United Nations voted to create UN Women, the United Nations Entity for Gender Equality and the Empowerment of Women, centralizing four existing programs for women in order to increase their visibility and effectiveness to help improve the status of women around the world:

> Gender equality is not only a basic human right, but its achievement has enormous socio-economic ramifications. Empowering women fuels thriving economies, spurring productivity and

> growth. Yet gender inequalities remain deeply entrenched in every society. Women lack access to decent work and face occupational segregation and gender wage gaps. They are too often denied access to basic education and health care. Women in all parts of the world suffer violence and discrimination. They are under-represented in political and economic decision-making processes. For many years, the UN has faced serious challenges in its efforts to promote gender equality globally, including inadequate funding and no single recognized driver to direct UN activities on gender equality issues. UN Women was created to address such challenges.[9]

In this prevailing environment, religions must do more. Christian churches already provide substantial social services to disenfranchised women globally, but reexamining how church teachings and ritual can support and not undermine women's empowerment is essential. In 2013, President Jimmy Carter and the Carter Center sponsored the conference "Mobilizing Faith for Women: Engaging the Power of Religion and Belief to Advance Human Rights and Dignity." As the Daughters of Wisdom have shown, how religious messages of women's empowerment are communicated in third world contexts may well be different from how they are taught and ritualized in the United States and Europe. The main teachings, however, that a woman's life reflects wisdom about God and that Christian women benefit from seeing themselves in God's image, offer powerful woman-positive messages in all settings. When nearly one-third of the world's population practices Christianity, these religious initiatives could have substantial global impact.

More than forty years have passed since the women's movement entered Christianity, and today the landscape has changed, much of it for the better. There are still many churches, however, that continue to discriminate against women in ways that are no longer acceptable in other sectors of society. Without new initiatives, future generations of men and women will continue to be born into these patriarchal sacred canopies and social settings. A religion that does not challenge sexism writ large in the heavens does not communicate gender equality on earth. Ritual has a role to play in communicating the sacred stories we believe about God, ourselves, and each other. Expressing female imagery of God is one way to affirm the "good news" that all humanity is made in the image of God.

Notes

Introduction

1. Sandra Schneider, "God Is More Than Two Men and a Bird," *U.S. Catholic* 55, no. 5 (May 1990): 20.

2. Grace Ji-Sun Kim, *The Grace of Sophia: A Korean North American Women's Christology* (Cleveland: Pilgrim Press, 2002), 82–96.

3. John J. Collins, *Jewish Wisdom in the Hellenistic Age* (Kentucky: Westminster John Knox Press, 1997), 1.

4. James L. Crenshaw, *Old Testament Wisdom: An Introduction* (Louisville, KY: Westminster John Knox Press, 1981), 19.

5. Words from Ecclesiastes 3:1. Music and additional words by Pete Seeger. New York: Melody Trails, 1954.

6. Silvia Schroer, *Wisdom Has Built Her House: Studies on the Figure of Sophia in the Bible*, trans. Linda M. Maloney and William McDonough (Collegeville, MN: Liturgical Press, 2000), 105–106.

7. Maria Rzepinska, "The Divine Wisdom of Michelangelo in *The Creation of Adam*," *Artibus et Historiae* 15, no. 29 (1994): 181–187.

8. See "Wisdom" and "Ecclesiasticus," in *The Bible: Authorized King James Version with Apocrypha* (New York: Oxford University Press, 1998), 93, 112.

9. *The HarperCollins Study Bible: New Revised Standard Version Bible with the Aprocryphal/Deuterocanonical Books* (New York: HarperCollins, 1993), 1508–1509.

10. The NSRV commentary notes, "Personified wisdom speaks similar words in Sir 24.19; 51.23."

11. Raymond Brown, *The Gospel According to John*, vol. 1, Anchor Bible 29 (Garden City, NY: Doubleday, 1966), cxii–cxv.

12. *The HarperCollins Study Bible: New Revised Standard Version with the Apocryphal/Deuterocanonical Books* (New York: HarperCollins, 1993), 1878.

13. James M. Robinson, "Jesus as Sophos and Sophia," in *Aspects of Wisdom in Judaism and Early Christianity*, ed. Robert L. Wilken (London: University of Notre Dame Press, 1975), 9–12. See also Kim, *The Grace of Sophia*, 114–115.

14. See Barbara Newman, *Sister of Wisdom: St. Hildegard's Theology of the Feminine* (Berkeley: University of California Press, 1987).

15. Matthew Fox, *Breakthrough: Meister Eckhart's Creation Spirituality in New Translation* (New York: Image Books, 1980), 219–220.

16. Rudolf Steiner, *Isis Mary Sophia: Her Mission and Ours: Selected Lectures and Writings by Rudolf Steiner*, ed. and introduction by Christopher Bamford (Herndon, VA: SteinerBooks, 2003), 21.

17. Rosemary Radford Ruether, *Goddesses and the Divine Feminine: A Western Religious History* (Berkeley: University of California Press, 2005), 244–245.

18. See Reb Zalman Schachter-Shalomi, *Paradigm Shift: From the Jewish Renewal Teachings of Reb Zalman Schachter-Shalomi*, ed. Ellen Singer (Lanham, MD: Jason Aronson, 2000).

19. Joyce Eisenberg and Ellen Scolnic, *The JPS Dictionary of Jewish Words* (Philadelphia: The Jewish Publication Society, 2001), 143; Charlotte Elisheva Fonrobert and Martin S. Jaffe, eds., *The Cambridge Companion to The Talmud and Rabbinic Literature* (Cambridge: Cambridge University Press, 2007), xix.

20. Gerard von Rad, *Wisdom in Israel* (Nashville: Abingdon Press, 1972), 153.

21. Mary Daly, *The Church and the Second Sex*, with the Feminist Post-christian Introduction and New Archaic Afterwords by the Author (Boston: Beacon Press, 1985), 8.

22. Ibid., 10.

23. Mary Daly, *Beyond God the Father: Toward a Philosophy of Women's Liberation*, with an Original Reintroduction by the Author (Boston: Beacon Press, 1973), 19.

24. Roger Finke and Rodney Stark, *The Churching of America, 1776–2005: Winners and Losers in Our Religious Economy* (New Brunswick, NJ: Rutgers University Press, 2005), 23.

25. Letty Russell and J. Shannon Clarkson, eds., *Dictionary of Feminist Theologies* (Louisville, KY: Westminster John Knox Press, 1996), xix–xxvii.

26. Susan Morrison, "From the Bishop," *United Methodist Reporter for Eastern Pennsylvania*, March 11, 1994.

27. Collins, *Jewish Wisdom in the Hellenistic Age*, 11.

28. See Elisabeth Schüssler Fiorenza, *In Memory of Her: A Feminist Theological Reconstruction of Christian Origins* (New York: Continuum, 1983), *Jesus: Miriam's Child, Sophia's Prophet: Critical Issues in Feminist Christology* (New York: Continuum, 1994); Susan Cady, Marian Ronan, and Hal Taussig, *Sophia: The Future of Feminist Spirituality* (San Francisco: Harper & Row, 1986), *Wisdom's Feast: Sophia in Study and Celebration* (San Francisco: Harper & Row, 1986); Schroer, *Wisdom Has Built Her House*.

29. Rosemary Radford Ruether, *Goddesses and the Divine Feminine: A Western Religious History* (Berkeley: University of California Press, 2005), 5.

30. Elisabeth Schüssler Fiorenza, *Wisdom Ways: Introducing Feminist Biblical Interpretation* (Maryknoll, NY: Orbis Books, 2001), 27–28.

31. Daly, *Beyond God the Father*, 19.

32. See Nancy J. Berneking and Pamela Carter Joern, eds., *Re-Membering and Re-Imagining* (Cleveland: Pilgrim Press, 1995).

33. Stewart M. Hoover and Lynn Schofield Clark, "Event and Publicity as Social Drama: A Case Study of the Re-Imagining Conference 1995," *Review of Religious Studies* 39, no. 2 (December 1997): 159–160.

34. Catherine Bell, *Ritual Theory Ritual Practice* (New York: Oxford University Press, 1992), 130.

35. Bruce Lincoln, *Discourse and the Construction of Society: Comparative Studies of Myth, Ritual, and Classification* (New York: Oxford University Press, 1989), 199.

36. Ronald L. Grimes, *Ritual Criticism: Case Studies in its Practice, Essays on Its Theory* (Columbia: University of South Carolina Press, 1990), 19.

37. Ibid., 119.

38. David Chidester and Edward T. Linenthal, eds., *American Sacred Space* (Bloomington: Indiana University Press, 1995), 16.

39. Greg Johnson, *Sacred Claims: Repatriation and Living Tradition* (Charlottesville: University of Virginia Press, 2007), 6.

40. Ronald L. Grimes, *Deeply Into the Bones: Re-Inventing Rites of Passage* (Berkeley: University of California Press, 2000), 2, 320–322.

41. Mary Farrell Bednarowski, *The Religious Imagination of American Women* (Bloomington: Indiana University Press, 1999), 16–21.

42. R. Marie Griffith, *God's Daughters: Evangelical Women and the Power of Submission* (Berkeley: University of California Press, 1997), 14.

CHAPTER 1

1. Patricia J. Thompson, "Called, Ordained but Not Equal until '56," http://audo.umc.org/interior.asp?ptid=43&mid=10996. Accessed January 25, 2014.

2. Susan Cole, phone interview, Philadelphia, PA, November 27, 2007.

3. Ibid.

4. Cole, March 10, 2008.

5. Ibid.

6. Cole, November 27, 2007.

7. Ibid.

8. Susan Cady, Marian Ronan, and Hal Taussig, *Wisdom's Feast: Sophia in Study and Celebration* (San Francisco: Harper & Row, 1986), 102–103.

9. Cady, Ronan, and Taussig, *Wisdom's Feast*, 104.

10. Cady, Ronan, and Taussig, *Wisdom's Feast*, 119.

11. Rev. Cynthia L. Davis, "Conference on Sophia to Be Held at Arch Street," *United Methodist Reporter for Eastern Pennsylvania*, February 17, 1984.

12. Academic Announcement List and Standing Order Preview (New York: Harper & Row Publishers, October, November, December 1986).

13. Art Brandenburg, "Sophia," *United Methodist Reporter for Eastern Pennsylvania*, November 20, 1987.

14. Nancy Waring, "Freudian Fantasies," *The Women's Review of Books* IV, no. 12 (September 1987).

15. Michael D. Schaeffer, "Women Creating Ritual to Fill Religious Void," *Philadelphia Inquirer*, February 19, 1989.

16. Ibid.

17. Eric M. Umile, "Here I Stand: Why Silence about Heresy?," *United Methodist Reporter*, October 6, 1989.

18. Hal Taussig, personal archive.

19. Hal Taussig interview, Philadelphia, PA, March 10, 2008.

20. *United Methodist Reporter*, October 20, 1989.

21. *Introducing Sophia: 1989 Courses and Resources from Sophia's House*, Sophia's House promotional pamphlet.

22. Eric M. Umile, Johana Stahl, and Rev. G. Paul Beck, "Dear Brothers and Sister in Jesus Christ," UMC of Huntington Valley letter, January 29, 1991.

23. "A Service of Empowerment and Courage," Worship aid, June 8, 1990.

24. "Jesus Christ Is Lord!" Newsletter 1, no. 2, June 1991.

25. Randy Petersen, "Wisdom's Feast of Gospel's Famine?," *Good News: The Bi-Monthly Magazine for United Methodists*, July/August 1990, 13.

26. James V. Heidinger II, "Editorial: Fairest Sophia," *Good News: The Bi-Monthly Magazine for United Methodists*, July/August 1990.

27. Eric M. Umile and thirty others, "An Open Letter about Our Common Crisis of Faith as United Methodists," December 1, 1990.

28. Virginia Burrus, "The Heretical Woman as Symbol in Alexander, Athanasius, and Jerome," *Harvard Theological Review* 84, no. 3 (1991): 232.

29. "Jesus Christ Is Lord!" Newsletter 1, no. 1, April 1991.

30. Rev. Mark Rains, "Specificity of Grievance: Dissemination of Doctrines Contrary to the Established Standards of Doctrine of the Church, as Outlined in the 1992 Book of Discipline of the UMC, Paragraph 2623 (f)," January 4, 1993.

31. Thomas Ogden, "Encountering the Goddess at Church," *Christianity Today*, August 16, 1993.

32. Stewart Hoover and Lynn Schofield Clark, "Event and Publicity as Social Drama: A Case Study of the Re-imagining Conference," *Review of Religious Research* 39, no. 2 (December 1997): 154. See also Joyce D. Sohl, Deputy Secretary General Women's Division, *Fact Sheet Concerning the "Re-Imagining" Conference and the Women's Division of the United Methodist Board of Global Ministries*, January 4, 1994.

33. "Event and Publicity as Social Drama: A Case Study of the Re-imagining Conference," 165.

34. Bill Broadway, "After 'RE-Imagining God" God: The Reality of Job Loss," *Washington Post*, July 2, 1994.

35. "Event and Publicity as Social Drama: A Case Study of the Re-imagining Conference," 160–161.

36. Ibid., 161.

37. Sohl, *Fact Sheet Concerning the "Re-Imagining" Conference.*

38. Susan Murch Morrison and eight others, "A Time of Hope—A Time of Threat," open letter, February 1994.

39. Susan M. Morrison, "From the Bishop: My Response," *United Methodist Reporter for Eastern Pennsylvania*, March 11, 1994.

40. Report of the Task Force on the Study of Wisdom, the Council of Bishops, "Biblical Wisdom & Current Theological Ferment (October 31–November, 1994)," *Circuit Rider*, March 1995, 35.

41. Richard D. Hecht, "Rites Require Rights: J. Z. Smith's To Take Place: Toward a Theory in Ritual after Twenty Years Space, Place, and Lived Experience in Antiquity Consultation," *Journal of the American Academy of Religion* 76, no. 3 (September 2008): 790–805.

42. Teresa Berger, ed., *Dissident Daughters: Feminist Liturgies in Global Context* (Louisville, KY: Westminster John Knox Press, 2001), 13; Starhawk, *The Spiral Dance: A Rebirth of the Ancient Religion of the Great Goddess*, 10th anniversary ed. (San Francisco: HarperCollins, 1989), 201–203; Kay Turner, "Contemporary Feminist Rituals," in *The Politics of Women's Spirituality: Essays on the Rise of Spiritual Power within the Feminist Movement*, ed. Charlene Spretnak (Garden City, NY: Anchor Books, 1982), 219.

43. Catherine Bell, *Ritual: Perspectives and Dimensions* (New York: Oxford University Press, 1997), 238.

CHAPTER 2

1. Daughter of Wisdom, phone interview, Mullins, WV, June 6, 2009.

2. Melissa J. Wilde, *Vatican II: A Sociological Analysis of Religious Change* (Princeton, NJ: Princeton University Press, 2007), 2–3.

3. Daughter of Wisdom, interview, Litchfield, CT, June 7, 2007.

4. Daughter of Wisdom, interview, Provincial House, Islip, NY, June 16, 2007.

5. Daughter of Wisdom, interview, Provincial House, Islip, NY May 23, 2006.

6. *History of Daughters of Wisdom in the United States 1904–1973* (Litchfield, CT: Wisdom House Heritage Room self-published archive), 243.

7. Rodney Starke and Roger Finke, "Catholic Religious Vocations: Decline and Revival," *Review of Religious Research* 42, no. 2 (2000): 125–145.

8. Daughter of Wisdom, interview, Provincial House, Islip, NY, May 23, 2006.

9. Daughter of Wisdom, interview, Provincial House, Islip, NY, May 23, 2006.

10. Former Daughter of Wisdom, interview, Provincial House, Islip, NY, June 15, 2007.

11. Daughter of Wisdom, interview, Provincial House, Islip, NY, June 10, 2007.

12. Daughter of Wisdom, interview, Provincial House, Islip, NY, June 14, 2007.

13. Daughter of Wisdom, interview, Provincial House, Islip, NY, May 23, 2006.

14. Daughter of Wisdom, interview, Provincial House, Islip, NY, May 26, 2006.

15. Daughter of Wisdom, interview, Provincial House, Islip, NY, May 25, 2006.

16. Daughter of Wisdom, interview, Provincial House, Islip, NY, May 29, 2007.

17. Daughter of Wisdom, phone interview, Mullins, WV, June 6, 2009.

18. Daughter of Wisdom, interview, Provincial House, Islip, NY, May 23, 2006.

19. Daughter of Wisdom, phone interview, Mullins, WV, June 6, 2009.

20. "Sophia Has a Long History," *The United Methodist Reporter*, October 27, 1989.

21. Pierre Humblet, *A Lover's Letter to Her Beloved: The Mystical Process of Transformation in Grignion De Montfort's "The Love of Eternal Wisdom,"* 2nd ed., trans. J. Vriend (Nijmegen, Netherlands: Titus Brandsma Institute, 1995), 18.

22. Theological Reflection, *Wisdom Circle Session I: The Wisdom We Have Come to Know* (Islip, NY: self-published, Daughters of Wisdom Archives, October 1992).

23. Commentary, *Wisdom Circle Session IX: Wisdom/Sophia: Teacher* (Islip, NY: self-published, Daughters of Wisdom Archives, June 1993).

24. Daughter of Wisdom, phone interview, Mullins, WV, June 6, 2009.

25. Louis Marie de Montfort, *God Alone: The Collected Writings of St. Louis Marie de Montfort* (Bay Shore, NY: Montfort Publications, 1999), 50.

26. Louis-Marie Grignion de Montfort, *Love of Eternal Wisdom: Volume: Chapters 1–8*, trans. Barbara Moore (Islip, NY: self-published, Daughters of Wisdom Archives, 1996), 28.

27. Cady, Ronan, and Taussig, *Wisdom's Feast*, 182.

28. Cady, Ronan, and Taussig, *Wisdom's Feast*, 182–183.

29. Elizabeth Johnson, "Mary of Nazareth: Friend of God and Prophet," *America* (June 17–24, 2000): 7–13.

30. Daughter of Wisdom, interview, Provincial House, Islip, NY, May 24, 2006.

31. Daughter of Wisdom, interview, Provincial House, Litchfield, CT, May 23, 2007.

32. *Daughters of Wisdom Centennial Booklet* (Islip, NY: Daughters of Wisdom Archives), 18.

33. "A Divorced Mother's New Vocation as a Nun," *New York Times: NY Region–Long Island Journal,* December 21, 2003.

34. Daughter of Wisdom, interview, Provincial House, Islip, NY, May 25, 2006.

35. Daughter of Wisdom, interview, Bayridge, NY, May 31, 2007.

36. *Religious Life in Wisdom's Way* Daughters of Wisdom International Novitiate—training material.

37. "Daughters of Wisdom Launch FireInOurHearts.Org," http://www.daughtersofwisdom.org/index.php?option=com_content&view=article&id=225:daughters-of-wisdom-launch-fireinourheartsorg&catid=38&Itemid=297, accessed May 4, 2013.

38. Fire in Our Hearts: A Ministry of the Daughters of Wisdom, http://fireinourhearts.org, accessed May 14, 2013.

39. Daughter of Wisdom, interview, Litchfield, CT, June 6, 2007.

40. Daughter of Wisdom, interview, Litchfield, CT, June 6, 2007.

41. Daughter of Wisdom, interview, Coram, NY, June 13, 2007.

42. Daughter of Wisdom, interview, Silver Springs, MD, May 29, 2006.

CHAPTER 3

1. Anne Hepburn, interview, Edinburgh, March 29, 2012.

2. Ibid.

3. Church of Scotland, *Assembly Report on Eldership,* 2003.

4. Anne Hepburn, *Memories of Malawi and Scotland* (Edinburgh: Anne Hepburn, 2011), 50.

5. Hepburn, *Memories of Malawi and Scotland,* 52.

6. Hepburn, *Memories of Malawi and Scotland,* 100–101.

7. *Glasgow Herald,* May 20, 1982.

8. Ann Allen, personal letter sent to Woman's Guild offices, May 3, 1982.

9. Hepburn, *Memories of Malawi and Scotland,* 68.

10. Alan E. Lewis, ed. *The Motherhood of God: A Report by a Study Group Appointed by the Woman's Guild and the Panel on Doctrine on the Invitation of the General Assembly of the Church of Scotland* (Edinburgh: Saint Andrew Press, 1984), 2.

11. *The Scotsman,* May 20, 1982.

12. V. A. Dickson, *The Scotsman,* May 31, 1982.

13. Margaret Macfarlane, *The Scotsman,* May 27, 1982.

14. Rev. James McL. Ritchie, *The Scotsman,* May 20, 1982.

15. Rev. S. Kennedy, *Life and Work,* October 1982.

16. Mrs. A. M. Mackay, *The Scotsman*, May 27, 1982.
17. Mrs. Alison Hunter, *Life and Work*, August 1982.
18. M. J. Browning, *Life and Work*, October 1982.
19. Robert A. Davis, *The Scotsman*, May 24, 1982.
20. Mrs. Elizabeth McEwan, *Life and Work*, October 1982.
21. G. N. Warnock, Elder, *The Scotsman*, May 27, 1982.
22. Rev. Angus Kerr, *Life and Work*, September 1982.
23. Mrs. Helen G. Johnstone, *The Scotsman*, May 24, 1982.
24. W. M. Beveridge, *The Scotsman*, May 26, 1982.
25. Frank Connell, *The Scotsman*, May 29, 1982.
26. Rev R. J. Stewart, *The Scotsman*, May 26, 1982.
27. Rev. Graeme Brown, *Life and Work*, October 1982.
28. G. N. Warnock, *Life and Work*, October 1982.
29. Hepburn, interview, May 21, 2012
30. Lewis, *The Motherhood of God*, 45–47.
31. Lewis, *The Motherhood of God*, v.
32. Hepburn, interview, April 4, 2012.
33. BBC, May 23, 1984.
34. Hepburn, interview, May 1, 2012.
35. Hepburn, interview, April 4, 2012.
36. John L. Bell, "Scottish Hymnody: An Ecumenical and Personal Perspective," in *Worship and Liturgy in Context: Studies and Case Studies in Theology and Practice*, ed. Duncan B. Forrester and Doug Gay (Norwich: SCM Press, 2009), 259.
37. Gordon Donaldson, "Reformation to Covenant," in *Studies in the History of Worship in Scotland*, 2nd ed., ed. Duncan Forrester and Douglas Murray (Edinburgh: T&T Clark, 1996), 37.
38. Gordon Donaldson, "Covenant to Revolution," in *Studies in the History of Worship in Scotland*, 2nd ed., ed. Duncan Forrester and Douglas Murray (Edinburgh: T&T Clark, 1996), 60.
39. www.pressandjournal.co.uk/Article.aspx/172446, accessed April 25, 2012.
40. *Church Hymnary*, ix.
41. *Life and Work*, June 2012.
42. Church of Scotland candidates for Ministry, group interview, April 3, 2012.
43. John L. Bell and Graham Maule, *God and Her Girls: A Celebration of the Giftedness of Forgotten Women* (Glasgow: Wild Goose Resource Group, 2010), 14–15
44. Ibid.
45. Bell and Maule, *God and Her Girls*, 16–17.
46. Finlay Macdonald, sermon, St. Giles Cathedral, Edinburgh, March 18, 2012.

47. Selwyn Hughes, *Every Day with Jesus: One Year Devotional Walking in His Ways* (Surrey: Crusade for World Revival, 2004), 324–325.

48. *The Scotsman*, March 31, 2012.

CHAPTER 4

1. Stacy Boorn, interview, herchurch, San Francisco, October 31, 2007.

2. www.herchurch.org.

3. Boorn, Faith and Feminism conference, introductory remarks, November 2, 2007

4. herchurch members, interview, May 3, 2009

5. Boorn, phone interview, April 8, 2008.

6. herchurch member, interview, herchurch, San Francisco, November 5, 2007.

7. herchurch members, interview, May 3, 2008

8. Boorn, interview, San Francisco, November 12, 2007

9. Boorn, interview, November 3, 2007

10. Boorn, interview, November 18, 2008.

11. www.herchurch.org.

12. Boorn, interview, San Francisco, November 5, 2007

13. Teresa Blythe, *50 Ways to Pray: Practices from Many Traditions and Times* (Nashville: Abingdon Press, 2006), 91.

14. herchurch Goddess rosary prayer card, 2007.

15. Stacy Boorn, interview, San Francisco, November 12, 2007.

16. Stacy Boorn, interview, November 12, 2007.

17. Stacy Boorn, Good Friday sermon, herchurch, March 23, 2008.

18. Sunday service, herchurch, San Francisco, May 3, 2008.

19. Sunday Service, herchurch, San Francisco, November 4, 2007.

20. Stacy Boorn, herchurch, interview, May 3, 2008.

21. herchurch member, interview, December 3, 2008.

22. herchurch member, interview, November 27, 2007.

23. Stacy Boorn, interview, November 11, 2007.

24. Faith and Feminism conference attendee, November 3, 2007.

25. Faith and Feminism conference attendee, November 3, 2007

26. Faith and Feminism, pre-conference participant, November 3, 2007.

27. Boorn, interview, November 5, 2007.

28. Faith and Feminism conference, herchurch, San Francisco, November 2, 2007.

29. Faith and Feminism conference responder, November 3, 2007.

30. Faith and Feminism conference responder, November 3, 2007.

31. Faith and Feminism conference responder, November 3, 2007.

32. herchurch member, interview, November 3, 2007.

33. Boorn, Faith and Feminism conference, November 4, 2007.

34. Nicole Teichman, *A Faith Journey at Ebenezer/Herchurch Lutheran*, http:// www.youtube.com, accessed November 10, 2009.

35. Ibid.

36. Ibid.

37. Ibid.

38. herchurch member, interview, November 14, 2008.

39. herchurch member, Faith and Feminism conference, November 7, 2008.

40. herchurch member, interview, November 6, 2007.

41. Faith and Feminism conference participant, November 8, 2008.

42. Carol Christ, Faith and Feminism conference, November 6, 2008.

43. Boorn, interview, May 3, 2009.

44. Ibid.

45. Ibid.

46. Boorn, interview, April 28, 2009

47. Boorn, interview, May 3, 2009.

CONCLUSION

1. Kristin R. Kelly, "What Shall We Call Her?," http://womanistinstitute.org/what-shall-we-call-her/, accessed 7-30-2013.

2. See David Chidester and Edward T. Linenthal, eds., *American Sacred Space* (Bloomington: Indiana University Press, 1995). See also Greg Johnson, *Sacred Claims: Repatriation and Living Tradition* (Charlottesville: University of Virginia Press, 2007).

3. Paul Young, "Why I Wrote *The Shack*," *Guideposts* (August 2009): 77–78.

4. See Ronald L. Grimes, *Rite out of Place: Ritual, Media, and the Arts* (New York: Oxford University Press, 2006). See also Steven Weitzman, "Reopening the Gates of J. Z. Smith's Temple: *To Take Place* in the Light of New Historicism," *Journal of the American Academy of Religion* 76, no. 3 (September 2008): 766–773.

5. Gloria Steinem, "The Progression of Feminism: Where Are We Going?," CSPAN American Perspectives (Nassau Community College, Garden City, NY: September 15, 2007).

6. Gloria Steinem, "Feminism for the 21st Century," *Feldt/Barbanell Women of the World Lecture* (Arizona State University, Tempe, AZ: October 18, 2007).

7. See Lesley A. Northup, *Ritualizing Women: Patterns of Spirituality* (Cleveland: Pilgrim Press, 1997).

8. Pat Julian, interview, Franciscan Renewal Center, Phoenix, AZ, January 14, 2010.

9. UN Women: the United Nations Entity for Gender Equality and the Empowerment of Women, www.unwomen.org, accessed August 24, 2013.

Bibliography

Adler, Rachel. *Engendering Judaism: An Inclusive Theology and Ethics.* Philadelphia: Jewish Publication Society, 1998.

Ahmed, Durre S., ed. *Gendering the Spirit: Women, Religion and the Post-Colonial Response.* New York: Zed Books, 2002.

Alberti, Johanna. *Gender and the Historian.* Harlow, UK: Longman, 2002.

Alcoff, Linda Martín, and John D. Caputo. *Feminism, Sexuality, and the Return of Religion.* Bloomington: Indiana University Press, 2011.

Alexander, Estrelda. *The Women of Azusa Street.* Cleveland: Pilgrim Press, 2005.

Anderson, Christine M. "Catholic Nuns and the Invention of Social Work: The Sisters of the Santa Maria Institute of Cincinnati, Ohio, 1897 through the 1920's." *Journal of Women's History* 12 (2000): 60–88.

Apffel-Marglin, Frederique. *Subversive Spiritualities: How Rituals Enact the World.* New York: Oxford University Press, 2012.

Armour, Ellen. *Bodily Citations: Religion and Judith Butler.* New York: Columbia University Press, 2006.

Armstrong, Karen. *The Spiral Staircase: My Climb Out of Darkness.* New York: Alfred A. Knopf, 2004.

Asad, Talal. *Genealogies of Religion: Discipline and Reasons of Power in Christianity and Islam.* Baltimore: Johns Hopkins University Press, 1993.

Askola, Irja, and Nicole Fischer-Duchable. *Living Letters: A Report of Visits to the Churches during the Ecumenical Decade—Churches in Solidarity with Women.* Geneva: World Council of Churches Publications, 1997.

Baird, Joseph L., and Ehrman, Radd K. *The Letters of Hildegard of Bingen.* New York: Oxford University Press, 2004.

Baker-Fletcher, Karen. *Dancing with God: The Trinity from a Womanist Perspective.* St. Louis, MO: Chalice Press, 2006.

Bamford, Christopher. *Isis Mary Sophia: Her Mission and Ours: Selected Lectures and Writings by Rudolf Steiner.* Herndon, VA: Steiner Books, 2003.

Banaszak, Lee Ann, ed. *The U.S. Women's Movement in Global Perspective.* Lanham, MD: Rowman & Littlefield, 2006.

Bayes, Jane H., and Nayereh Tohidi, eds. *Globalization, Gender, and Religion: The Politics of Implementing Women's Rights in Catholic and Muslim Contexts.* New York: Palgrave, 2001.

Beattie, Tina. *Eve's Pilgrimage: A Woman's Quest for the City of God.* London: Burns & Oates, 2002.

———. *New Catholic Feminism: Theology and Theory.* London: Routledge, 2006.

Bednarowski, Mary Farrell. *The Religious Imagination of American Women.* Bloomington: Indiana University Press, 1999.

Bell, Catherine M. *Ritual: Perspectives and Dimensions.* New York: Oxford University Press, 1997.

———. *Ritual Theory, Ritual Practice.* New York: Oxford University Press, 1992.

Bell, John L. "Scottish Hymnody: An Ecumenical and Personal Perspective." Edited by Duncan B. Forrester and Doug Gay. *Worship and Liturgy in Context: Studies and Case Studies in Theology and Practice.* Norwich: SCM Press, 2009.

Bell, John L., and Graham Maule. *God and Her Girls: A Celebration of the Giftedness of Forgotten Women.* Glasgow: Wild Goose Resource Group, 2010.

Bendroth, Margaret Lamberts. *Fundamentalism and Gender, 1875 to the Present.* New Haven: Yale University Press, 1993.

Bendroth, Margaret Lamberts, and Virginian Lieson Brereton, eds. *Women and Twentieth-Century Protestantism.* Chicago: University of Illinois Press, 2002.

Bergant, Dianne. *Israel's Wisdom Literature: A Liberation-Critical Reading.* Minneapolis, MN: Fortress Press, 1997.

———. *What Are They Saying about Wisdom Literature?* New York: Paulist Press, 1984.

Berger, Helen A., Evan A. Leach, and Leigh S. Shaffer. *Voices from the Pagan Census: A National Survey of Witches and Neo-Pagans in the United States.* Columbia: University of South Carolina Press, 2003.

Berger, Peter L. *The Sacred Canopy: Elements of a Sociological Theory of Religion.* Garden City, NY: Doubleday, 1967.

Berger, Teresa. *Fragments of Real Presence: Liturgical Traditions in the Hands of Women.* New York: Crossroad, 2005.

———. *Dissident Daughters: Feminist Liturgies in Global Context.* Edited by Teresa Berger. Louisville, KY: Westminster John Knox Press, 2001.

———. *Women's Ways of Worship: Gender Analysis and Liturgical History.* Collegeville, MN: Liturgical Press, 1999.

Berneking, Nancy J., and Pamela Carter Joern, eds. *Re-Membering and Re-Imagining.* Cleveland: Pilgrim Press, 1995.

The Bible: Authorized King James Version with Apocrypha. New York: Oxford University Press, 1998.

Bielo, James S. "The 'Emerging Church' in America: Notes on the Interaction of Christianities." *Religion* 39, no. 3 (September 2009): 219–232.

Blythe, Teresa. *50 Ways to Pray: Practices from Many Traditions and Times.* Nashville, TN: Abingdon Press, 2006.

Bradley, Ian. *Believing in Britain: The Spiritual Identity of "Britishness."* London: I.B. Tauris, 2007.

Braude, Ann. *Sisters and Saints: Women and American Religion.* New York: Oxford University Press, 2007.

———. *Transforming the Faiths of our Fathers: Women Who Changed American Religion.* New York: Palgrave Macmillan, 2004.

Brekus, Catherine A., ed. *The Religious History of American Women: Reimagining the Past.* Chapel Hill: University of North Carolina Press, 2007.

Brenner, Athalya. *A Feminist Companion to Wisdom Literature.* Sheffield, UK: Sheffield Academic Press, 1995.

Brenner, Athalya, and Carole Fontaine. *A Feminist Companion to Reading the Bible: Approaches, Methods and Strategies.* Sheffield, UK: Sheffield Academic Press, 1997.

Brock, Rita Nakashima, Jung Ha Kim, Kwok Pui-Lan, and Seung, Ai Yank, eds. *Off the Menu: Asian and Asian North American Women's Religion and Theology.* Louisville, KY: Westminster John Knox Press, 2007.

Brown, Dan. *The Da Vinci Code: A Novel.* New York: Doubleday, 2003.

Brown, Delwin, Sheila Greeve Davaney, and Kathryn Tanner, eds. *Converging on Culture: Theologians in Dialogue with Cultural Analysis and Criticism.* New York: Oxford University Press, 2001.

Brown, Karen McCarthy. *Mama Lola: A Vodou Priestess in Brooklyn.* Berkeley: University of California Press, 1991.

Brown, Raymond. *The Gospel According to John,* vol. 1, Anchor Bible 29. Garden City, NY: Doubleday, 1966.

Butler, Judith. *Gender Trouble: Feminism and The Subversion of Identity.* New York: Routledge, 1990.

Burrus, Virginia. "The Heretical Woman as Symbol in Alexander, Athanasius, and Jerome." *Harvard Theological Review* vol. 84 issue 3 (1991): 229–248.

Bynum, Caroline Walker. *Holy Feast and Holy Fast: The Religious Significance of Food to Medieval Women.* Berkeley: University of California Press, 1987.

Byrne, Julie. *O God of Players: The Story of the Immaculata Mighty Macs.* New York: Columbia University Press, 2003.

Cady, Linell. "Loosening the Category That Binds: Modern 'Religion' and the Promise of Cultural Studies." *Converging on Culture: Theologians in Dialogue with Cultural Analysis and Criticism.* Edited by Sheila Greeve Davaney and Kathryn Tanner. New York: Oxford University Press, 2001.

Cady, Susan, Marian Ronan, and Hal Taussig. *Sophia: The Future of Feminist Spirituality.* San Francisco: Harper & Row, 1986.

Cady, Susan, Marian Ronan, and Hal Taussig. *Wisdom's Feast: Sophia in Study and Celebration.* Lanham, MD: Sheed & Ward, 1997.

Campion, Nardi Reeder. *Mother Ann Lee: Morning Star of the Shakers.* Hanover, NH: University Press of New England, 1990.

Caron, Charlotte. *To Make and Make Again: Feminist Ritual Theology.* New York: Crossroad, 1993.

Carter, Jimmy. "Losing My Religion for Equality." *The Age* (July 15, 2009).

Casanova, José. *Public Religions in the Modern World.* Chicago: University of Chicago Press, 1994.

Castelli, Elziabeth A., ed. *Women, Gender, Religion: A Reader.* New York: Palgrave, 2001.

Certeau, Michel de. *The Practice of Everyday Life.* Translated by Steven F. Rendall. Berkeley: University of California Press, 1984.

Chappell, Louise, and Lisa Hill, eds. *The Politics of Women's Interests: New Comparative Perspectives.* New York: Routledge, 2006.

Charles, Nickie, and Helen Hintjens, eds. *Gender, Ethnicity and Political Ideologies.* New York: Routledge, 1998.

Chidester, David, and Edward T. Linenthal, eds. *American Sacred Space.* Bloomington: Indiana University Press, 1995.

Chopp, Rebecca S. *Saving Work: Feminist Practices of Theological Education.* Louisville, KY: Westminster John Knox Press, 1995.

Chopp, Rebecca S., and Sheila Greeve Davaney. *Horizons in Feminist Theology: Identity, Tradition, and Norms.* Minneapolis: Fortress Press, 1997.

Christ, Carol P. *Diving Deep and Surfacing: Women Writers on Spiritual Quest.* Boston: Beacon Press, 1980.

———. *Rebirth of the Goddess: Finding Meaning in Feminist Spirituality.* Reading, MA: Addison-Wesley, 1997.

———. *She Who Changes: Re-imagining the Divine in the World.* New York: Palgrave Macmillan, 2003.

Christ, Carol P., and Judith Plaskow, eds. *Womanspirit Rising: A Feminist Reader in Religion.* New York: Harper & Row, 1979.

Church Hymnary Trust. *Church Hymnary: Melody and Words 4: Melody Version.* Norwich: Canterbury Press, 2005.

Chwe, Michael Suk-Young. *Rational Ritual: Culture, Coordination, and Common Knowledge.* Princeton, NJ: Princeton University Press, 2013.

Clifford, Richard J. *The Wisdom Literature.* Nashville, TN: Abingdon Press, 1998.

Cochran, Pamela. *Evangelical Feminism: A History.* New York: New York University Press, 2005.

Collins, John J. *Jewish Wisdom in the Hellenistic Age.* Louisville, KY: Westminster John Knox Press, 1997.

Collins, Randall. *Interaction Ritual Chains.* Princeton, NJ: Princeton University Press, 2005.

Cone, James H. *Black Theology and Black Power.* New York: Seabury Press, 1969.

Connelly, Joan Breton. *Portrait of a Priestess: Women and Ritual in Ancient Greece.* Princeton, NJ: Princeton University Press, 2007.

Corrington, Gail. *Her Image of Salvation: Female Saviors and Formative Christianity*. Louisville, KY: Westminster John Knox Press, 1992.

Crandall, Barbara. *Gender and Religion: The Dark Side of Scripture*. 2nd ed. New York: Continuum, 2012.

Creegan, Nicola Hoggard. *Living on the Boundaries: Evangelical Women, Feminism and the Theological Academy*. Downers Grove, IL: InterVarsity Press, 2005.

Crenshaw, James L. *Old Testament Wisdom: An Introduction*. Louisville, NY: Westminster John Knox Press, 1981.

Cud, Ann E., and Robin O. Andreasen, eds. *Feminist Theory: A Philosophical Anthology*. Malden, MA: Blackwell Publishing, 2005.

Cyre, Susan. "Special Report: Mainline Denial—How Our churches Are Responding to *Re-Imagining*." *Good News* (March/April 1994): 12–14.

Dahlberg, Lana. *Birthing God: Women's Experiences of the Divine*. Woodstock, VT: SkyLight Paths Publications, 2013.

Daly, Mary. *Beyond God the Father: Toward a Philosophy of Women's Liberation*, with an Original Reintroduction by the Author. Boston: Beacon Press, 1985.

———. *The Church and the Second Sex*, with the Feminist Postchristian Introduction and New Archaic Afterwords by the Author. Boston: Beacon Press, 1985.

Davidson, Robert, M. A. *Wisdom and Worship*. Philadelphia: Trinity Press International, 1990.

DeCrane, Susanne M. *Aquinas, Feminism, and the Common Good*. Washington, DC: Georgetown University Press, 2004.

Delgadillo, Theresa. *Spiritual Mestizaje: Religion, Gender, Race, and Nation in Contemporary Chicana Narrative*. Durham, NC: Duke University Press, 2011.

Dell, Katharine J., and Margaret Barker, eds. *Wisdom: The Collected Articles of Norman Whybray*. Burlington, VT: Ashgate, 2005.

de Montfort, Louis Marie. *God Alone: The Collected Writings of St. Louis Marie de Montfort*. Translated by the Order of Montfort Missionaries. Bay Shore, NY: Montfort Publications, 1999.

de Montfort, Louis-Marie Grignion. *Love of Eternal Wisdom*. Translated by Barbara Moore. Islip, NY: Daughters of Wisdom Archives, 1996.

Devlin-Glass, Frances, and Lyn McCredden, eds. *Feminist Poetics of the Sacred: Creative Suspicions*. New York: Oxford University Press, 2001.

Dietrich, Julia. "The Visionary Rhetoric of Hildegard of Bingen." In *Listening to Their Voices: The Rhetorical Activities of Historic Women*. Edited by Molly Meijer Wertheimer. Columbia: University of South Carolina Press, 1997.

DiNovo, Cheri. *Qu(e)erying Evangelism: Growing a Community from the Outside In*. Cleveland: Pilgrim Press, 2005.

Dixon, Joy. *Divine Feminine: Theosophy and Feminism in England*. Baltimore: Johns Hopkins University Press, 2001.

Dolan, Jay P. *In Search of an American Catholicism: A History of Religion and Culture in Tension*. New York: Oxford University Press, 2002.

Douglass, Jane Dempsey, and James F. Kay, eds. *Women, Gender, and Christian Community.* Louisville, KY: Westminster John Knox Press, 1997.

Dresser, Marianne, ed. *Buddhist Women on the Edge: Contemporary Perspectives from the Western Frontier.* Berkeley, CA: North Atlantic Books, 1996.

Durkheim, Émile. *The Elementary Forms of Religious Life.* Translated and with an introduction by Karen E. Fields. New York: Free Press, 1995.

Early, Joseph E. *A Texas Baptist Power Struggle: The Hayden Controversy.* Denton: University of North Texas Press, 2005.

Eaton, J. H. *The Contemplative Face of Old Testament Wisdom: In the Context of World Religions.* Philadelphia, PA: Trinity Press International, 1989.

Ebaugh, Helen Rose. "The Growth and Decline of Catholic Religious Orders of Women Worldwide: The Impact of Women's Opportunity Structures." *Journal for the Scientific Study of Religion* 32 (1993): 68–75.

Eisenberg, Ronald L. *The JPS Guide to Jewish Traditions.* Philadelphia: The Jewish Publication Society, 2004.

Eller, Cynthia. *Living in the Lap of the Goddess: The Feminist Spirituality Movement in America.* New York: Crossroad, 1993.

———. *The Myth of Matriarchal Prehistory: Why an Invented Past Won't Give Women a Future.* Boston: Beacon Press, 2000.

Elliott, Dyan. *Proving Woman: Female Spirituality and Inquisitional Culture in the Later Middle Ages.* Princeton, NJ: Princeton University Press, 2004.

Epple, Angelika, and Angelika Schaser, eds. *Gendering Historiography: Beyond National Canons.* New York: Campus Verlag, 2009.

Evans, Frederick William. *Shakers: Compendium of the Origin, History, Principles, Rules and Regulations, Government, and Doctrines of the United Society of Believers in Christ's Second Appearing.* New York: AMS Press, 1975.

Farrell, Michael J. "Jesus 2000 Is the Whole Point of It." *National Catholic Reporter* 36, no. 9 (December 1999): 24.

Fedele, Anna. *Gender and Power in Contemporary Spirituality: Ethnographic Studies.* New York: Routledge, 2013.

———. *Looking for Mary Magdalene: Alternative Pilgrimage and Ritual Creativity at Catholic Shrines in France.* New York: Oxford University Press, 2012.

Fialka, John J. *Sisters: Catholic Nuns and the Making of America.* New York: St. Martin's Press, 2003.

Finke, Roger, and Rodney Stark. *The Churching of America, 1776–2005: Winners and Losers in Our Religious Economy.* New Brunswick, NJ: Rutgers University Press, 2005.

Finkelhor, David. "Current Information on the Scope and Nature of Child Sexual Abuse." *Sexual Abuse of Children* 4, no. 2 (Summer/Fall 1994): 31.

Fletcher, Jeannine Hill. *Motherhood as Metaphor: Engendering Interreligious Dialogue.* Bronx, NY: Fordham University Press. 2013.

Flinders, Carol. *At the Root of This Longing: Reconciling a Spiritual Hunger and a Feminist Thirst.* San Francisco: HarperSanFrancisco, 1998.

Floyd-Thomas, Stacey M., ed. *Deeper Shades of Purple: Womanism in Religion and Society.* New York: New York University Press, 2006.

Foley, Edward, and Robert Schreiter, eds. *The Wisdom of Creation.* Collegeville, MN: Liturgical Press, 2004.

Fonrobert, Charlotte Elisheva, and Martin S. Jaffee, eds. *The Cambridge Companion to the Talmud and Rabbinic Literature.* Cambridge: Cambridge University Press, 2007.

Ford, David. *Christian Wisdom: Desiring God and Learning in Love.* New York: Cambridge University Press, 2007.

Forrester, Duncan B., and Doug Gay, eds. *Worship and Liturgy in Context: Studies and Case Studies in Theology and Practice.* London: SCM Press, 2009.

Forrester, Duncan B., and Douglas Murray, eds. *Studies in the History of Worship in Scotland.* Edinburgh: T & T Clark, 1996.

Fox, Matthew. *Breakthrough: Meister Eckhart's Creation Spirituality in New Translation.* New York: Image Books, 1980.

Fox, Thomas C. "Controversial Questions Stricken from Religious Study." *National Catholic Reporter,* November 10, 2009.

Francis, Richard. *Ann, the Word: The Story of Ann Lee, Female Messiah, Mother of the Shakers, the Woman Clothed with the Sun.* New York: Arcade Publishing, 2001.

Frazer, James George. *The Golden Bough: A Study in Magic and Religion.* New York: Macmillan Company, 1935.

Freedberg, David. *The Power of Images: Studies in the History of Theory of Response.* Chicago: University of Chicago Press, 1989.

Freedman, Estelle B. *No Turning Back: the History of Feminism and the Future of Women.* New York: Ballantine Books, 2002.

Fulkerson, Mary McClintock. *Changing the Subject: Women's Discourses and Feminist Theology.* Minneapolis: Fortress Press, 1994.

Fuss, Diana. *Essentially Speaking: Feminism, Nature and Difference.* New York: Routledge, 1989.

Garza, Jennifer. "A Mother to Some, an Outcast to Vatican." *The Sacramento Bee* (February 1, 2010): B2.

Geertz, Clifford. *The Interpretation of Cultures: Selected Essays.* New York: Basic Books, 1973.

George, Mark K. "Jonathan Z. Smith's To Take Place: Toward Theory in Ritual After 20 Years." *Journal of the American Academy of Religion* 76, no. 3 (September 2008): 781–782.

Gibbs, Eddie. *ChurchMorph: How Megatrends Are Reshaping Christian Communities.* Ada, MI: Baker Academic, 2009.

Gilgoff, Dan. *The Jesus Machine: How James Dobson, Focus on the Family, and Evangelical America are Winning the Culture War.* New York: St. Martin's Press, 2007.

Goff, Philip, and Paul Harvey, eds. *Themes in Religion and American Culture.* Chapel Hill: University of North Carolina Press, 2004.

Gonzalez, Michelle A. *Created in God's Image: An Introduction to Feminist Theological Anthropology.* New York: Orbis, 2007.

Good, Deirdre, ed. *Mariam, the Magdalen, and the Mother.* Bloomington: Indiana University Press, 2005.

Gorey, Kevin M., and Donald R. Leslie. "The Prevalence of Child Sexual Abuse: Integrative Review Adjustment for Potential Response and Measurement Biases." *Child Abuse and Neglect* 21, no. 4 (April 1997): 391.

Gottschalk, Stephen. *The Emergence of Christian Science in American Religious Life.* Berkeley: University of California Press, 1973.

Gould, Graham. *The Desert Fathers on Monastic Community.* New York: Oxford University Press, 1993.

Graves, Robert. *The White Goddess: A Historical Grammar of Poetical Myth.* New York: Octagon Books, 1976.

Greene-McCreight, Kathryn. *Feminist Reconstructions of Christian Doctrine: Narrative Analysis and Appraisal.* New York: Oxford University Press, 2000.

Griffith, Elisabeth. *In Her Own Right: The Life of Elizabeth Cady Stanton.* New York: Oxford University Press, 1984.

Griffith, R. Marie. *God's Daughters: Evangelical Women and the Power of Submission.* Berkeley: University of California Press, 1997.

Griffith, R. Marie, and Barbara Dianne Savage. *Women and Religion in the African Diaspora: Knowledge, Power, and Performance.* Baltimore: Johns Hopkins University Press, 2006.

Griffin, Wendy, ed. *Daughters of the Goddess: Studies of Healing, Identity, and Empowerment.* Walnut Creek, CA: Alta Mira Press, 2000.

Grigg, Richard. *When God Becomes Goddess: The Transformation of American Religion.* New York: Continuum, 1995.

Grimes, Ronald L. *Deeply Into the Bones: Re-Inventing Rites of Passage.* Berkeley: University of California Press, 2000.

———. *Rite Out of Place: Ritual, Media, and the Arts.* New York: Oxford University Press, 2006.

———. *Ritual Criticism: Case Studies in Its Practice, Essays on Its Theory.* Columbia: University of South Carolina Press, 1990.

Grimes, Ronald L., Ute Husken, Udo Simon, and Eric Venbrux. *Ritual, Media, and Conflict.* New York: Oxford University Press, 2011.

Grimes, William. "The Man Who Rendered Jesus for the Age of Duplication." *New York Times.* October 12, 1994.

Gross, Rita M. *Feminism and Religion: An Introduction.* Boston: Beacon Press, 1996.

———. *A Garland of Feminist Reflections: Forty Years of Religious Exploration.* Berkeley: University of California Press, 2009.

Gross, Rita M., and Rosemary Radford Ruether. *Religious Feminism and the Future of the Planet: A Christian-Buddhist Conversation.* New York: Continuum, 2001.

Halbertal, Tova Hartman. *Appropriately Subversive: Modern Mothers in Traditional Religions.* Cambridge, MA: Harvard University Press, 2002.

Hall, David D, ed. *Lived Religion in America: Toward a History of Practice.* Princeton, NJ: Princeton University Press, 1997.

Hall, Donald E., ed. *Muscular Christianity: Embodying the Victorian Age.* New York: Cambridge University Press, 1994.

Hammond, Phillip E. *Religion and Personal Autonomy: The Third Disestablishment in America.* Columbia: University of South Carolina Press, 1992.

Hampson, Daphne. *Theology and Feminism.* Cambridge, UK: Blackwell Publishers, 1990.

Haraway, Donna Jeanne. *Simians, Cyborgs, and Women: The Reinvention of Nature.* London: Free Association Books, 1991.

Hardesty, Nancy. *Women Called to Witness: Evangelical Feminism in the Nineteenth Century.* Knoxville: University of Tennessee Press, 1999.

———. *Your Daughters Shall Prophesy: Revivalism and Feminism in the Age of Finney.* Brooklyn, NY: Carlson Publishing, 1991.

Harding, Sandra, ed. *The Feminist Standpoint Theory Reader: Intellectual and Political Controversies.* New York: Routledge, 2004.

Harper, Keith, ed. *Send the Light: Lottie Moon's Letters and Other Writings.* Macon, GA: Mercer University Press, 2002.

Hartman Halbertal, Tova. *Appropriately Subversive: Modern Mothers in Traditional Religions.* Cambridge, MA: Harvard University Press, 2002.

Hartman, Susan M. "Expanding Feminism's Field and Focus: Activism in the National Council of Churches in the 1960s and 1970s." In *Women and Twentieth-Century Protestantism.* Edited by Margaret Lamberts Bendroth and Virginia Lieson Brereton. Urbana: University of Illinois Press, 2002.

Hartsock, Nancy C. M. *The Feminist Standpoint Revisited and Other Essays.* Boulder, CO: Westview Press, 1998.

Harvey, Andrew, and Anne Baring. *The Divine Feminine: Exploring the Feminine Face of God throughout the world.* Berkeley, CA: Conari Press, 1996.

Haskins, Susan. *Mary Magdalen: Myth and Metaphor.* London: HarperCollins, 1993.

Hassey, Janette. *No Time for Silence: Evangelical Women in Public Ministry Around the Turn of the Century.* Grand Rapids, MI: Academie Books, 1986.

Hawley, John Stratton. *Fundamentalism and Gender.* New York: Oxford University Press, 1994.

Hecht, Richard D. "Rites Require Rights: J. Z. Smith's To Take Place: Toward a Theory in Ritual After Twenty Years Space, Place, and Lived Experience in Antiquity Consultation." *Journal of the American Academy of Religion* 76, no. 3 (September 2008): 790–805.

Heidinger II, James V. "Editorial: Fairest Sophia." *Good News: The Bi-Monthly Magazine for United Methodists* (July/August 1990).

Henderson, Sarah, and Alana S. Jeydel. *Participation and Protest: Women and Politics in a Global World.* New York: Oxford University Press, 2007.

Hepburn, Anne. *Memories of Malawi and Scotland.* Edinburgh: Anne Hepburn, 2011.

Herberg, Will. *Protestant, Catholic, Jew: An Essay in American Religious Sociology.* Garden City, NY: Doubleday, 1955.

Heron, Barbara. *Desire for Development: Whiteness, Gender, and the Helping Imperative.* Waterloo, ON: Wilfrid Laurier University Press, 2007.

Hesse-Biber, Sharlene Nagy, ed. *Handbook of Feminist Research: Theory and Praxis.* Thousand Oaks, CA: SAGE Publications, 2007.

Higginbotham, Evelyn Brooks. *Righteous Discontent: The Women's Movement in the Black Baptist Church, 1880–1920.* Cambridge, MA: Harvard University Press, 1993.

Hogan, Linda. *From Women's Experience to Feminist Theology.* Sheffield, UK: Sheffield Academic Press, 1995.

Hoge, Dean R., Benton Johnson, and Donald A. Luidens. *Vanishing Boundaries: The Religion of Mainline Protestant Baby Boomers.* Louisville, KY: Westminster John Knox Press, 1994.

Holmes, Emily A., and Wendy Farley. *Women, Writing, Theology: Transforming a Tradition of Exclusion.* Waco, TX: Baylor University Press, 2011.

hooks, bell. *Ain't I a Woman: Black Women and Feminism.* Boston: South End Press, 1981.

———. *Feminism Is for Everybody: Passionate Politics.* Cambridge, MA: South End Press, 2000.

Hoover, Stewart M., and Lynn Schofield Clark. "Event and Publicity as Social Drama: A Case Study of the Re-Imagining Conference 1995." *Review of Religious Studies* 39, no. 2 (December 1997): 153–172.

Hughes, Selwyn. *Every Day with Jesus: One Year Devotional Walking in His Ways.* Surrey: Crusade for World Revival, 2004.

Humblet, Pierre. *A Lover's Letter to Her Beloved: The Mystical Process of Transformation in Grignion De Montfort's "The Love of Eternal Wisdom."* 2nd ed. Translated by J. Vriend. Nijmegen, Netherlands: Titus Brandsma Institute, 1995.

Husken, Ute, and Frank Neubert. *Negotiating Rites.* New York: Oxford University Press, 2011.

Hyatt, Irwin T. *Our Ordered Lives Confess: Three Nineteenth-Century American Missionaries in East Shantung.* Cambridge, MA: Harvard University Press, 1976.

Ingersoll, Julie. *Evangelical Christian Women: War Stories in the Gender Battles.* New York: New York University Press, 2003.

Isasi-Diaz, Ada Maria. *La Lucha Continues: Mujerista Theology.* Maryknoll, NY: Orbis Books, 2004.

Jay, Nancy B. *Throughout Your Generations Forever: Sacrifice, Religion, and Paternity.* Chicago: University of Chicago Press, 1992.

John Paul II. *Ad Teundam Fidem*: Apostolic Letter Motu Proprio by which certain norms are inserted into the *Code of Canon Law* and into the *Code of Canons of the Eastern Churches.* May 18, 1998.

———. *Ordinatio Sacerdotalis: Apolostolic Letter to the Bishops of the Catholic Church on Reserving Priestly Ordination to Men Alone.* Vatican, May 22, 1994.

Johnson, Elizabeth A., ed. *The Church Women Want: Catholic Women in Dialogue.* New York: Crossroad, 2002.

———. *Consider Jesus: Waves of Renewal in Christology.* New York: Crossroad, 1990.

———. *Friends of God and Prophets: A Feminist Theological Reading of the Communion of Saints.* New York: Continuum, 1998.

———. "Mary of Nazareth: Friend of God and Prophet." *America* (June 17–24, 2000): 7–13.

———. *She Who Is: The Mystery of God in a Feminist Theological Discourse.* New York: Crossroad, 1992.

Johnson, Greg. *Sacred Claims: Repatriation and Living Tradition.* Charlottesville: University of Virginia Press, 2007.

Jones, Serene. *Feminist Theory and Christian Theology: Cartographies of Grace.* Minneapolis: Fortress Press, 2000.

Jung, C. G. *Aspects of the Feminine.* Translated by R. F. C. Hull. Princeton, NJ: Princeton University Press, 1982.

Kamitsuka, Margaret D. *Feminist Theology and the Challenge of Difference.* New York: Oxford University Press, 2007.

Katsuno-Ishii, Lynda, and Edna J. Orteza, eds. *Of Rolling Waters and Roaring Wind: A Celebration of the Woman Song.* Geneva: World Council of Churches Publications, 2000.

Katz, Melissa R., and Robert Orsi A., eds. *Divine Mirrors: The Virgin Mary in the Visual Arts.* New York: Oxford University Press, 2001.

Katzenstein, Mary Fainsod. *Faithful and Fearless: Moving Feminist Protest Inside the Church and Military.* Princeton, NJ: Princeton University Press, 1998.

Keller, David G. R. *Oasis of Wisdom: The Worlds of the Desert Fathers and Mothers.* Collegeville, MN: Liturgical Press, 2005.

Keller, Rosemary Skinner, Rosemary Radford Ruether, and Marie Cantlon, eds. *Encyclopedia of Women and Religion in North America.* Bloomington: Indiana University Press, 2006.

Kelley, Carl Franklin. *Meister Eckhart on Divine Knowledge.* New Haven, CT: Yale University Press, 1977.

Kern, Kathi. *Mrs. Stanton's Bible.* Ithaca, NY: Cornell University Press, 2001.

Kidd, Sue Monk. *The Dance of the Dissident Daughter: A Woman's Journey from Christian Tradition to the Sacred Feminine.* San Francisco: HarperSanFrancisco, 1995.

Kienzle, Beverly Mayne, and Pamela J. Walker, eds. *Women Preachers and Prophets through Two Millennia of Christianity.* Berkeley: University of California Press, 1998.

Kim, David Kyuman. *Melancholic Freedom: Agency and the Spirit of Politics.* New York: Oxford University Press, 2007.

Kim, Grace Ji-Sun. *The Grace of Sophia: A Korean North American Women's Christology*. Cleveland: Pilgrim Press, 2002.

King, Karen L. *The Gospel of Mary of Magdala: Jesus and the First Woman Apostle*. Santa Rosa, CA: Polebridge Press, 2003.

Kinsley, David R. *Hindu Goddesses: Visions of the Divine Feminine in the Hindu Religious Tradition*. Berkeley: University of California Press, 1986.

Knight, Jennie S. *Feminist Mysticism and Images of God*. Atlanta: Chalice Press, 2011.

Kosmin, Barry A., and Ariela Keysar. *American Religious Identification Survey (ARIS) 2008*. Hartford, CT: Trinity College, 2009.

Kripal, Jeffrey John. *The Serpent's Gift: Gnostic Reflections on the Study of Religion*. Chicago: University of Chicago Press, 2007.

Kripal Jeffrey J., and Glenn W. Shuck, eds. *On the Edge of the Future Esalen and the Evolution of American Culture*. Bloomington: Indiana University Press, 2005.

Kristof, Nicholas D., and Sheryl WuDunn. *Half the Sky: Turning Oppression into Opportunity for Women Worldwide*. New York: Alfred A. Knopf, 2009.

Krondorfer, Bjorn. *Male Confessions: Intimate Revelations and the Religious Imagination*. Stamford, CA: Stanford University Press, 2009.

Lawless, Elaine J. *Handmaidens of the Lord: Pentecostal Women Preachers and Traditional Religion*. Philadelphia: University of Pennsylvania Press, 1988.

Lehman, Edward C. *Gender and Work: The Case of the Clergy*. Albany: State University of New York Press, 1993.

Lerner, Gerda. *The Creation of Feminist Consciousness: From the Middle Ages to Eighteen-Seventy*. New York: Oxford University Press, 1993.

Lewis, Alan E., ed. *The Motherhood of God: A Report by a Study Group Appointed by the Woman's Guild and the Panel on Doctrine on the Invitation of the General Assembly of the Church of Scotland*. Edinburgh: Saint Andrew Press, 1984.

Lewis, James R. *The Oxford Handbook of New Religious Movements*. New York: Oxford University Press, 2004.

Lincoln, Bruce. *Discourse and the Construction of Society: Comparative Studies of Myth, Ritual, and Classification*. New York: Oxford University Press, 1989.

Lincoln, Bruce. *Emerging from the Chrysalis: Studies in Rituals Women's Initiation*. Cambridge, MA: Harvard University Press, 1981.

Mack, Burton. "Social Locations." *Journal of the American Academy of Religion* 76, no. 3 (September 2008): 782–789.

Maddux, Kristy. *The Faithful Citizen: Popular Christian Media and Gendered Civic Identities*. Waco, TX: Baylor University Press, 2010.

Madigan, Kevin, and Carolyn Osiek. *Ordained Women in the Early Church: A Documentary History*. Baltimore: Johns Hopkins University Press, 2005.

Maffly-Kipp, Laurie F. *Religion and Society in Frontier California*. New Haven, CT: Yale University Press, 1994.

Maffly-Kipp, Laurie F., Leigh E. Schmidt, and Mark Valeri, eds. *Practicing Protestants: Histories of Christian Life in America, 1630–1965*. Baltimore: Johns Hopkins University Press, 2006.

Magliocco, Sabina. *Neopagan: Sacred Art and Altars: Making Things Whole*. Jackson: University Press of Mississippi, 2001.

Mahmood, Saba. *Politics of Piety: The Islamic Revival and the Feminist Subject*. Princeton, NJ: Princeton University Press, 2005.

Manning, Christel. *God Gave Us the Right: Conservative Catholic, Evangelical Protestant, and Orthodox Jewish Women Grapple with Feminism*. New Brunswick, NJ: Rutgers University Press, 1999.

Marler, Joan. "The Myth of Universal Patriarchy: A Critical Response to Cynthia Eller's *Myth of Matriarchal Prehistory*." *The Journal of the Britain and Ireland School of Feminist Theology* 14, no. 2 (January 2006): 163–187.

Martos, Joseph, and Pierre Hégy, eds. *Equal at the Creation: Sexism, Society, and Christian Thought*. Toronto: University of Toronto Press, 1998.

McDannell, Colleen. *Material Christianity: Religion and Popular Culture in America*. New Haven, CT: Yale University Press, 1995.

McEnroy, Carmel Elizabeth. *Guests in Their Own House: The Women of Vatican II*. New York: Crossroad, 1996.

McFague, Sallie. *The Body of God: An Ecological Theology*. Minneapolis: Fortress Press, 1993.

McGrath, Elsie Hainz, Bridget Mary Meehan, and Ida Raming, eds. *Women Find a Way: The Movement and Stories of Roman Catholic Womenpriests*. Virtualbookworm.com Publishing, 2008.

McGreevy, John T. *Catholicism and American Freedom: A History*. New York: W.W. Norton, 2003.

McKnight, Scot. "Five Streams of the Emerging Church." *Christianity Today* 51, no. 2 (February 2007): 34–39.

McLoughlin, William Gerald, and Robert N. Bellah, eds. *Religion in America*. Boston: Houghton Mifflin, 1968.

Meeks, Wayne A., ed. *The HarperCollins Study Bible: New Revised Standard Version with the Apocryphal/Deuterocanonical Books*. New York: HarperCollins, 1993.

Mehegan, David. "Personal Jesus." *Boston Globe*, January 17, 2004.

Milmine, Georgine. *The Life of Mary Baker G. Eddy and the History of Christian Science*. Grand Rapids, MI: Baker Book House, 1971.

Mollenkott, Virginia R. *The Divine Feminine: The Biblical Imagery of God as Female*. New York: Crossroad, 1983.

———. *Sensuous Spirituality: Out from Fundamentalism*. New York: Crossroad, 1992.

Moore, R. Laurence. *Selling God: American Religion in the Marketplace of Culture*. New York: Oxford University Press, 1994.

Moore, R. Laurence. *Touchdown Jesus: The Mixing of Sacred and Secular in American History*. Louisville, KY: Westminster John Knox Press, 2003.

Morgan, David, ed. *Icons of American Protestantism: The Art of Warner Sallman.* New Haven, CT: Yale University Press, 1996.

———. *The Lure of Images: A History of Religion and Visual Media in America.* New York: Routledge, 2007.

Morgan, David T. *Southern Baptist Sisters: In Search of Status, 1845–2000.* Macon, GA: Mercer University Press, 2003.

Morgan, Sue. *The Feminist History Reader.* New York: Routledge, 2006.

Morrison, Susan. "From the Bishop." *United Methodist Reporter for Eastern Pennsylvania,* March 11, 1994.

Murphy, Cullen. *The Word According to Eve: Women and the Bible in Ancient Times and Our Own.* Boston: Houghton Mifflin, 1998.

Murphy, Roland E. *The Tree of Life: An Exploration of the Biblical Wisdom Literature.* New York: Doubleday, 1990.

Nabhan-Warren, Kristy. *The Virgin of El Barrio: Marian Apparitions, Catholic Evangelizing, and Mexican American Activism.* New York: New York University Press, 2005.

Nesbitt, Paula D. *Feminization of the Clergy in America: Occupational and Organizational Perspectives.* New York: Oxford University Press, 1997.

Newman, Barbara. *From Virile Woman to Woman Christ: Studies in Medieval Religion and Literature.* Philadelphia: University of Pennsylvania Press, 1995.

Newman, Barbara, *God and the Goddesses: Vision, Poetry, and Belief in the Middle Ages.* Philadelphia: University of Pennsylvania Press, 2003.

Newman, Barbara. *Sister of Wisdom: St. Hildegard's Theology of the Feminine.* Berkeley: University of California Press, 1987.

Northup, Lesley A. *Ritualizing Women: Patterns of Spirituality.* Cleveland: Pilgrim Press, 1997.

O'Connor, Kathleen M. *The Wisdom Literature.* Collegeville, MN: The Liturgical Press, 1990.

Ogden, Thomas. "Encountering the Goddess at Church." *Christianity Today,* August 16, 1993.

Olson, Laura R., Sue E. S. Crawford, and Melissa M. Deckman. *Women with a Mission: Religion, Gender, and the Politics of Women Clergy.* Tuscaloosa: University of Alabama Press, 2005.

Orsi, Robert A. *Between Heaven and Earth: The Religious Worlds People Make and the Scholars Who Study Them.* Princeton, NJ: Princeton University Press, 2005.

———. *Thank You, St. Jude: Women's Devotion to the Patron Saint of Hopeless Causes.* New Haven, CT: Yale University Press, 1996.

———. *The Madonna of 115th Street: Faith and Community in Italian Harlem.* New Haven, CT: Yale University Press, 1985.

Pagels, Elaine. *Adam, Eve, and the Serpent.* New York: Random House, 1988.

———. "What Became of God the Mother?" In *Womanspirit Rising: A Feminist Reader in Religion.* Edited by Carol P. Christ and Judith Plaskow. San Francisco: Harper & Row, 1979.

Paglia, Camille. *Sexual Personae: Art and Decadence from Nefertiti to Emily Dickinson*. New Haven, CT: Yale University Press, 1990.

Palmer, Susan B. "Women in New Religious Movements." In *The Oxford Handbook of New Religious Movements*. Edited by James R. Lewis. Oxford: Oxford University Press, 2004.

Parsons, Susan Frank, ed. *The Cambridge Companion to Feminist Theology*. Cambridge: Cambridge University Press, 2002.

Pasture, Patrick, Jan Art, and Thomas Buerman. *Gender and Christianity in Modern Europe: Beyond the Feminization Thesis*. Belgium: Leuven University Press, 2012.

Pears, Angela. *Feminist Christian Encounters: The Methods and Strategies of Feminist Informed Christian Theologies*. Burlington, VT: Ashgate, 2004.

Peay, Pythia. "Feminism's Fourth Wave: A New Activist Movement Is Gathering Women Across Faiths." *Utne Reader* 128 (March/April 2005): 59–60.

Perdue, Leo G. *Wisdom and Cult: A Critical Analysis of the Views of Cult in the Wisdom Literatures of Israel and the Ancient Near East*. Missoula, MT: Scholars Press for the Society of Biblical Literature, 1977.

Pike, Sarah M. *Earthly Bodies, Magical Selves: Contemporary Pagans and the Search for Community*. Berkeley: University of California Press, 2001.

———. *New Age and Neopagan Religions in America*. New York: Columbia University Press, 2004.

Plaskow, Judith. *Standing Again at Sinai: Judaism from a Feminist Perspective*. New York: Harper & Row, 1990.

Plaskow, Judith, and Carol P. Christ, eds. *Weaving the Visions: New Patterns in Feminist Spirituality.* San Francisco: Harper & Row, 1989.

Plate, Brent S., ed. *Religion, Art, and Visual Culture: A Crosscultural Reader*. New York: Palgrave, 2002.

Powell, Robert. *The Sophia Teachings: The Emergence of the Divine Feminine in Our Time*. Great Barrington, MA: Lindisfarne Books, 2001.

Pramuk, Christopher. *Sophia: The Hidden Christ of Thomas Merton*. Collegeville, MN: Liturgical Press, 2009.

Procter-Smith, Marjorie. *In Her Own Rite: Constructing Feminist Liturgical Tradition*. Memphis: Order of Saint Luke Publications, 2000.

———. *Praying with Our Eyes Open: Engendering Feminist Liturgical Prayer*. Nashville: Abingdon Press, 1995.

Prothero, Stephen. *American Jesus: How the Son of God Became a National Icon*. New York: Farrar, Straus and Giroux, 2003.

Proudfoot, Wayne. *Religious Experience*. Berkeley: University of California Press, 1985.

Putney, Clifford. *Muscular Christianity: Manhood and Sports in Protestant America, 1880–1920*. Cambridge, MA: Harvard University Press, 2001.

Quiñonez, Lora Ann, and Mary Daniel Turner. *The Transformation of American Catholic Sisters*. Philadelphia: Temple University Press, 1992.

Rad, Gerhard von; *Wisdom in Israel*. Nashville: Abingdon Press, 1972.

Radford Ruether, Rosemary. *Goddesses and the Divine Feminine: A Western Religious History*. Berkeley: University of California Press, 2005.

Rae, Eleanor, and Bernice Marie-Daly. *Created in Her Image: Models of the Feminine Divine*. New York: Crossroad, 1990.

Reed, Wendy, and Jennifer Horne. *All Out of Faith: Southern Women on Spirituality*. Tuscaloosa: University of Alabama Press, 2006.

Reeves, Thomas C. *The Empty Church: Does Organized Religion Matter Anymore?* New York: Simon & Schuster, 1998.

Report of the Task Force on the Study of Wisdom, the Council of Bishops; "Biblical Wisdom & Current Theological Ferment (Oct. 31–Nov.4, 1994)." *Circuit Rider* (March 1995): 2–40.

Riswold, Caryn D. *Feminism and Christianity: Questions and Answers in the Third Wave*. Cambridge: The Lutterworth Press, 2009.

Robinson, James M. "Jesus as Sophos and Sophia." In *Aspects of Wisdom in Judaism and Early Christianity*. Edited by Robert L. Wilken. London: University of Notre Dame Press, 1975.

Ronan, Marian. *Tracing the Sign of the Cross: Sexuality, Mourning, and the Future of American Catholicism*. New York: Columbia University Press, 2009.

Roof, Wade Clark. *A Generation of Seekers: The Spiritual Journeys of the Baby Boom Generation*. San Francisco: HarperSanFrancisco, 1993.

———. *Spiritual Marketplace: Baby Boomers and the Remaking of American Religion*. Princeton, NJ: Princeton University Press, 1999.

Ruether, Rosemary Radford, ed. *Feminist Theologies: Legacy and Prospect*. Minneapolis: Fortress Press, 2007.

———. *Gender, Ethnicity, and Religion: Views from the Other Side*. Minneapolis: Fortress Press, 2002.

———. *Goddesses and the Divine Feminine*. Berkeley: University of California Press, 2005.

———. *Sexism and God-talk: Toward a Feminist Theology*. Boston: Beacon Press, 1983.

———. *Visionary Women: Three Medieval Mystics*. Minneapolis: Fortress Press, 2002.

———. *Women-church: Theology and Practice of Feminist Liturgical Communities*. San Francisco: Harper & Row, 1985.

Rupp, Joyce. *Prayers to Sophia*. Philadelphia: Innisfree Press, 2000.

———. *The Star in My Heart: Experiencing Sophia, Inner Wisdom*. San Diego: Luramedia, 1990.

Russell, Letty M., and J. Shannon Clarkson, eds. *Dictionary of Feminist Theologies*. Louisville, KY: Westminster John Knox Press, 1996.

Rzepinska, Maria. "The Divine Wisdom of Michelangelo in *The Creation of Adam*." *Artibus et Historiae* 15, no. 29 (1994): 181–187.

Sahlins, Marshall David. *Culture in Practice: Selected Essays*. New York: Zone Books, 2000.

Salganik, M. J., and D. D. Heckathorn. "Sampling and Estimation in Hidden Populations Using Respondent-Driven Sampling." *Sociological Methodology* 34 (2004): 193–239.

Sawyer, Deborah F., and Diane M. Collier. *Is There a Future for Feminist Theology?* Sheffield: Sheffield Academic Press, 1999.

Say, Elizabeth A. *Evidence on Her Own Behalf: Women's Narrative as Theological Voice.* Savage, MD: Rowman & Littlefield Publishers, 1990.

Schachter-Shalomi, Zalman. *Paradigm Shift: From the Jewish Renewal Teachings of Reb Zalman Schachter-Shalomi.* Edited by Ellen Singer. Lanham, MD: Jason Aronson, 2000.

Schaef, Anne Wilson. *Women's Reality: An Emerging Female System in the White Male Society.* Minneapolis: Winston Press, 1981.

Schäfer, Peter. *Mirror of His Beauty: Feminine Images of God from the Bible to the Early Kabbalah.* Princeton, NJ: Princeton University Press, 2004.

Schmidt, Alvin J. *Veiled and Silenced: How Culture Shaped Sexist Theology.* Macon, GA: Mercer University Press, 2000.

Schmidt, Frederick W. *A Still Small Voice: Women, Ordination, and the Church.* Syracuse, NY: Syracuse University Press, 1996.

Schmidt, Leigh Eric. *Consumer Rites: The Buying and Selling of American Holidays.* Princeton, NJ: Princeton University Press, 1995.

Schmidt, Leigh Eric. *Restless Souls: The Making of American Spirituality.* San Francisco: HarperSanFrancisco, 2005.

Schneider, Carl J., and Dorothy Schneider. *In Their Own Right: The History of American Clergywomen.* New York: Crossroad, 1997.

Schneider, Laurel C. *Re-Imagining the Divine: Confronting the Backlash against Feminist Theology.* Cleveland: Pilgrim Press, 1998.

Schneider, Sandra. "God Is More Than Two Men and a Bird" *U.S. Catholic* 55, no. 5 (May 1990): 20–27.

Schoepflin, Rennie B. *Christian Science on Trial: Religious Healing in America.* Baltimore: Johns Hopkins University Press, 2003.

Schroer, Silvia, ed. *Images and Gender: Contributions to the Hermeneutics of Reading Ancient Art.* Fribourg, Switzerland: Academic Press, 2006.

———. *Wisdom Has Built Her House: Studies on the Figure of Sophia in the Bible.* Translated by Linda M. Maloney and William McDonough. Collegeville, MN: Liturgical Press, 2000.

Schumacher, Michelle M., ed. *Women in Christ: Toward a New Feminism.* Cambridge: William B. Eerdmans, 2004.

Schüssler Fiorenza, Elizabeth. *Changing Horizons: Explorations of Feminist Interpretation.* Minneapolis: Fortress Press, 2013.

———. *Discipleship of Equals: A Critical Feminist Ekklesia-logy of Liberation.* New York: Crossroad, 1993.

———. *In Memory of Her: A Feminist Theological Reconstruction of Christian Origins.* New York: Continuum, 1983.

———. *Jesus: Miriam's Child, Sophia's Prophet: Critical Issues in Feminist Christology*. New York: Continuum, 1994.

———. *Wisdom Ways: Introducing Feminist Biblical Interpretation*. Maryknoll, NY: Orbis Books, 2001.

Seligman, Adam B., Robert P. Weller, Michael J. Puett, and Bennett Simon. *Ritual and Its Consequences: An Essay on the Limits of Sincerity*. New York: Oxford University Press, 2008.

Sered, Susan Starr. *Priestess, Mother, Sacred Sister: Religions Dominated by Women*. New York: Oxford University Press, 1994.

Shapiro, Rami M. *The Divine Feminine in Biblical Wisdom Literature*. Woodstock, VT: SkyLight Paths Publications, 2005.

Sharma, Arvind. *Methodology in Religious Studies: The Interface with Women's Studies*. Albany: State University of New York Press, 2002.

Sheikh, Naveed S., ed. *Engendering the Politics of Religion: Women, Identity and Agency in Global Religio-Politics*. New York: Routledge, 2013.

Shepherd, Loraine MacKenzie. *Feminist Theologies for a Postmodern Church: Diversity, Community, and Scripture*. New York: P. Lang, 2002.

Shepherd, Loraine MacKenzie. *Feminist Theologies for a Postmodern Church: Diversity, Community, and Scripture*. New York: Peter Lang, 2002.

Sheppard, Gerald T. *Wisdom as a Hermeneutical Construct: A Study in the Sapientializing of the Old Testament*. New York: W. de Gruyter, 1980.

Short, Roy H. *The Episcopal Leadership Role in United Methodism*. Nashville: Abingdon Press, 1985.

———. *History of the Council of Bishops of the United Methodist Church, 1939–1979*. Nashville: Abingdon Press, 1980.

Silberger, Julius. *Mary Baker Eddy, an Interpretive Biography of the Founder of Christian Science*. Boston: Little, Brown, 1980.

Slee, Nicola. *Women's Faith Development: Patterns and Processes*. Burlington, VT: Ashgate, 2004.

Smith, Christian, ed. *The Secular Revolution: Power, Interests, and Conflict in the Secularization of American Public Life*. Berkeley: University of California Press, 2003.

Smith, Dorothy E. *The Conceptual Practices of Power: A Feminist Sociology of Knowledge*. Boston: Northeastern University Press, 1990.

Smith, Jonathan Z. "The Bare Facts of Ritual." *History of Religion* 20, nos. 1–2 (1980): 125.

———. *Imagining Religion: From Babylon to Jonestown*. Chicago: University of Chicago Press, 1982.

———. *Map Is Not Territory: Studies in the History of Religions*. Chicago: University of Chicago Press, 1993.

———. *To Take Place: Toward Theory in Ritual*. Chicago: University of Chicago Press, 1987.

Smith, Yolanda Y. *Women's Spirituality and Education in the Black Church*. New York: Palgrave Macmillan, 2013.

Soble, Alan. *The Philosophy of Sex and Love: An Introduction*. St. Paul: Paragon House, 2008.

Spivak, Gayatri Chakravorty. "Can the Subaltern Speak?" *Marxism and the Interpretation of Culture*. Edited by Cary Nelson and Lawrence Grossberg. Urbana: University of Illinois Press, 1988.

Spongberg, Mary. *Writing Women's History since the Renaissance*. New York: Palgrave Macmillan, 2002.

Spretnak, Charlene. *Missing Mary: The Queen of Heaven and Her Re-emergence in the Modern Church*. New York: Palgrave Macmillan, 2004.

Spretnak, Charlene, ed. *The Politics of Women's Spirituality: Essays on the Rise of Spiritual Power within the Feminist Movement*. Garden City, NY: Anchor Books, 1982.

Stanley, Susie C. *Holy Boldness: Women Preachers' Autobiographies and the Sanctified Self*. Knoxville: University of Tennessee Press, 2002.

Stanton, Elizabeth Cady. *The Woman's Bible*. New York: Arno Press, 1972.

Starbird, Margaret. *Mary Magdalene, Bride in Exile*. Rochester, VT: Bear, 2005.

Starhawk. *The Spiral Dance: A Rebirth of the Ancient Religion of the Great Goddess*, 10th anniversary ed. San Francisco: HarperCollins, 1989.

Stark, Rodney, and Roger Finke. "Catholic Religious Vocations: Decline and Revival." *Review of Religious Research* 42, no. 2 (2000): 125–145.

Steinem, Gloria. *Outrageous Acts and Everyday Rebellions*. New York: Holt, Rinehart and Winston, 1983.

———. *Revolution from Within: A Book of Self-Esteem*. Boston: Little, Brown, 1992.

Steiner, Rudolf. *Isis Mary Sophia: Her Mission and Ours: Selected Lectures and Writings by Rudolf Steiner*. Edited by Christopher Bamford. Great Barrington, MA: Steiner Books, 2003.

Stratton, Kimberly B. *Naming the Witch: Magic, Ideology, and Stereotype in the Ancient World*. New York: Columbia University Press, 2007.

Streufert, Mary J. *Transformative Lutheran Theologies: Feminist, Womanist, and Mujerista Perspectives*. Minneapolis: Fortress Press, 2010.

Suchocki, Marjorie. *God, Christ, Church: A Practical Guide to Process Theology*. New York: Crossroad, 1982.

Swidler, Leonard J. *Jesus Was a Feminist: What the Gospels Reveal About His Revolutionary Perspective*. Lanham, MD: Sheed & Ward, 2007.

Tannen, Ricki Stefanie. *The Female Trickster: The Mask That Reveals*. New York: Routledge, 2007.

Taussig, Hal. *In the Beginning Was the Meal: Social Experimentation and Early Christian Identity*. Minneapolis: Fortress Press, 2009.

———. *A New Spiritual Home: Progressive Christianity at the Grass Roots*. Salem, OR: Polebridge Press, 2006.

Taylor, Sarah McFarland. *Green Sisters: A Spiritual Ecology*. Cambridge, MA: Harvard University Press, 2007.

Teel, Karen. *Racism and the Image of God.* New York, NY: Palgrave Macmillan, 2011.

Thomas, Christine M. "Place and Memory: Response to Jonathan Z. Smith on To Take Place, on the Occasion of Its Twentieth Anniversary." *Journal of the American Academy of Religion* 76, no. 3 (September 2008): 773–781.

Thumma, Scott, and Edward R. Gray, eds. *Gay Religion.* Walnut Creek, CA: AltaMira Press, 2005.

Tomberg, Valentin. *Christ and Sophia: Anthroposophic Meditations on the Old Testament, New Testament, and Apocalypse.* Great Barrington, MA: SteinerBooks, 2006.

Tomm, Winnie. *Bodied Mindfulness: Women's Spirits, Bodies and Places.* Waterloo, Ontario: Wilfrid Laurier University Press, 1995.

Torjesen, Karen Jo. *When Women Were Priests: Women's Leadership in the Early Church and the Scandal of their Subordination in the Rise of Christianity.* San Francisco: HarperSanFrancisco, 1993.

Tracy, Steven R. *Mending the Soul: Understanding and Healing Abuse.* Grand Rapids, MI: Zondervan, 2005.

Trethowan, Illtyd. *Process Theology and the Christian Tradition: An Essay in Post Vatican II Thinking.* Still River, MA: St. Bede's, 1985.

Tuckett, Christopher Mark. *The Gospel of Mary.* New York: Oxford University Press, 2007.

Tuell, Jack M. *The Organization of the United Methodist Church.* Nashville: Abingdon Press, 1997.

Turner, Kay. *Beautiful Necessity: The Art and Meaning of Women's Altars.* New York: Thames & Hudson, 1999.

———. "Contemporary Feminist Rituals." In *The Politics of Women's Spirituality: Essays on the Rise of Spiritual Power within the Feminist Movement.* Edited by Charlene Spretnak. Garden City, NY: Anchor Books, 1982.

Turner, Victor. *Dramas, Fields and Metaphors: Symbolic Action in Human Society.* Ithaca, NY: Cornell University Press, 1974.

———. *The Ritual Process: Structure and Anti-structure.* Chicago: Aldine, 1969.

Tweed, Thomas A., ed. *Retelling U.S. Religious History.* Berkeley: University of California Press, 1997.

Twitchell, James B. *Shopping for God: How Christianity Went from in Your Heart to in Your Face.* New York: Simon & Schuster, 2007.

Versluis, Arthur. *Wisdom's Children: A Christian Esoteric Tradition.* Albany: State University of New York Press, 1999.

Wallace, Ruth A. *They Call Her Pastor: A New Role for Catholic Women.* Albany: State University of New York Press, 1992.

Walsh, Mary-Paula. *Feminism and Christian Tradition: An Annotated Bibliography and Critical Introduction to the Literature.* Westport, CT: Greenwood Press, 1999.

Waring, Nancy. "Freudian Fantasies." *The Women's Review of Books* IV, no. 12 (September 1987).

Watson, Natalie K. *Feminist Theology.* Grand Rapids, MI: W.B. Eerdmans, 2003.

Waylen, Georgina. *Engendering Transitions: Women's Mobilization, Institutions, and Gender Outcomes.* Oxford: Oxford University Press, 2007.

Weaver, Mary Jo. *New Catholic Women: A Contemporary Challenge to Traditional Religious Authority.* Bloomington: Indiana University Press, 1995.

Weigel, George. *Witness to Hope: The Biography of Pope John Paul II.* New York: Cliff Street Books, 1999.

Weitzman, Steven. "Reopening the Gates of J. Z. Smith's Temple: *To Take Place* in the Light of New Historicism." *Journal of the American Academy of Religion* 76, no. 3 (September 2008): 766–773.

Wellman, Judith. *Grass Roots Reform in the Burned-Over District of Upstate New York: Religion, Abolitionism, and Democracy.* New York: Garland, 2000.

———. *The Road to Seneca Falls: Elizabeth Cady Stanton and the First Woman's Rights Convention.* Urbana: University of Illinois Press, 2004.

Wertheimer, Molly Meijer, ed. *Listening to Their Voices: The Rhetorical Activities of Historic Women.* Columbia: University of South Carolina Press, 1997.

Wessinger, Catherine, ed. *Religious Institutions and Women's Leadership: New Roles inside the Mainstream.* Columbia, SC: University of South Carolina Press, 1996.

Wilcox, Melissa M. *Coming Out in Christianity: Religion, Identity, and Community.* Bloomington: Indiana University Press, 2003.

Wilcox, Melissa M. *Queer Women and Religious Individualism.* Bloomington: Indiana University Press, 2009.

Wilde, Melissa J. *Vatican II: A Sociological Analysis of Religious Change.* Princeton: Princeton University Press, 2007.

Wilken, Robert L., ed. *Aspects of Wisdom in Judaism and Early Christianity.* Notre Dame, IN: University of Notre Dame Press, 1975.

Williams, Delores. "The Color of Feminism." *Christianity and Crisis* 45 (1985).

———. *Sisters in the Wilderness: The Challenge of Womanist God-Talk.* Maryknoll, NY: Orbis Books, 1993.

Winkelmann, Carol Lea. *The Language of Battered Women: A Rhetorical Analysis of Personal Theologies.* Albany: State University of New York Press, 2003.

Wootton, Janet. *Introducing a Practical Feminist Theology of Worship.* Cleveland: Pilgrim Press, 2000.

Wootton, Janet. *This Is Our Song: Women's Hymn-Writing.* Eugene, OR: Wipf & Stock, 2013.

Wren, Brian. *What Language Shall I Borrow?: God-Talk in Worship: A Male Response to Feminist Theology.* London: SCM Press, 1989.

Wuthnow, Robert. *Creative Spirituality: The Way of the Artist.* Berkeley: University of California Press, 2001.

Yoder, Christine Roy. *Wisdom as a Woman of Substance: A Socioeconomic Reading of Proverbs 1–9 and 31:10–31*. Berlin: Walter de Gruyter, 2001.

Young, Paul. "Why I Wrote *The Shack*." *Guideposts* (August 2009): 74–78.

Young, William Paul. *The Shack: Where Tragedy Confronts Eternity*. Los Angeles: Windblown Media, 2007.

INDEX